The Last Jewish Joke

The Last Jewish Joke

MICHEL WIEVIORKA

Translated by Cory Stockwell

polity

Originally published in French as *La dernière histoire juive* © Éditions Denoël, 2023. The text has been revised and updated by the author for the English edition.

This English translation © Polity Press, 2025

This work received support for excellence in publication and translation from Albertine Translation, a program created by Villa Albertine and funded by Albertine Foundation.

Polity Press
65 Bridge Street
Cambridge CB2 1UR, UK

Polity Press
111 River Street
Hoboken, NJ 07030, USA

ISBN-13: 978-1-5095-6465-1 – hardback

A catalogue record for this book is available from the British Library.

Library of Congress Control Number: 2024949655

Typeset in 11 on 14pt Warnock Pro
by Cheshire Typesetting Ltd, Cuddington, Cheshire
Printed and bound in Great Britain by CPI Group (UK) Ltd, Croydon

The publisher has used its best endeavours to ensure that the URLs for external websites referred to in this book are correct and active at the time of going to press. However, the publisher has no responsibility for the websites and can make no guarantee that a site will remain live or that the content is or will remain appropriate.

Every effort has been made to trace all copyright holders, but if any have been overlooked the publisher will be pleased to include any necessary credits in any subsequent reprint or edition.

For further information on Polity, visit our website: politybooks.com

Contents

Acknowledgments

I would like to thank my sisters Annette and Sylvie, as well as Alain Geismar and Régis Meyran for reading a first draft of this book: I benefited greatly from their valuable comments. I would also like to thank Dorothée Cunéo for her confidence and fruitful suggestions.

Instructions for Use

This book deals with a unique genre of humor and with the history of this genre: "Jewish jokes," which should not be confused with anti-Semitic jokes.

The era of "Jewish jokes" has a prehistory, which goes back to the 1960s and originates, above all, in a movement from East to West and, in a very secondary way, on the shores of the Mediterranean – this is the first phase of its development. Its zenith, the second phase, takes place in the United States and France, and lasts barely a half-century. And finally, in its closing phase, it enters into a state of decline.

This book is interested above all in the content of these jokes, which it contextualizes, though it must sometimes (very rarely and only when necessary) hide the identity of a person or their surroundings. In doing so, it sheds a light that is broader than it may seem on Jewish sociology and history, and not only on the collective unconscious that they reveal.

Since its author is a researcher in the social sciences, this book also provides an occasion to reflect upon the way it was constructed – the path it took, the ideas and intellectual engagements it contains, and its specific approach, which essentially lies at the crossroads of political sociology and history.

1

The American Invention of
Jewish Jokes

The Jewish mother

There was a time when the cafeteria of the Maison des sciences de l'homme was a marvelous place, where students, CNRS researchers, professors, and lecturers from the École des hautes études en sciences sociales all crossed paths, not to mention guests from all over the world. You might run into Jacques Derrida or another living incarnation of "French Theory," important sociologists such as Pierre Bourdieu, Alain Touraine, and many others, famous historians such as Fernand Braudel (leading light of the Annales School of historiography), François Furet, and Jacques Le Goff, and countless figures from the social sciences and humanities in America, Britain, and elsewhere.

I often had coffee there with the historian Gilles Veinstein, who had a neighboring office on the eighth floor of the building people called the "54" (because it was located at 54 boulevard de Raspail in Paris). Gilles, who died in 2013, and who was a noted specialist of Turkish and Ottoman history, had a dramatic experience in the second part of the 1990s. From the moment he entered the Collège de France as a professor, with the procedure still not complete, he was the target of a violent polemic because, in 1995, in the magazine *L'Histoire*, he had taken the side of Bernard Lewis, a world-famous specialist of Islam who, in the pages of *Le Monde*, had refused to classify the massacre of Armenians by Turks in 1915 as a genocide.

Along with several others, I defended Gilles publicly, because the controversy came to take the form of unacceptable *ad hominem* attacks, even though his arguments were those of a historian participating in a debate, not those of a politically motivated denier. My personal position wasn't easy to maintain. I was on a knife edge, because, while I clearly supported him, it was also important for me to display, no less clearly, my support for the Armenian cause and for demands to recognize the genocide. Gilles and I often, and at great length, spoke about this affair, which deeply and lastingly wounded him. We also had other conversation topics, of course.

My mother would come to have lunch with me from time to time in the canteen of the "54," in the basement, and nothing pleased her more than when she found herself, afterwards, seated at a table in the cafeteria on the main floor with me and one or another of my friends, including Gilles, who, reflecting one day on the relationship between my mother and myself (her eldest son), told us the following joke:

A bit of bad news, a bit of good news
  Two Jewish mothers often meet over a cup of tea, and their conversations revolve, for the most part, around the respective merits of their eldest sons.
  "Guess what? Something incredible is happening with my son," one of them declares.
  "What is it? I hope it's good news," exclaims the other, who obviously wants it to be bad news.
  "Actually, there's good news and bad news."
  "Start with the bad news."

"My son is living with another man! They're going to get married."

"I'm sorry to hear! And the good news?"

"He's a doctor!"

The invasive Jewish mother is no mere myth. I've come across several, including at the boundaries of my own family. In fact, we have distant Latin American relatives with whom I crossed paths in Argentina; I visited them at the end of the 1980s when I was passing through Buenos Aires. One of them, a cousin of my mother, lived with her husband in a luxury condominium where children were forbidden. The path they'd taken to get there was anything but commonplace. Her husband, after having left Nazi-invaded Poland in his youth, did business in the USSR in wartime. He then made his way to Palestine, where he met my mother's cousin, before going to Italy toward the end of the war and working for the American army. They then migrated to North America, hoping to make money, and from there they finally opted for Argentina, where he had a few contacts.

They then made a fortune in the import–export business. When I visited, I was able to observe how my mother's cousin kept a close watch on her two sons and two daughters-in-law. She bought each couple a superb house less than a kilometer away from her own home, one to the west, the other to the east. Clearly, both sons followed her wishes, and she intervened in many aspects of their lives. They all welcomed me warmly: family is sacred. But deep down I had the sense of an incommensurable distance; their world, heavily controlled by the mother of the family, dominated by money and very pro-Israeli, was foreign to me.

One day, in November 2022, I'm walking in a street in Paris with my sister Sylvie; we've just done our shopping together. I give her news from our own mother, whom, as a good eldest son, I phone every evening in her retirement care home, and all of a sudden, through an association of ideas, I share with her the joke about the two Jewish mothers told to me by Gilles Veinstein. It then turns out that Sylvie also had a good joke about a Jewish mother. Here it is:

> *A young Jewish man has decided to get married, and is hesitating between two women. He likes them both, but lacks confidence and can't make up his mind. He confides in his mother and asks for her help. Finally, they agree that she'll invite both potential spouses over to her home, one after the other, and then tell her son the right thing to do.*
>
> *Immediately after meeting both women, the mother calls her son.*
>
> *"My dear, I've seen your two friends, and I can tell you that I've made my choice, it's clear and obvious."*
>
> *"So quickly?"*
>
> *"Yes, yes, you have to marry the tall blond one."*
>
> *"How can you be so sure?"*
>
> *"I already hate her!"*

This joke isn't specifically Jewish, and could in fact apply to many non-Jewish mothers, except that the stereotype includes the complete submission of the son to the choice made by his mother, who is supposed to know what's best for him. And therefore the role of the submissive son is also a stereotype – you can't have one without the other.

The issue of the relationship between mothers and daughters-in-law is much broader. Here as well, if the joke touches me, or concerns me, it is above all because it pushes the caricature to the point of absurdity. What's true in this joke isn't solely or even particularly Jewish, and yet it needs to be qualified as "Jewish" to make me laugh.

Our own mother has nothing to do with this kind of character, whom she also laughs about. She brought up her three children in material conditions that were difficult, and, like many other mothers, she placed demands on us, but she was never invasive or overprotective; she didn't get involved in everything. I think I can say with confidence that she didn't turn me into a character comparable in any way to Alex Portnoy from Philip Roth's novel *Portnoy's Complaint*, whom I'll speak about below. My father dreamed of seeing me attend a top university, but only vaguely, without any real fervor. My mother was no more obsessed by success than he was, especially the way people imagined this obsession in the 1960s and 1970s, in the figure of the doctor; it's true that her brother, Roger Perelman, embodied this success beyond all measure, as he was certainly one of the best French pediatricians of his generation and was recognized as such. The stereotype of the Jewish mother is that she crushes the father, or causes him to vanish; my parents functioned more like a balanced couple from the standpoint of the influence each exercised on their children.

I like these jokes about Jewish mothers precisely because they contrast with my own lived experience. I was able to laugh about them with my own mother, or with a friend like Gilles Veinstein, because in a way we have one foot inside them and one foot outside: our personal experience allows us to see what is excessive about them. I'll just add that if the doctor appears as the highest symbol of success, including financial success, this doesn't really apply to my family, because we placed the greatest value on intellectual life, and on morals or ethics – never on money. It certainly wasn't to get rich that my uncle Roger and my sister Sylvie chose medicine.

But why, or how, has the Jewish mother become the main character of so many jokes? Why does she have to be "Jewish" when so many non-Jewish mothers are abusive, invasive, stifling, guilt-inducing, and excessively anxious about their children, above all their sons?

To understand, you have to consider the American context of the 1960s, when a stereotypical version of the Jewish mother

appeared before a large audience in the United States, popularized in 1964 by Dan Greenburg's bestseller *How to Be a Jewish
Mother: A Very Lovely Training Manual*, a very funny book
that was adapted for the theater. A study by Aldo Naouri, Sylvie
Angel, and Philippe Gutton, entitled *Les Mères juives n'existent
pas . . . mais alors, qu'est-ce qui existe?* ["Jewish mothers don't
exist . . . but then, what does?"],[1] opens convincing lines of
inquiry: the arrival of the Jewish mother on the stage of Jewish
humor owes a great deal to Dan Greenburg, but also to Philip
Roth and his novel *Portnoy's Complaint*, in which, during a
monologue in the office of his psychoanalyst, the narrator
describes a caricature of a Jewish mother. The "Jewish mother"
was wildly successful because it arose in a context of empathy
for an increasingly visible Jewish culture and history, and at
the same time evoked a development whereby women attained
emancipation while paternal authority declined. Philip Roth's
book, an immense success in the United States and around the
world, proved to be subversive in its raw treatment of sex, but
also in dealing with how a Jew might feel a sense of belonging
to American modernity, giving a jolt of sorts to the context of
stifling puritanism. Alex, the blaspheming main character, is
a sexual obsessive who spends his time dreaming of beautiful
non-Jewish blonds. He's at war with religious and familial constraints, but he never makes a complete break, never detaches
himself from his Jewish identity.

Among the main figures of the trailblazing feminism of the
1960s, Betty Friedan and Gloria Steinem identified as Jews,
and others as well, such as Bella Abzug, to the point that they
were seen by the American far right as leaders of the "Jewish
conspiracy," the supposed plot against the Christian family
and its values. On the other hand, feminism also exercised
an influence at the heart of the Jewish world, which came up
against resistance from the heritage of a traditional Jewish
culture in which men studied and were breadwinners, while
women managed family life.

The thrust of feminist modernity could also be found in France in the same era, and with the same effects where the Jewish mother is concerned. The actress Marthe Villalonga played the role of a Jewish mother who was very invasive toward her son, played by the comedian Guy Bedos, in two films from the 1970s, *Pardon Mon Affaire* and *Pardon Mon Affaire, Too!*, which, fittingly, spoke of the transformations of French society, its interrogations of masculinity, but also developments that owe a great deal to the women's movement.

In this context, people felt perfectly entitled to import the American theme of the "Jewish mother" onto French soil, and to read with relish Jewish literature from the United States (above all from New York) which dealt with the traditional Jewish family, and Jewish life more generally, as they existed in the European past or in their contemporary American forms, where they were jostled by modernity and above all by the women's movement. A global readership, which wasn't necessarily Jewish, demonstrated broad empathy, conquered by Isaac Bashevis Singer, Saul Bellow, Chaïm Potok, and Bernard Malamud.

In its contemporary version, the character of the Jewish mother is similar to more general ideas about mothers-in-law, demonstrating the continued existence of a prior culture, but also the breaches being opened in this culture, including the Jewish world, by the contestation of patriarchy and the recognition of women's rights and feminism. This stereotype holds less and less for the present day. Today's mothers are certainly not indifferent to the sexual orientation of their children, but they are far less able to impose their traditional conceptions of marriage and family upon them than they were in the past.

The Jewish mother has lost – she is doomed. The joke that my friend Gilles Veinstein told my mother and me is dated: it belonged to a historical period that is ending, and only those belonging to aging generations – my generation, not that of my children – still laugh at it. These aging generations, however, nonetheless perceived and appreciated the importance of cultural mutation brought by new, or renewed, political struggles and demands, such as those of women.

The era of Jewish communities from Eastern Europe is over, and the Jewish mother is one of the last echoes of their decomposition, while at the same time it is enough of a caricature to also express a change, the entry into a new phase of modernity. But this caricature will not endure. In the Jewish cinema and literature of the United States in the 1970s – Woody Allen, Erica Jong,[2] Philip Roth, and many others – the Jewish mother gave rise to neuroses and even (though this is debatable) psychoses; she created good clients for psychoanalysis, which at the time was beginning to play an important role in the lives of American Jews, especially those in New York, as illustrated by *Portnoy's Complaint*. For in the end, there exists a paranoiac aspect to certain Jewish jokes, which sometimes display a sentiment of persecution, and a world in which right reasoning is built on false (or at least seriously twisted) premises.

Has this time really come to an end? It certainly seems like it, at least where mothers are concerned. But the Jewish mother can only be fully understood in her relationship with a hypochondriac son, at once sexually obsessed and vaguely romantic, a misfit who is nonetheless capable of success, etc. – this is a character that may indeed endure.

When history goes beyond tears

"Jewish jokes" haven't been around long, but Jewish witticisms are an ancient genre, and are at the heart of an apparent paradox: while Jewish history, according to the historian Salo Baron, is almost always "tearful," made up of tragic events that systematically call forth tears, which is something he criticized for a long time before moderating his point of view late in life, and while it is always heavy with suffering and drama –

persecutions, expulsions, massacres – the Jewish people, including in the writings and pronouncements of certain of their religious representatives, also identify with a form of humor that is all its own. Indeed, the genre we know as "Jewish jokes" was only able to develop because these people refused to limit themselves to a history of victimhood and to the evocation of the Shoah, and instead foregrounded their culture and their positive contributions to the life of ideas.

Obviously, witticisms were already very present in Freud's era, in the Vienna of the early twentieth century, and the father of psychoanalysis recounts an abundance of them.[3] But the flourishing of "Jewish jokes" as a singular genre, which include jokes such as the one I've just related about the Jewish mother, originates to a great extent in the United States of the late 1960s. Their humor, at the heart of which the Jewish mother plays a decisive role, flourished considerably in this time and place, as testified to in particular by literature and cinema.

It must be said that, at this moment, the world of American Jews undergoes a considerable and indeed wholesale transformation. Certainly, we're still speaking about a minority group, as the first research in the sociology of health demonstrates. The work of Irving Zola, for instance, which is seen as pioneering, compares the ways in which the members of various minority groups, including Jews, express their suffering when they are sick.[4] Jews have a specific way of doing so, as do the Irish and the Italians, for instance; Blacks and Native Americans are not taken into account in the research of this period, as they do not yet belong to the public space of groups that count in the same way as the minorities stemming from European migration. Only later will they enter the fray of comparative work of this kind.

Broadly speaking, these studies claim that Jewish men who have taken ill moan and groan in a way that reinforces their power over the rest of their family, which is distinct, for instance, from Irish men, who grit their teeth without complaining. Furthermore, sickness and death are frequent subjects of American Jewish literature – it's true, as Judith Stora-Sandor notes, that "Jewish humor finds its source in misfortune. If the highest value is life, the highest misfortune is death, which means that, more than any other theme, it merits an ironic treatment."[5] And hypochondria has been an important feature of male Jewish characters in American literature and cinema since at least the 1960s.

By that time, American Jews had already played a major role in the cultural life of their country for almost a century, in theater, music, publishing, and, more recently, television. They brought to these domains a humor whose origins lay in their own history, but this was usually not explicit because they didn't present themselves as Jews. They were cautious to anchor themselves on the side of universalism, which, for them, meant masking or minimizing their belonging to a community, perhaps to favor their civic participation in collective life. It is thus that Hollywood, which owes a great deal to Jews, long avoided producing films with explicitly Jewish themes or characters, or featuring even the slightest Jewish specificity. And even though many Jewish democrats, mainly from northern states, had participated just a few years earlier in the struggle for civil rights and the defense of universal values alongside Black Americans, they hadn't done so in the name of promoting this or that identity.

The philosopher Michael Walzer, who was an active participant in debates that once opposed communitarians (who place more value on specific identities) and liberals (who privilege political citizenship), says somewhere that most American Jews in the 1960s, at least the progressive ones, generally lined up behind "liberal," i.e. civic, values. During this period, the discrimination from which Jews had traditionally suffered hadn't yet disappeared, but it was in its death throes. As such, David Apter, a political sociologist respected around the world, especially for his work on the politics of modernization, told me that when he joined the faculty of Yale University in 1969 (later he would chair the sociology department), he was told that he was the first Jew to whom such a position had ever been offered. The end of more or less disguised quotas that prevented Jews from entering the university as students or instructors (and also kept them out of high-ranking government positions, the army, and the diplomatic corps) went hand in hand with the removal of restrictions on entering high-society clubs that had been the purview of WASPs [White Anglo-Saxon Protestants]. In order to explain why he'd resigned from one of these, the Friars' Club, Groucho Marx made this famous quip: "I don't want to belong to any club that would accept me as one of its members."

While it is true that, in the 1930s, anti-Semitic violence exploded in the context of the New Deal (which anti-Semites called the "Jew Deal"), things had changed by the 1950s, when the "Jewish Renaissance," as the sociologist Nathan Glazer called it, began. Glazer describes its religious and educational aspects (with the establishment of synagogues and schools), and views it as a result of the strong contribution made by Jews to the country's growing prosperity. He also notes that anti-Semitism seems, in this period, to "have almost entirely disappeared,"[6] though he also points to the appearance, at the heart of Black resistance movements, of worrisome expressions of anti-white radicalism, which could potentially take Jews as its target.

This "Renaissance" intensified at the end of the 1960s, with 1967 marking a turning point, according to Glazer, because of the Six-Day War: American Jews suddenly started to take an interest in the State of Israel, which developed not because they themselves felt insecure, but rather from the idea that a genocide of the Jews was once more possible. This fear was also fed by the fact that black and white extremists were hostile to Israel, which actively cooperated with South Africa's apartheid regime. The risk that the Jewish state would be isolated suddenly began to worry the American diaspora. The history of relations between Blacks and Jews in the United States is complex and ever-changing, and the interactions between these communities, right up to the present day, have continually oscillated, as Édith Bruder has shown, between identification, cooperation, and rivalry, which contains a share of anti-Semitism.[7]

While the opinion of the diaspora remained largely favorable toward Israel, certain critical voices began to be heard, most often on the left. Since then, we've seen the contours of a general decoupling of American Jews from Israel, from which fear often springs up here and there. The 1960s were therefore not entirely optimistic. But by and large, the development of the situation nonetheless favored genuine confidence in the future, a feeling that real progress was being made, as evidenced by the growing visibility of Jews in American public life. Compared with other minorities, the economic and social success of American Jews, helped along by the growth of the postwar years, is clear, even if there still exist poor Jews, of course. Jews began to bring a great deal to the cultural vitality of the United States, and did so explicitly as Jews – I'll return to this point – in literature, fine arts, and cinema. They were able to move people with stories of their past, all the while remaining part of the general progress of their society. They were more and more willing to express themselves without hiding their identity.

Even before the emotion aroused by the Six-Day War, and the enthusiasm with which Israel's quick and complete victory was welcomed, the State of Israel was viewed kindly not only by Jews, but in the general opinion, especially since Israel put the Nazi Adolf Eichmann on trial in 1961–2 in a highly mediatized event, after its secret service agents had captured him in Argentina. The philosopher Hannah Arendt would report on his trial in her 1963 book *Eichmann in Jerusalem*, which had vast reverberations and gave rise to lively debates. The very existence of the Hebrew State was a source of pride, though it was not attractive enough to lead many American Jews to opt for the *aliyah*, a Hebrew word that means "ascension" and refers to the return to the Holy Land.

Pioneers in the age of victimhood

This era also witnessed a rising awareness of the destruction of European Jews by the Nazis, an awareness that to this point had been limited to the Jewish world, which was quickly accelerated and reinforced by a significant number of cultural productions. The television series *Holocaust*, a saga consisting of four episodes that related the life of a Jewish family in the face of Nazism, was broadcast in 1978, and was incredibly successful. Similarly, the graphic novel *Maus*, by Art Spiegelman, which was published first serially in a magazine and then as a book, enjoyed phenomenal success, with millions of copies sold and translations in about thirty languages. *Maus*, which appeared from 1981 to 1991, joins in a single narrative thread the story of Spiegelman's father, starting in Poland in the 1930s, including his deportation, and the trajectory of the author, marked by a tense relationship with his father. *Maus* also draws its force from the fact that its characters are represented by animals: the Poles appear as pigs, the Nazis as cats, and the Jews as mice. This sort of thing is generally undertaken by racists and anti-Semites, but here it is similar to George Orwell's *Animal Farm*, in a metaphoric vein that sidesteps essentialism or animalization.

Toward the end of this period, the understanding of the Shoah reached its apex with the global success of Steven Spielberg's film *Schindler's List* (based on Thomas Keneally's 1982 novel *Schindler's Ark*), released in 1993. The film tells the story of how a German industrialist, Oskar Schindler, rescued around 1,200 Jews destined for death in a concentration camp.

Within this context, which was the same for other minorities who were mobilizing, in particular the Black community, American Jews are the most advanced representation of what would become the age of victimhood. Indeed, a historical period was beginning in which various collective actors, especially African Americans, were calling for their cultural or ethnic specificity, which to that point had been mistreated, derided, or denied, to be recognized. It was then, in the 1970s, that a politics demanding multiculturalism came into being, proposing measures of recognition and justice, with forms of compensation for those belonging to marginalized communities, in the form of social assistance or scholarships for students who were eligible to enroll in universities that had previously been barred to them. This would give rise to Affirmative Action measures, which aimed to compensate for injustice and social inequality by allocating rights and supplemental means to the members of groups at a structural disadvantage, beginning with Black Americans.

As Jean-Michael Chaumont showed, in a dissertation that I supervised, which was then published in a series I edited,[8] the uniqueness of the Shoah – at the time, people called it the genocide or the Holocaust; the term "Shoah" was not popularized until Claude Lanzmann's film of that name, which was released in 1985 – was the fact around which the first great debate of the age of victimhood took shape.

The starting point for this was a statement made by Elie Wiesel in 1967, when he demanded, during a seminar in which George Steiner also participated, that the Holocaust no longer be considered as a shameful page of Jewish history. This was followed by major mobilizations or protests, the former driven by women's movements (which were increasingly active), the latter pointing to historical suffering on the part of minority groups other than Jews, in particular African Americans, who had first become active as a group with the civil rights movement at the end of the 1950s, and who demanded social measures and the recognition of their own identity, culture, and history.

American Jews were the pioneers in an era that came more and more to be organized around identity, which does not necessarily equate to exclusivity. The climate – with the growing awareness of the extermination of Jews in Europe, the positive image of Israel, and declining discrimination – was very favorable to them.

The success of literary reflections of this development, with Saul Bellow, Bernard Malamud, and Philip Roth, bears witness to a sensitivity or an increased interest for what happened in Europe, or for how immigrants from Europe lived in America, and this also concerned non-Jewish Americans. In 1979, William Styron published *Sophie's Choice*, a bestseller on which a 1982 film, also a huge success, would be based. People were coming to take stock of the Shoah, which had turned Jews into the victims of a crime the likes of which had never been seen; Jews were thought of as deserving compassion for having been subjected to barbarism, the inhumanity of genocide, and the worst horrors imaginable. It was as a result of this that, in 1978, Jimmy Carter, then president, created a commission whose aim was to write a report on the creation and financing of a Holocaust memorial, and the proclaiming of a day of remembrance. In 1980, Congress unanimously voted for the creation of a memorial museum in Washington, DC. It was inaugurated in April 1996. At the same time, the context of the 1980s and 1990s allowed American Jews to emphasize those aspects of their experience that are different from mere victimhood: the link between the American diaspora and the State of Israel, and, more broadly, a great cultural vitality, a taste for life, an ancestral sense of humor, and a capacity for political and intellectual mobilization that was very progressive, especially at that time. It became possible for non-Jews to find points in common with Jews, even – perhaps especially – when they alluded to their shortcomings with humor or incontestable literary talent.

Hence the strong presence of Jewish humor in the media, especially with Woody Allen's first films: *Annie Hall*, *Zelig*, *Hannah and her Sisters*, and *Radio Days*; indeed, we see this same Jewish humor, in the years between 1970 and 1990, in a much later film, *Whatever Works*, by the same Woody Allen. This vein of humor was perpetuated in the films of the Coen brothers, Joel and Ethan, with their very colorful Jewish characters. In particular, *A Serious Man* (2010) puts the Jewish community on display, and even if you need some understanding of Jewish culture to understand the film's fine points, it was intended for – and was able to reach – a broad audience.

Throughout the 1990s, the comedian Jerry Seinfeld won fame on NBC on a sitcom steeped in Jewish humor that was all the rage. Seinfeld, who was born in Brooklyn, often mentioned in interviews his personal experience as a Jew, the son of an artist who had collected innumerable jokes when he fought in the Second World War – the *Witz*, the witticism, as is well known, existed long before the rise of "Jewish jokes." This sitcom, perhaps the most successful from a financial standpoint in the entire history of American television, whose final episode was watched by 76.3 million spectators, makes Seinfeld's Jewish milieu seem very appealing, as it demonstrates that those in this milieu do not hesitate to make fun of the Jewish religion, even on television.

Another series, *The Nanny*, equally well known in other countries, also had an immense success in the United States, where it was launched in 1993 on CBS; the lead actress, Fran Drescher, confided during an interview that she had fought to make the character of the nanny explicitly Jewish, and not Italian, as the sponsor, Proctor and Gamble, had initially wanted.[9]

Finally, the lived memory of the European past, if not of the shtetl then at least of *Yiddishland*, of Jewish life in Central and Eastern Europe, was still alive at the end of the twentieth century, as was that of other minorities, especially the Italians and the Irish. Hence, when Ellis Island ceased to serve as a federal processing center for immigrants arriving by boat to New York (as it did from 1892 to 1954) and became the Ellis Island Immigration Museum, which opened its doors in 1990, visitors arrived in droves. Among them, many Jews originally from Central Europe, along with their descendants, arrived in a state of heightened emotion to search for traces of a migration that belongs to a not-yet distant past, and that brings back a great many memories, among them the list of the names of all those who passed through this center. Georges Perec, in his beautiful 1994 book *Ellis Island*, found, during his visit, not so much roots or direct evidence of this Jewish past, which was not his aim, but rather a site at which "exhausted officials baptize new Americans by the shovelful," a "dumping ground" that marks the rupture of an exile coming to a close, which for him is "very confusedly but very intimately linked to the very fact of being Jewish." As for me, I've taken the ferry to Ellis Island several times, which has given me a palpable sense of the memories such a visit can kindle for those Jews who began arriving from the Old World (so well described by Irving Howe in his 1976 bestseller *The World of Our Fathers*) beginning in the late nineteenth century, and for their descendants. I also have a palpable sense of exactly what aspects of this "dumping ground" bear witness to the human and intellectual qualities of those who passed through it, such as those of a young girl whose story the visitor can read. Since she arrived during a period of anti-immigrant pressure, she underwent a tense interrogation, including tests intended to measure her skills and intelligence. I cite from memory the following fragment of this interrogation:

"If you had to wash a staircase thoroughly, would you begin at the top or the bottom?"

"I hope you don't think I'm applying to enter the United States so I can be a cleaner!"

An entire cluster of factors that led to the blossoming of a relatively happy Jewish life formed in the United States during the final thirty years of the twentieth century, which gave rise to interest and goodwill coming from well beyond the Jewish world alone. So it's not surprising to read, on one of those postcards you can buy at souvenir stands to send to parents or friends, that being Jewish is "a marvelous experience." Nor is it surprising that American humor came to be marked by what Wallace Markfield calls a "Yiddishization."[10] This was already taking shape in the work of the Marx brothers (who stopped performing together in films in 1950), especially in Groucho's Yiddish-inflected slang.

The American prehistory of the era of "Jewish jokes" can also be found in the "Borscht Belt," dealt with by Adam Biro,[11] those counties in the Catskills where, from the 1920s until 1960, thousands of Jews vacationed to "breathe the air of Jewish comedians," and which constituted an incubator through which many important figures passed, including the actors Jerry Lewis and Mel Brooks. Starting in the 1970s, several of Mel Brooks's films illustrate the development that turned him into a "disobedient Jew," to cite the title of the book that Jeremy Dauber wrote about him.[12] This is particularly true of *Blazing Saddles*, in which Brooks plays the role of an Indian chief who speaks Yiddish. His film *The History of the World, Part I* gave rise, in 2023, to a series, *The History of the World, Part II*, where we find the same humor, sprinkled with Jewish jokes. A form of humor aimed at a broad audience, not just a Jewish one.

It is not surprising that, from 1970 to 2000, many Jewish jokes emerged that were able to cross the Atlantic, jokes that could be enjoyed – this goes to the heart of how I'm defining them in this book – as much by non-Jews as by Jews. It is also not surprising that a 2013 study by the Pew Research Center showed that 42 percent of American Jews considered humor essential to their Jewish identity,[13] and that several recent books, including academic books, have dealt with Jewish humor, such as *Jewish Comedy: A Serious History*, by Jeremy Dauber,[14] *Jewish Humor*, by the rabbi Joseph Telushkin,[15] *The Big Book of Jewish Humor*, by William Novak,[16] etc.

But at the same time we must be nuanced. Let us not underestimate the fact that Jews in the United States have often felt a strong sense of guilt, for having survived the Shoah, and indeed for having avoided it, when so many others suffered and perished. We find echoes of this on several occasions in Spiegelman's *Maus*. The Franco-American literary critic George Steiner, who died in 2020, also took note of this in an anguished interview with Laura Adler on the radio station France Culture.[17] We can also note, in what may at first glance appear as a golden age – and not for the first time in Jewish history – signs of a loss of traditional points of reference, which may owe something to the appearance of new forms of contestation, the most important of which is feminism. The weakening of Jewish identity is also linked to the accelerated Americanization of American Jews, to a rise in mixed marriages, and to the beginnings of a dilution and fragmentation, and indeed exploding, of identity, as discussed by Françoise Ouzan.[18] The Jewish jokes of the United States from 1970 to 2000 draw on a past that has ended, at least in part, and therefore carry a vague sense of nostalgia, even as they still make sense in a relatively happy present. But they do so without constantly invoking the segregated existence that gave meaning to the jokes from Yiddishland, when the latter was still alive; and in those cases when they do invoke it, they do so less tenderly and a bit more critically. These jokes should also be read retrospectively as the symptom of a period that has ended, or is ending, and as so many expressions of an entrance into the age of modern individualism, for Jews and for everyone else, and of a resurgence of identities: Jews, in all of this, are just one actor among many, and not necessarily the most capable of confronting the ravages of time. There's no guarantee that success will last.

2

Prolegomena

Some Jewish jokes bring us back to a world that has disappeared and become some sort of fantasy world, from which it is nonetheless possible to derive lessons that have a timeless value. The prehistory of Jewish jokes thus interweaves with the present time, as their humor brings us back to the past while at the same time featuring seemingly structural traits that are inherent to the Jewish experience in general.

The watch

A few months before his death, my father told the following joke to anyone who would listen – and there was no more avid listener than me!

> *This joke takes place in a shtetl, a little Jewish town in pre-war Poland. One day, Moshe comes upon a rabbi in the street. They exchange greetings and tell each other their news. Moshe says:*
> *"Everything would be fine if my beautiful gold watch, which I wear as a pocket watch, hadn't been stolen."*

"What?" exclaims the rabbi. "Do you have any idea who could have taken it?"

"Of course! It so happens that every week, I get together with about a dozen friends to talk about one thing or another. Last week, when I was leaving, I noticed that my watch was gone. It had to be one of my friends. But I hate being suspicious of any of them! I do have an inkling of who did it, but what can I do?"

"I have an idea!" the rabbi cries out. "Next time you meet, casually introduce the theme of the Ten Commandments – after all, it's a great discussion topic. And when you get to 'Thou shalt not steal,' look straight into the eyes of the person you suspect. Perhaps he'll get upset and behave strangely."

Moshe warmly thanks the rabbi for his advice, and they go their separate ways. Several weeks pass. The rabbi notices that on two occasions, just as they're about to cross paths, Moshe manages to avoid him. Finally they come face to face, and the rabbi seizes the chance to ask Moshe about his watch. Moshe, clearly embarrassed, tries to sidestep the question, and then finally explains:

"I followed your advice."

"And?"

"When we got together, I suggested to my friends that we discuss the Ten Commandments, and they agreed."

"And did you do what I told you?"

"No, it wasn't necessary. Because when we arrived at 'Thou shalt not commit adultery,' I remembered where I'd left my watch."

This joke wasn't necessarily new when my father told it to me in 1990. I came across it later on in a book by Joseph Klatzmann, *Jewish Humor*.[1] There are various versions – sometimes the watch is replaced by a bicycle. If I tell the joke here, it's because it's one of the last two memories I have of my father's final months, before he stupidly died of a heart attack because he decided to stop taking his daily medication (it was useless, he said, because his blood pressure was back to normal).

The other memory, which for me is inseparable from the first, is his meeting with Elie Wiesel, who won the Nobel Peace Prize in 1986, and was the author of a body of work marked by his experience of the Shoah, and his knowledge of the lost world of Central and Eastern Europe's *Yiddishland*. Émile Malet, manager of the journal *Passages*, put me in charge of the international conference, "Three Days on Racism," in Créteil, from June 5 to 7, 1991 (I later edited the proceedings of the colloquium, which appeared under the title *Racisme et modernité*),[2] and Elie Wiesel accepted my invitation to give the keynote address on the opening night. My father had a pleasant interaction with him at the reception, during which they spoke Yiddish together, one on one, for quite some time, which brought my father a great deal of joy.

Winds from the east

I associate the exchange between my father and Wiesel with the joke about Moshe and the rabbi because, for me, they both evoke the Jewish pre-war past in Poland. My father, not least as the translator of stories and novels linked to this past, often by great authors – Shalom Asch, Ozer Warschawski, Mendele Moïkher Sforim (as a young man, before the war, he had also translated into French a few stories by his father, Wolf) – continually reminisced about this era, all the while expressing gratitude for living in France. The world of the shtetl, of which Rachel Ertel gives an account in a book published in 1982,[3] had in truth been in decline since the middle of the nineteenth century, and perhaps even before that, as the historian Jacob Katz has shown (for example in his book *Out of the Ghetto: The Social Background of Jewish Emancipation 1770–1870*).[4] And my father's nostalgia blends this faraway past with the pre-war past that's much closer to us, during which time he lived in Paris, with his family, in a dynamic universe of Jewish immigrants from Central Europe.

With the war, the shtetl disappeared completely, as did the Parisian world that my father had known. And even if the Yiddish language has survived in spite of Nazism and Stalinism, it is certainly not as a national language – indeed, the State of Israel has never supported it. It survives mainly because of pious Jews, such as ultraorthodox Hassidic Jews in Brooklyn, New York, in Mea Shearim in Jerusalem, and in a few other large cities, such as Antwerp and Montreal. These pious Jews use this language in their daily lives, reserving Hebrew for their relations with God. This saddened my father, who was a left-wing atheist. I remember when my parents, in the late 1950s, asked Rachel Ertel's mother to instill in me the rudiments of Yiddish. This quickly turned out to be unsuccessful, as I preferred the modernity of my school friends, soccer, cycling, and parties. And my state-run high school, with its republican values, wasn't exactly fertile ground for distinct identities.

I had some contact with Yiddish culture, which I never found oppressive, but I was only moderately interested in it. My parents spoke Yiddish to each other when they didn't want their children to understand – usually when they were getting ready to go out at night. My maternal grandfather, whom I knew well, only knew a few words of French, but I still saw him often, and was happy to do so. And since this chapter deals with watches, I've just remembered something about him: he'd promised to give me his beautiful gold watch, which also served as a pocket watch attached to a chain, and in 1987, when he died, my cousins and I realized that he had in fact promised it to all his male grandchildren – girls were far less important than boys in the culture of *Yiddishland*, a subject I discussed earlier in my chapter on Jewish mothers.

Much later, having always been interested in the tension between distinct cultures and French republicanism, I would place myself alongside those who seek to connect, rather than oppose, universalism and unique minority identities, and I would favor a moderate multiculturalism for France, one capable of reconciling the recognition of particularity with respect for universal values. I've inherited a very specific political experience, one that has been able to unite the love for universal values with an affirmation of belonging to a minority, one that is both social (in the past, it was working class, made up of laborers and artisans) and cultural, with its own language, Yiddish, and its own history, dramatically interrupted by Nazism. I want to state from the outset that this book, often written in the first person singular, is nonetheless not a pure autobiographical exercise or a reflection on my own journey. It's true that, in contextualizing "Jewish jokes" in sociological or historical terms, I point at the same time to what they mean for me, and interested readers will have no trouble finding the thousand and one threads linking my own path with these jokes. The choice I made in the wake of May '68 to become a sociologist and work in an academic setting, even though my studies to that point should have led me to a career in business, management, or marketing (I went to a prestigious business school and then took a doctorate in management), no doubt owes something to the value my family and circle of friends placed on books and the life of ideas. And indeed, I'm not alone in this, since my sisters Annette and Sylvie, and my brother Olivier, form, along with me, an exceptional family: all four of us write books! And since we all uphold republican values, we've all chosen to work in public service, higher learning, research, or public health.

I had a passionate desire to become a researcher. And the subjects to which I've been drawn for an entire half-century, not to mention the way I've approached them – social movements, racism, anti-Semitism, multiculturalism, democracy, and also violence or terrorism – are linked in countless ways with the experiences of my childhood and youth. Not, however, in a deterministic way: on the one hand, life could have led me down a different path, and, on the other, scientific rigor has its own demands, such as rational thinking, argumentation, demonstration, and providing evidence.

But let's return to what the watch joke tells us. The shtetl of Moshe and the rabbi is a place that is alive and deeply human, where people meet and have discussions, and where stealing and adultery are always possible, as they are in other places. It forms a collectivity of coreligionists of whom the rabbi is a manifestation. He is able to give sensible advice and has a close relationship with the everyday lives of people. The world of the shtetl contains several characters: other than the rabbi, and sometimes a beadle, we also find the *schadken*, who arranges marriages by bringing families together – Freud dealt at length with this subject and this figure in his analysis of the relationship between jokes and the unconscious – and the *schnorrer*, with whom Freud also deals, a beggar through whom local bonds are formed, and for which a better translation might be "scrounger."

My father liked to refer to an example of wordplay. In the interwar period, there was a brand of cigarettes in France called "Senoritas," which could be an object of begging: scrounging one from someone you knew meant asking for a "Schnoritas." This also brings me back to Freud, who describes, with the help of numerous examples, this technique for forming witticisms that works by way of condensation, as in the joke about a rather poor man who delights in having been spoken to by Rothschild, whom he found himself sitting next to, in a "familionnaire" way – familiar, as his equal, and millionaire, which he wasn't.[5] The humoristic realm of *Yiddishland* also included shopkeepers, craftsmen, tailors, etc., and various figures from the non-Jewish world, the world of goys (plural: goyim). It was diverse, except for the fact that sexual themes, which are so central to jokes in general, had barely any place in Jewish jokes, as we'll see, even though sexuality would later be decisive in

Jewish literature, with Philip Roth, for example, or Woody
Allen in cinema. At most, like in the joke about the watch,
there are vague allusions to adultery or marriage, aspects of
which sometimes contravene modesty, as in the following
joke:

> A schadken *proposes to a man of a rather ripe age a young
> woman who possesses every desirable quality: she cooks well,
> knows how to run a household, and comes from a respected
> family. In bed? She is, the* schadken *specifies, "like a fish."*
>
> *The marriage takes place, and a few weeks later, the husband
> comes to complain to the matchmaker: he's been sold fraudulent
> merchandise:*
>
> *"You promised me a woman who is like a fish in bed, but you
> didn't tell me she was pregnant, obviously by another man."*
>
> *"But I told you the truth: like a fish in bed. A* gefilte fish!*[6]*

Speaking in Paris about the Jewish life of yesteryear, after the
Second World War, with humor, in the form of jokes, meant
creating a bond between the past and a present that didn't have
much to do with this past. It meant implicitly recalling what
had been destroyed, perhaps while flouting historical reality;
my maternal grandparents, for example, left Poland in part
for economic reasons, like many other migrants. And also so
as to be no longer subjected to the anti-Semitism that was
so powerful in that country; and finally, in part, not so much
to flee stifling village communities as to leave behind large
cities where the prevailing Jewish life was often oppressive
and above all religious. For them, the shtetl was already just a
memory, albeit a very dear one. And while many planned to go
to America, some of them, like my paternal grandfather, had
acted from a passionate desire to reach France, the land of the
Enlightenment, Victor Hugo, and Guy de Maupassant, and
also of an intellectual and artistic life that was intense, modern,
and open.

The shtetl, including even those urban universes of Central Europe when they were still infused with the cultures of particular communities, was already in steep decline when the Second World War began, and for many Jews in this part of the world – those who lived, for example, in Vilnius, Warsaw, and other large cities – modernity's influence was increasingly important. Which didn't mean that religion's influence had become negligible. The work of Marc Chagall forcefully expresses these traditional and religious universes, while blending them with elements drawn from Russian culture.

Beginning in the eighteenth century, the Jews of Central and Eastern Europe found themselves caught between two main movements: Hasidism, which sought to renew religion by way of mysticism, and the *Haskalah*, which incorporated its followers in line with modernity and Enlightenment currents, steering them toward assimilation. A joke like the one about the watch certainly owes something to this tension. I think my grandparents, both paternal and maternal, fled Poland principally to get away from Hasidism. Which doesn't lead me to conclude that their humor was one-sided. Hasidic communities granted an important place, beginning in the eighteenth century, to the *badchen*, an actor who was charged with the task of amusing people at weddings and certain celebrations, a sort of clown who performed without fear and, when necessary, slipped into vulgarity.

In the funny stories that my father liked, the Jews of the shtetl remain steeped in religion, and the rabbi is a central character. In the joke about the watch, the rabbi embodies a certain common sense, a down-to-earth intelligence, and not only some sort of sacred relationship with God. In the many other jokes that come from this era, from this part of the world, God Himself is present, often in the form of a dialogue in which, as Judith Stora-Sandor notes, He is "the main interlocutor,"[7] capable of irony with regard to Himself. He is thus lively, a familiar presence, and is expected to settle matters in the earthly realm. Sometimes this familiarity leads to criticism, but "this verbal violence, whether in the form of reproaches, invective, or anger, has trouble concealing the love that lies beneath it," continues Stora-Sandor.[8]

A working-class genre

Here are two more jokes my father used to tell. Both take place in a synagogue.

In the first joke, a man is praying out loud and begs God insistently and repetitively:

"God, let me win the lottery, let me win, I can't take it anymore."

After a while, God, exasperated, in a loud voice that fills the entire synagogue, responds:

"Maybe try buying a ticket!"

And in the second joke, a poor man is praying, and asks God for a bit of money so he can buy some food.

Another man, clearly well off, is also praying.

The poor man is noisy, which annoys the richer man, who takes a few bills from his pocket and gives them to him:

"And now, stop bothering God, wasting His time and monopolizing Him, for a few złotys. After all, I'm asking for a hundred thousand złotys!"

There was nothing of the believer in my father; indeed, the Bundist tradition was rather unreligious, if not antireligious. But like many of his friends, the universe that he liked to evoke, his universe, included God, who still had a place within it, by way of Yiddish literature and in jokes of this kind. There's something amazing about this persistence, which contains no animosity but a great deal of tenderness; as Judith Stora-Sandor correctly noted: "Even when God no longer exists, He still continues to haunt the Jewish imagination, both in its literary and non-literary forms."[9] Perhaps this is a sign of the great difficulty of remaining a Jew when you have left the ghetto, the shtetl, entered into modernity, and cut yourself off from religion as faith and belief.

The fact remains that speaking about a rabbi (or several rabbis) in a humorous tone persists to this day. In Joann Sfar's 2011 graphic novel and subsequent animated film *The Rabbi's Cat*, for example, we find a joke about a cat belonging to the rabbi of Algiers who obtained the power of speech after eating a parrot, and who is eager to have his bar mitzvah. Another example is the sketch by Édouard Baer, no less absurd, about the rabbi's hen – "a rabbi hen is funny, isn't it?"

My paternal grandfather, Wolf, who died at Auschwitz, wrote wonderful stories that my uncle Méni, his son, had translated from Yiddish and published in French.[10] He allows the reader to feel the tension, for migrants like himself, of living between a Polish past that was in many ways unbearable, and was also ending, but nonetheless made him nostalgic, and an uncertain future, with a Parisian present lying between them, in which, as one reads on the back cover, one comes across "parvenus and failures, utopians, spongers and artists . . . as well as young women grappling with ideals that affect their love life."

The shtetl disappeared long ago. What motivated my father wasn't only the disappearance of this faraway world in the east. It was also the disappearance of his own childhood, in the bohemian space that his parents had created. His form of humor maintained real links with the Talmudic thought found in the Yiddish literature that he adored, but it also owed a great deal to his social environment, which was working class. At times, this humor was in poor taste, coarse and even vulgar. The following joke, which my father used to tell, is indeed a tad vulgar; I hesitated to bring it up here, but I had to, because it's part of the overall picture.

> *The action takes place in a working-class restaurant. The client has just finished eating, and the waiter comes over to add up the bill.*
>
> *He looks at the man's shirt, and what he sees allows him to figure out what he has had for lunch without needing to consult his note pad. Indeed, the various stains reveal the contents of the meal. The client had the matzo ball soup, with flour and egg dumplings, calves' foot jelly, and a piece of cheesecake, along with red wine. The waiter adds up the bill, scribbles the total on a piece of paper, and gives it to the client, who promptly lets out a booming and smelly burp.*
>
> *Which leads the waiter to exclaim:*
>
> *"Sorry, but I forget about your appetizer, the* zibele.*"*[11]

This joke obviously shouldn't be told to an elegant and stylish audience, as it might annoy people due to its vulgarity; even though it deals with Jews, it's best suited for an audience of working-class Jews, who are poor and proletarian, workers and craftspeople, more on the side of the "pariahs" than that of the very assimilated "parvenus" with whom Hannah Arendt contrasts them – her distinction is of use, even if it is basic and binary, and warrants discussion and critique, as Michel Dreyfus has shown.[12] Before the war, my father's family owned a restaurant whose clientele was not particularly well off, consisting of a bohemian crowd of students, intellectuals, and artists. A cafeteria, in other words, in which a scene like the one in the joke could easily be imagined, reminding us that the humor of many Jewish jokes is rooted in a living culture.

The only people who can fully understand the joke about Moshe and the rabbi (this is perhaps even truer of the joke about the bill in the restaurant) are those who have some idea, even if only a fleeting and sentimental one, of the cultural complexity that these jokes come to condense and simplify. My generation never experienced the real world of the shtetl, having merely rubbed shoulders with the generation that preceded it, which originated from this world and held a more or less mythical or idealized memory of it. This memory is especially meaningful for survivors, as the genocide destroyed many of those who had come from these worlds of Eastern Europe, along with the culture they had recreated, but also invented, as a result of their migration.

And since placing rabbis in humorous situations can also lead us to North Africa – the film *The Rabbi's Cat* takes place in Algiers – it strikes me that the Ashkenazi world, with its *Yiddishkeit* and its memory of the shtetl, doesn't hold a monopoly on this absurd humor involving rabbis. And furthermore, to remain with this film and the graphic novel from which it is adapted, Joann Sfar comes from a Sephardic family from Sétif, Algeria, on his father's side, and an Ashkenazi family from Ukraine on his mother's side. A lovely synthesis!

3

In France, in the 1960s and 1970s

Sale with receipt

What follows takes place in Paris, around Réaumur-Sébastopol, in the Sentier neighborhood. A client has just walked into a wholesale clothing store, and hands a large order to the assistant: about a hundred pairs of men's pants, forty jackets, two hundred shirts, etc. After which the client barks out:

"I'll need a receipt."

"A receipt?" repeats the dumbstruck assistant.

"That's right," the client calmly confirms.

"I'll see what I can do."

The assistant heads for the boss's office, and explains, while pointing a finger toward the client through the glass window:

"That client over there wants a receipt."

Perplexed, and indeed bewildered, the boss replies:

"A receipt? What kind of scam is he trying to pull?"

This joke was told to me in the 1970s by André Kunstlinger, who died in 2022. He was a family friend, but in a slightly distant way because he'd chosen to live not in and around Paris, like them, but in Lyon, where his relatives had already settled during the war, and where he ran a wholesale clothing business with his wife Régine on the rue Longue – the shortest street in the city, as he liked to say.

He was one of those cultured Jews who live in an economic universe that isn't very intellectually demanding (and thus far below their own level), that of the *schmattes*, the making and selling of clothes, if you like. In the past he'd been a radical, perhaps a Trotskyist, and his brother Henri had played a role in the Resistance. He was a great reader and an informed lover of classical music; when I was still very young, he introduced me to both Raoul Vaneigem's *Revolution of Everyday Life* and Carl Orff's *Carmina Burana*.

The joke I just quoted belongs to a world that developed essentially after the Second World War in France, and then withered, or moved elsewhere, starting in the 1980s. In it, one perceives not a nostalgia for a past that is more or less over, but an amused and incisive take on this world of the *schmattes*, with its incredible mixture of business and Jewishness that is usually focused far more on trading than on producing, and in which great fortunes were made after the war, often by circumventing taxes and social security charges. I know a little about this, because I witnessed my maternal aunt Berthe and my uncle Raoul, who ran a women's clothing factory, and who to that point had been the richest members of the family – they had a maid and drove a Versailles, the French version of the Cadillac – suddenly declare bankruptcy and lose everything in the 1960s because they'd neglected to pay their social benefits charges to the appropriate authorities.

Some within this world were uncultured and coarse, interested above all in money. But most of them cared about culture, and hence led rather schizophrenic lives: at work, far from any intellectual demands, they focused on selling clothes, but outside work, they spent time with their families and engaged intensely in political and cultural activity and the life of ideas. Almost all of them monitored their children's studies and encouraged their social advancement; many introduced their children to music and paid for piano or violin lessons. It was important to my father that I learn to play the piano, which is why, on the recommendation of his friend Serge Pludermacher, I began lessons at the age of six or seven with "Madame Olga," a demanding woman from Russia who also taught Serge's son, Georges Pludermacher. He would become an immensely important pianist, renowned and beloved the world over. The comparison between myself and "Jojo" obviously didn't work to my advantage, however much my father might have wished it to be otherwise.

If the joke about the "sale with receipt" rang so true when one of these *schmattes* salesmen told it to me, it's because it so perfectly conveyed his somewhat schizophrenic (or at least divided) yet amused take on his own professional universe, in which what is normal in one place is abnormal in another. And in which people avoided the tax authorities (obviously I'm not referring to André Kunstlinger himself) all the while feeling a deep attachment to the French Republic and respect for its institutions, happy as they were to live in a state governed by the rule of law. I had the good fortune of being in contact with this friendly world in which many earned their living from the *schmattes*, taking vacations in large groups in the mountains, going camping in an atmosphere of constant friendship and solidarity, and where there was always a special place for humor. People were able to relativize their daily problems in these settings, perhaps because the experience of the destruction of the Jews by the Nazis was still fresh in their minds, and because they were swept along by the economic dynamism of the postwar years. As Freddy Raphaël, the great sociologist from Strasbourg, puts it, "rigidity is no match for humor."[1]

This friendly universe has persisted in the general imagination in France, but today it refers much more to the Sephardic Jews who mostly came from North Africa following decolonialization, and who were showcased in films such as *The Big Pardon* and *Would I Lie to You?*. The joke about the sale with receipt has a place in this Sephardic world as well, where people poke fun at and stand at a distance from themselves, and where illegal acts and tax evasion are not necessarily foreign.

Ashkenazim and Sephardim

Initially, "Jewish jokes" arose from a relationship with the East, with Central Europe, and was hence a sort of fantasy relationship, because what it harks back to has disappeared. But another axis has now been added to this relationship – a Mediterranean axis, if you like – with decolonization and the arrival in France of a considerable number of Sephardic Jews, who are themselves very different from the very small number of Sephardic Jews who arrived from the Iberian Peninsula after their expulsion in 1492, and followed by the Inquisition, the "purity of blood" statutes, and persecutions of those who had converted.

Until my teenage years, my personal universe, at least the Jewish aspect of it, was almost exclusively Ashkenazi. This was also true of the majority of Jews whom I noticed in the intellectual and political life of the 1950s and '60s. A little later, in the 1970s and '80s, those familiar with Trotskyist organizations such as Alain Krivine's Revolutionary Communist League, a number of whose leaders were Jewish, joked that they could have held their board meetings in Yiddish, which only Ashkenazi Jews speak, if there hadn't been a notable Sephardic exception in the person of Daniel Bensaïd, who came from a Jewish family from Oran. It was only much later that I discovered the Sephardic origins of Edgar Morin, who was a Salonica Jew – he speaks about it magnificently in his book *Vidal and His Family*.[2] Before that, I'd never have imagined that he wasn't Ashkenazi.

The existence of two great but separate traditions within Judaism often gives rise to polemical remarks, more or less humorous, which sometimes reflect a rivalry. One symptomatic illustration comes to me from a dentist who worked in the sixth arrondissement, in a neighborhood marked by a strong institutional Catholic presence – convents, places of worship, etc. This presence was on the decline, but still alive. I went to him as much for the pleasure of chatting as for my teeth, and we became friends. He always had good jokes to tell, which shows that a Sephardic dentist and an Ashkenazi sociologist can appreciate the same humor. The following joke is a true story, with one or two modifications to protect the anonymity of those involved.

> One day, a new patient knocks on the door of the dentist's office. The man, rather old, is a priest named Lévy. At first, the dentist doesn't ask him any questions, and the exchanges between them are limited to what is necessary for the dentist's work. The contact between them then becomes more frequent, and one day the dentist works up the courage to say:
>
> "'Lévy,' that's a surprising name for a man of the church. It's Jewish, not Catholic."
>
> "That's not a problem. I'm Jewish and Catholic. Before the war, I began to believe, and decided to convert to Catholicism; later I went to seminary, but decided not to break with my Jewish origins. And also to continue to accept myself as a Jew. And I became a priest."
>
> "Like Monseigneur Lustiger?!"
>
> The priest, losing his temper, retorts:
>
> "Not at all! Absolutely not! He's an Ashkenazi. I'm Sephardic!"

This story deals with two great branches of the Jewish world, and outsiders might find little interest in it. Monseigneur Lustiger[3] was someone who aroused complex and ambivalent feelings in Catholic circles, but also with Jews, especially those

from Central and Eastern Europe who immigrated in the inter-
war period, which was the case for my parents' circle of family
and friends. Alex Derczansky, a researcher at the CNRS – a
specialist in oral rather than written Yiddish – knew this universe well. Indeed, he's the only person I've ever known, aside
from my father and my paternal uncle, to have personally met
my paternal grandfather – in Strasbourg, he told me, probably
at the end of the 1930s – and to have told me a little about him.
Alex Derczansky was a friend of Monseigneur Lustiger. And
they liked to speak Yiddish together. He would have liked this
joke.

Can you convert to Christianity while remaining a Jew? In
the Iberian Peninsula or in Latin America, beginning in the
sixteenth century, the Marranos, forced to convert in order
to survive without emigrating, tried to live their Jewishness in
secret, within the familial realm. Traces sometimes remained
after very long periods. But this isn't the same thing as fully and
publicly taking on a double appearance. The issue, it seems to
me, can only interest a small number of people, as it is almost
theological in nature. I'll simply recall here that, for centuries,
the hatred of Jews, this stubborn people, "stiff-necked" as the
Torah calls them (in the Book of Exodus), was fed by their
refusal to convert to Christianity – a religion that, for its part,
viewed Judaism as deicidal. They killed Jesus: this affirmation
accompanied many pogroms and other massacres, especially
during the crusades; it operated not in a racial but in a religious
mode, even if the purity of blood statues, in a Spain determined
to get rid of the Jews, introduced a biological dimension, natu-
ralizing and thus racializing Jewishness.

The curiosity revealed by the joke I've just told resides in the
possibility that is offered today to important people, including
those at the highest levels of the ecclesiastical hierarchy, to be
explicitly and openly Jewish and Catholic at the same time. To
not have to choose. And also in the fact that this possibility
functions within a prelate that is mostly conservative. Because

even though he can in no way be lumped together with the reactionary minds of far-right Christianity, Monseigneur Lustiger waged war on the legacy of the Enlightenment. Jean-Louis Missika and Dominique Wolton, who interviewed him at length,[4] succeeded in bringing out the hostility toward the Enlightenment on the part of this anti-modern convert who remained explicitly Jewish.

The distinction between the Ashkenazi world, from which I hail, and the Sephardic world is interesting for at least two reasons. On the one hand, this is because of a change within the French diaspora: a stereotype (which deserves analysis) exists which posits that the leading figures of this diaspora, at least from an intellectual and artistic standpoint, were Ashkenazi until the 1990s or 2000s, and that this time has passed. This idea, however, is somewhat limited, and overlooks the contributions made by many people from old Sephardic communities, the Jews of the Pope, for instance, in the Comtat Venaissin in southern France – and on this topic I'll confine myself to referring to the work of the historian Pierre Vidal-Naquet, my former colleague at the École des hautes études en sciences sociales in Paris, a specialist on ancient Greece, and a tireless campaigner against torture during the Algerian War, against dictatorship, against Holocaust denial, and for a just peace in the Middle East. And on the other hand, it is because this distinction sheds a light (one that also deserves analysis) on the stages of development of the State of Israel, the origins of which, according to the same stereotype, were progressive, universalist, democratic, open, and also socialist as long as the dominant currents were of Ashkenazi origin, all of which is far less true today due to the predominance of Sephardim. This also calls for corrections that are anything but minor: in Israel, the massive presence of Ashkenazim from Russia, above all starting with Gorbachev's arrival in power, contributed to the rise of extremist or reactionary currents, and, in the history of the creation of the State of Israel, the purveyors of extremist nationalism were also, at times, Ashkenazi – Vladimir Zeev Jabotinsky, for example, an extreme-right figure in the Zionism of the 1920s and '30s and the main leader of the Irgun, whom David Ben Gurion, Prime Minister of Israel from 1948 to 1954 and again from 1955 to 1963, compared to Hitler, was born in Odessa, a major Ashkenazi city.

The joke about the priest Levy reflects a phenomenon whose importance should nonetheless not be exaggerated. It takes place within a universe of faith and religion in which the age-old tensions between Jews and Christians are abating because of the increasing compatibility of these groups. But it doesn't say a lot about the content and workings of the distinction between Ashkenazi Jews, who in France belong to a world that lost a great deal of its vitality from the 1970s until 2000, and Sephardic Jews, whose dynamism – whether from the standpoint of their group identity, their religiosity, or their support for the State of Israel – is clear. And it tells us even less about the way these two groups blend together in ways that are shifting, for instance with the appearance of numerous religious subdivisions within not only orthodox branches, but liberal and reformed ones as well. The distinction between Ashkenazi and Sephardic Jews reflects differences (which should not be exaggerated) that are ritual but also linguistic (Judeo-Spanish and other similar languages differ considerably from Yiddish), and even seems at times to oppose a culture that is Mediterranean and indeed maritime (from the standpoint of diet, for instance) to one that is European or continental. But this doesn't fully determine reality.

In both France and Israel in the 1960s and '70s, the arrival of Sephardic Jews, whose conceptions and values are somewhat distinct from those of Ashkenazi tradition, brought about changes. The joke about the priest emphasizes above all the existence of an image that has become a stereotype, that of a fault line running between the two groups. By making us laugh, it authorizes a kind of reconciliation between these groups.

But it is only partially a "Jewish joke" in the sense I'm using the term in this book: because it can be understood by two distinct audiences rather than just one, and because it does not confine the narrator to a single identity group – in this it is typical of "Jewish jokes," which require an audience that goes beyond the group to which the narrator belongs. It's simply that both of the groups in question here are Jewish, and each one is diverse in and of itself.

4

What Counts as a Jewish Joke and What Doesn't

One morning, a Jew drops his toast, on the buttered side, of course.

He anxiously wonders how he should interpret this sign. What is going to happen to him? He worries about it all day. And by the evening, he's so stressed that he decides to go see a rabbi to ask for some advice or an explanation. He asks his question in a state of worry. The rabbi plunges into his books, buries himself, looks in the Torah, the Mishnah, the Gemara, the Midrash . . . and after an hour, he finds the answer and triumphantly states: "I've got it! This morning, you buttered your toast on the wrong side!"

This joke, told to me by Michel Rocard, one of my best friends, a non-Jew to whom I mentioned that I was writing this book, sheds a light that reinforces or completes that of the watch jokes, and the one from the Sentier, the sale with receipt. Once again, there's a rabbi who steps in and tries to help a fellow Jew who is dealing with a difficult situation in his daily life. This joke has the added benefit of belonging to the realm of the absurd, which is typical of Jewish humor.

Everything we've just spoken about derived less from recent history than from the prehistory of the era of Jewish jokes. The reader already knows enough for me to be able to specify the meaning of this book before I jump right into this era. It's true that from time to time I'm trying to make people smile and even laugh by telling a few of these jokes, which I've carefully chosen from a repertoire of thousands. But in contextualizing them, in looking at them with a critical distance, in putting forth the analyses they inspire in me, I'm taking the risk of also making people sad, nostalgic, worried, or preoccupied. I also risk asking questions that are at once existential and historical about Jewish identity in today's world, its evolution over the last 75 years, and the way that all of us, whether Jewish or not, can try to respond.

In the United States, just as in France, Jewish jokes began to enter public life toward the end of the 1960s, becoming accessible to audiences that were not exclusively Jewish. They sprang neither from a humor destined to remain within the sole confines of the Jewish community, nor from anti-Semitism, which is still present in many jokes that only those driven by hate, contempt, conspiracy theories, or prejudice find funny. They really emerged in the 1970s, this time moving from West to East, and hence from America to Europe, but also from one shore of North America to the other; their audience reached its height at the end of the twentieth century, before going into a decline that may be irreversible.

Jokes, or humorous stories, whatever name we give them, are generally self-sufficient. They don't need to be contextualized to be understood at the moment they're told. This is why special pages or sections are set aside for them in certain newspapers and magazines, and why indeed in France an entire radio station, "Rires et chansons," has specialized in mediocre and occasionally anti-Semitic jokes. Recently I happened to tune into this station when a "joke" was being told about a serious car accident. It included a taxi passenger who was Jewish and thus, in this joke, stingy. She kept yelling even though she was stunned and wounded from the accident, but not because of the pain she felt: she was worried because the meter kept running, and insisted that it be stopped.

Where do Jewish jokes end and anti-Semitic jokes begin?

When we feel like telling a Jewish joke, it's because a specific context makes us think of it – an association of ideas, whether conscious or unconscious, is at work. When a group of friends gets together, jokes spring forth one after another; each person has one to add, which means the whole thing comes to resemble a chain, even though we don't know what's making up the links. At some point someone says he can never remember jokes, which means he can't contribute to the sequence. Is this a feature of his character, his personality? Perhaps he generally dislikes associating humor with anything deriving from his personal reality, his lived experience – or, if he does do this, he doesn't share it with others. Which doesn't prevent him from laughing at jokes told by others, indeed from being moved by these jokes, which call up memories, recollections of moments, events, people who are close to him.

The man or woman (though this is mostly a masculine genre, even if we're seeing more and more equality, here as elsewhere, between the sexes) who is good at telling jokes knows how to move those listening to them by giving the sense of being personally involved or concerned, in one way or another, sometimes to the point of including themselves. He or she shares not just the joke itself, but what it awakens, what it reminds people of, what it makes them think about. He or she has something in common with the listeners, and comes closer to them if only for a moment, unless they are already very close.

It happens, for example in English humor, that self-derision, which is so important in Jewish humor, also has a place in jokes of various origins. But in British jokes, this dimension presents something aristocratic, even imperial, while Jewish self-derision derives more from the life of common people.

Many jokes are based on stereotypes, and include a dose, even if only a small one, of malicious intent, contempt, or even hatred, which denigrates the target of the joke to increase the value of the one telling the joke and his audience – for Baudelaire, laughter always contains "a small share of meanness."[1] But this is not the case for Jewish jokes, whose humor should be distinguished from irony and all forms of "meanness."

Jokes that convey stereotypes based on hatred or contempt toward a group without distancing themselves from those sentiments are not part of the repertoire of that group. The Belgian jokes that flourished in France in the 1980s, whose main trait was to illustrate the supposed hopeless stupidity of their characters, didn't make Belgians laugh; Corsicans ignore jokes based on the stereotype of their laziness, just as the Scots do with jokes that describe them as tightfisted. As the comedian Pierre Desproges once said (this is also quoted by Daniel Grojnowski), "you can laugh about anything, but not with anyone."[2] Belgian, Corsican, or Scottish jokes essentialize their characters, which they reduce to a single trait (stupidity, laziness, stinginess), while Jewish jokes set forth a great diversity of issues and of human qualities or flaws, whether they deal with religion, everyday life, money, illness, business, food, marriage, or family (including the mother–son relationship), etc.

When the Soviet Union was in decline, and as some dissidents embodied the honor of thought and human rights, many political jokes, including Jewish ones, began to circulate, some of which eventually found some resonance in the West. But this was never due to the regime and its apparatchiks, or those satisfied by the compromises of the era: the population agreed to a tacit pact whereby it didn't ask too much of the regime, which ensured, come what may, that everyone's basic needs were fulfilled – jobs, food, housing, health, education, a few leisure activities, etc. In return, they agreed not to publicly criticize the system or those in power. And thus anti-Soviet jokes were, for those who enjoyed them, a way of discreetly taking an imaginary distance from an oppressive reality: laughing about it allowed them to put up with it more easily. A well-known mechanism is at work here, nicely described in the realm of popular culture by Richard Hoggart, an important professor of English Studies (and not sociology, as claimed by those, such as Pierre Bourdieu and Jean-Claude Passeron, who introduced his work to France), in a classic book entitled *The Uses of Literacy: Aspects of Working-Class Life.*

In France, these Soviet jokes enjoyed a certain success, linked above all to what turned out to be the collapse of communism and the communist party. This makes me think of an extreme example. In the mid-1970s, I attended one of Alain Touraine's classes; at the time, he was supervising my dissertation in sociology. At one point, he invited Louis Althusser, the star philosopher of Marxist structuralism and communism, to teach a class. Althusser was no fool. It would have been impossible for him not to perceive the decomposition of "real" communism in the East, and the decline of the communist party in France. Several times during this class, to the surprise of those in attendance, he told anti-Soviet and anti-communist jokes. A few years later, in 1980, he would assassinate his wife, manifesting in the most awful way a disturbance whose origins were certainly prior and foreign to the political developments of this era, but which found a means of expression in the context it provided.

Can a group take pleasure in laughing at itself, displaying its own stereotypes and difficulties of all kinds that weigh it down, without feeding or expressing hatred and contempt? Jewish jokes bring a positive and indeed spectacular response to this question, for, with them, a form of humor that is not necessarily tender toward Jews turns out to be acceptable not only among them, but also for non-Jews, so long as they are empathetic.

When a comedian places emphasis on his origins (with an accent, for instance) or his physical or cultural appearance (the color of his skin, for example), he opens himself to accusations of being alienated or self-hating, and of corresponding to racist ideas of his ethnic, racial, or national features. Of being the "non-threatening Black," for instance, who has interiorized the negative attributes that define him according to racist frameworks. Or, conversely, of provoking the indignation and wrath of the "politically correct." In the United States, the current success of stand-up comedians is in part due to Blacks who, in ironic gestures, make fun of racism by conforming completely to every possible cliché. But as an aptly titled article – "Stand-Up Gets Laughs but Walks a Fine Line" (December 26, 2019) – in the French newspaper *Libération* put it, it's a delicate exercise, and often it doesn't work out. In this regard, French comedians are surely in the lead when it comes to laughing at themselves (and making others laugh at them too) without giving in to self-loathing.

Jewish jokes can only be told by a Jew – if not, anti-Semitism soon surfaces. And becomes acceptable. In France, for instance, the comedian Popeck (his real name is Judka Herpstu), who spoke with a strong Jewish accent from Central Europe (which makes you think that he learned well from his familial milieu) made people laugh on stage in the 1960s, and then in the cinema in the 1970s, notably in Gérard Oury's 1973 film *The Mad Adventures of Rabbi Jacob*, in which he played the role of Moïshe Shmoll, the father of a boy preparing for his bar mitzvah. His character moans and groans and is incredibly tightfisted; his features are so exaggerated that we end up finding them touching. But if Popeck's sketches and numbers had been thought up by Jean-Marie Le Pen, founder of the Front National, they would be viewed as anti-Semitic, and rightly so. For Jewish and well-meaning non-Jewish spectators, Popeck generates a certain tenderness, a vague sense of complicity, through the sheer excess of his characters. No one sought to shut him down: on the contrary, he was embraced because of how he appropriated stereotypes by pushing them so far that they became absurd. But when the comedian Dieudonné, during a performance in 2013, said the following of a French radio host: "When I hear him speak, Patrick Cohen, I say to myself, you know, the gas chambers . . . too bad," his "humor" led the authorities to charge him with incitement to racial hatred, and to saddle him with a hefty fine three years later.

These are clear and obvious cases, but things are often more complex, which makes enjoyment more difficult. As Daniel Grojnowski writes: "When I was a teenager, I once laughed at a drawing by the cartoonist Siné published in *L'Express* during the Christmas holidays. It showed someone wearing an armband with a swastika, getting ready to put his Christmas chicken in the crematorium. I hadn't had the same experiences as my parents, who were immigrants from Central Europe, and had lost many family members in a crematorium."[3]

This story, and the drawing it deals with, remind me that, in 2009, the journalist Claude Askolovitch asked me to testify for him in a trial that was making a lot of noise in the media. The same Siné, in a column published in *Charlie Hebdo*, said the following of Jean Sarkozy, son of then–French president Nicolas Sarkozy: "He had just said that he wanted to convert to Judaism before marrying his fiancée, who is Jewish and one of the heirs to the Darty fortune.[4] This young man will go a long way in life!" The cartoonist rebuked Askolovitch for having unjustly accused him of anti-Semitism because of this statement. My testimony in support of the journalist had a real impact on the decision of the judges, who finally ruled in his favor. As he told me at the time, I no doubt helped him to avoid a lot of problems, including professional ones, by explaining that "the new anti-Semitism in France is based on the idea that Jews succeed in society while Arabs and Muslims don't." But I'm fully aware that the case of Siné, against whom a complaint has also been filed by LICRA (the International League against

Racism and Anti-Semitism) for incitement to racial hatred, should not be confused with the later one against Dieudonné. The cartoonist was an anarchist who was not to my taste, and this wasn't his first slide into anti-Semitism, but I would distinguish him from the extreme right.

The supposed "axiological neutrality" of the sociologist

This book is born out of a Jewish joke, the last Jewish joke, which I'll tell later. It's a joke that gave me a lot to reflect on. I started to realize that, in my own journey, the private and personal one but also my professional journey as a sociologist, jokes, and the humor of certain stories, had played a very significant role, to which I'd never paid attention. We usually consider everything funny as anecdotal. Sociologists try to give a broad view of things or to analyze them in detail, while jokes relax people at a surface level, for the time it takes to laugh. They don't belong to the realm of the serious and have no place in treatises and works in the social sciences, unless they themselves are the object of research. In this vein, David Le Breton has proposed an anthropology of laughter, or rather of the laugher [see e.g. https://www.booksfromfrance.fr/titles/3053.pdf?locale=en].[5] Others have reflected on ironic humor from a metaphysical or philosophical standpoint. In 1900, Henri Bergson developed a theory of laughter;[6] Sigmund Freud as well, at the beginning of the twentieth century, examined the relationship between witticisms and the unconscious[7] – a line of questioning that the father of psychoanalysis took up once again in his article "Humor."[8]

Bergson takes no interest in Jewish jokes, referring only to authors and works known to and accepted by his educated readership; nothing inflammatory or transgressive ever arises, even at the margins of his work. For him, laughing, when all is said and done, plays a role in social regulation. Unlike Bergson,

Freud is no conformist, dealing with that which gives rise to psychic conflicts, drives, and tensions, and how these can be resolved or at least warded off by laughter; he showcases jokes invented by Jews, and writes of witticisms thought up by non-Jews, which take Jews and their particularities as their object, that they are "for the most part examples of brutal foolishness." On the whole, Freud is not particularly interested in the social dimension of the Jewish jokes he mentions.

Jewish jokes as I have just defined them are invented by Jews – even if one can only rarely identify their author. They have nothing to do with foolishness or brutality. They are the very opposite of anti-Semitism.

I'm constantly recalling Jewish jokes and stories laden with Jewish humor, which are inseparable from my personal experience of a half-century of intellectual and professional engagement. I'm trying to think about the meaning of the emotion and the pleasure I feel when I hear them in good company. In real-life situations, they relate and solidify my belonging to a historical or intellectual collective, romanticized though this may be, as funny stories often do. But unlike most of these, the jokes and stories with which I'm dealing do not oppose the collective in reference to others: one of their functions is to authorize a certain integration into a broader universe, thanks to the relationship of understanding that they establish with those outside this collective.

For Jews from Central Europe before the Shoah, the written and spoken words, oral narratives, and books all formed a whole which both survivors and their immediate descendants took as a reference point; the Yiddish language was written and read, and infused spoken narratives with a means of expression, intonation, the thickness of reality and shared experience; when it was spoken, it was often accompanied by gestures that brought listener and narrator together. This richness is almost lost. Rare exceptions survive, like my friend, the singer Talila, to whom my mother loved listening.

All this belonged above all to the realm of common people. Even if, starting at the end of the eighteenth century, a small well-off fringe was able to constitute itself, and even if there existed Jewish courtiers and bankers, as well as a Jewish intelligentsia, European Jews were almost all poor and, indeed, destitute. They often formed a large proletariat in those places in Central Europe that were becoming industrialized, especially Poland. This is why the opposition between "pariahs" and "parvenus," so dear to Hannah Arendt, is questionable: it is more political and intellectual than social. The philosopher does not really take into consideration the working masses or small craftspeople who nonetheless constituted the vast majority. The Jewish jokes that resonate throughout this book make much more sense for the descendants of these categories than for others. Particularly in France, the children of poor immigrants from Central Europe appreciate them much more than the "Israelites" who had been present for a long time, and are more or less settled.

For a researcher in the social sciences and humanities, stories and writings that are laden with Jewish humor remind him that real life cannot be reduced to the analyses he might produce, especially as humor never appears in these analyses. Why not focus on social facts, cultural realities, and the movement of history in the light shed by humor – from the standpoint of what these humorous narratives and writings express, which allows one to see things, if not better, then at least differently? And at the same time, why not see in them the fruit of a history, of situations, of a social and political functioning that define their space and make their expression possible? These questions make it necessary to explain how I'm also concerned as a sociologist, and to demonstrate how I'm trying to at once articulate personal subjectivity as well as a concern for objectivity and rigor.

You'd have to be naive to think that research in the social sciences and humanities – and my research is no exception

– respects "axiological neutrality" as a dogma. This notion has been analyzed and developed much more than it has been adopted unequivocally by sociologists, including some of the most important, such as Max Weber and Norbert Elias. It means that the researcher must seek to avoid the bias that can arise from confusion between scientific judgment and an unconscious application of one's own values, opinions, and political orientations, among other factors. In truth, no researcher can remain unaware of the fact that his publications cannot express everything that he studies. A simple joke can say something that the researcher's requirement for complete neutrality forbids him to explore; it can inflect his analysis, complete his thoughts, and open up new perspectives.

The image of the researcher in the social sciences and humanities who takes a position of uncompromising exteriority with regard to his object is a delusion that holds fast in the same manner as an ideology, in the way Hannah Arendt defines it – as the pursuit of an idea. But humor often turns out to be particularly caustic. It causes things to shift, and at the same time it brings the narrator into the story he tells, giving it a depth that this narrative would otherwise lack. This is why, contrary to university protocol, I'm writing this book mostly in the first person singular. I'm moving between, on the one hand, my personal experience, my memories, things that have brought me joy and things that have disappointed me, and my subjectivity, all of which are products of, and at the same time produce, a history that includes a collective dimension, but also others that touch on my private life, and, on the other hand, my place as a researcher, a sociologist attentive, if not to "science," then at least to objectivity, rigor, and seriousness.

I would never have conducted my research on multiculturalism if I'd positioned myself in accordance with methods that are, admittedly, open, reasonable, and well thought out; nor would I have studied movements in which social demands blend with expectations of cultural recognition, as in certain regional struggles, or the Solidarność union, which was so profoundly attached to the Polish nation, if I hadn't been sensitized, in my family environment, to the experience of the Bund, the Jewish workers' movement in Lithuania, Poland, and Russia. In its time, the Bund was able to bring social and political engagement together with the affirmation of a Jewish culture, with its common language, Yiddish. A culture laden with humor.[9]

As such, if I have devoted many years to research on anti-Semitism and racism, it started from a personal experience in which, from very early on, I mixed what I'd learned from my family with my love of ideas, truth, and knowledge, with my integration in the French Republic and its secular schools, and a profound awareness of what produces the hatred of Jews. I nourished myself on all this, which is how I attained my sensitivity for everything that touches on alterity, collective life, history, and the personal experience of those who live all of this.

The Bund is a dreamlike reference insofar as there is almost nothing left of it in Paris, other than a club that is not always careful about sticking to the orientations that gave birth to it, or the collective vault in the Bagneux Cemetery where many of those who aligned themselves with it are buried. But this movement also brought another solution to the dilemma that often constituted the political horizon of diaspora Jews: Zionism or assimilation. It allowed people to participate in a Jewish movement that also took part in social struggles that transcended it without negating or invalidating it. It is appropriate for me to foreground all of this because of the role I played as a sociologist who participated, from the 1980s to the 2000s, in the public debate around multiculturalism, and who today participates in the debate around a "wokeness" that some claim is challenging the French Republic and its secularism – when in fact it seems to me, on the contrary, that it is the most engaged "anti-woke" who are proposing an inflexible vision, one that is ineffective because it is based on empty formulas. For a researcher in the social sciences, it is better to reflect upon what links him to his project than to demand an "axiological neutrality" that would obscure everything that might explain his interest for certain issues, and the methods and categories he employs to address them in a knowledge-producing process.

I recently read a booklet claiming that confusion arises when "activists without any academic qualifications are invited to take part in seminars." On the contrary, I've always found it useful to put my students in contact with social, political, and cultural actors who are engaged. Everyone comes out a winner because the exchange between such actors and researchers or students raises everyone's capacity for analysis. I've also found, in this misleading promotion of an "axiological neutrality" that would bring light to research through its supposed rigor, that I myself am an active contributor to the so-called influence of "Islamo-leftism"[10] in universities, and that I am "blind to context to the point of being incapable of differentiating between private and public." I dealt with these claims, which quickly turn sectarian and include *ad hominem* attacks, in a little book called *Racisme, antisémitisme et antiracisme*.[11] The fact remains that the problem is not one of "differentiating" private from public, which is within everyone's capability, but rather of considering the relationship between them, of going back and forth between them in an unconfused way, and of evaluating what makes up the relationship between the researcher and that which – or above all those whom – he studies. As Immanuel Wallerstein emphasized – in a very useful way, one that had a broad global impact – in his book *Open the Social Sciences: Report of the Gulbenkian Commission on the Restructuring of the Social Sciences*,[12] these disciplines are interested in humans, their interactions, their ability to debate what is said about them and what sometimes transforms them, at the same time as the researcher himself will likely undergo changes. The disciplines in question distinguish thought from action even as they examine their connections, neither sepa-rating them nor confusing them. This is why, in this book, I'm foregrounding the way my personal trajectory feeds my activi-ties as a researcher, and vice versa.

This book is not a collection of funny stories dealing with a specific theme – Jewish jokes, on which there is a considerable body of work, and whose humor goes back a long way – since this can already be found, for example, in Israel Zangwill's clas-sic and extremely funny 1894 novel *The King of the Schnorrers*. Its author, as social science researchers who specialize in immigration know well, is also behind the success of the term "melting pot," often used with regard to the integration of immigrants: this term was popularized by Zangwill's 1908 play *The Melting Pot*, and designates the mixture of ethnicities in a society in the process of cultural homogenization. In this regard, one can also cite, among other works, the three-volume collection, in Yiddish, written by Alter Druyanov in the inter-war period, and also, for work written in French, two books by Raymond Geiger: *Histoires juives* (1923) and *Nouvelles histoires juives* (1925).

The jokes and funny stories I'm considering offer a point of departure toward horizons other than that of mere laughter: they open a path to a reflection on memory (one that happens to be Jewish) but also to an understanding of the great develop-ments that for the past half-century have affected the world of the Jewish diaspora, including its relationship with the state of Israel. By evoking the jokes and funny stories that have moved me, I'm navigating between personal experience and sociological or historical analysis, and also between the child-hood and adolescence that shaped my personality, tastes, and interests, especially those that I inherited from my family and their circle of friends, and my adult life, which itself combines the hopes of yesterday and the depression that takes hold of me today when I think about the contemporary Jewish world, the anti-Semitism that affects the diaspora, or the developments in the State of Israel.

What remains when nothing remains

In the book for which she was awarded the Prix Femina for non-fiction, *Tombeaux*, my sister Annette Wieviorka reconstitutes what is known of our family history, on both the paternal and the maternal sides.[13] I descend from Jewish immigrants from Poland who arrived in France after the First World War fleeing desperate poverty, who were then decimated by the Nazis with the help of collaborators from the Vichy regime during the Second World War. My parents conceived me in 1945, and I'm the oldest of the siblings – whence, perhaps, my appreciation of jokes that feature Jewish mothers, for whom the eldest son takes precedence over all the other children. My education was based on values that were more republican and socialist than Jewish, and in any case was never religious, which gives me all the more liking for jokes that include a rabbi, and perhaps other members of the clergy, especially when their behavior includes some irreverence. This does not mean that my commitments in favor of secularism are antireligious. On the contrary, they are in line with everything that followed from the law of 1905, which guarantees freedom of conscience and religion. Along with Jean-Louis Bianco and Nicolas Cadène, I'm part of the collective that created the *Vigie de la laïcité*, the Monitor for Secularism, after the powers that be dissolved, in June 2021, the *Observatoire de la laïcité*, the Observatory for Secularism, despite the fact that it was very useful; one of the instigators of this destruction, Marlène Schiappa, who was then Secretary of State, became embroiled in a case of embezzlement of public funds, and exposed herself on the cover of *Playboy* in April 2023. This no doubt says something significant about the fight against "Islamo-Leftism."

Jewish consciousness is unique in that it has several dimensions: national (the feeling of belonging to a single people, a single nation); religious (but not necessarily); that which relates to Israel, and which runs from unconditional support for the Israeli government to anti-Zionist detestation; memorial; and related, finally, to the way others, especially those who are anti-Semites, regard it. It can thus assume different forms, depending on the person or changing with time in the same person. I'm obviously no exception.

I've always seen the universe of priests, pastors, imams, or rabbis as one that is foreign to my existence. In addition, up until 1967 and the Six-Day War, my family environment and my parents' circle of friends were, if not anti-Zionist, at least non-Zionist: Dany Cohn-Bendit, leader of the May '68 protests in France, sometimes uses the term "a-Zionist," and this is pertinent. From this derives my resistance to statements that associate, in an unnuanced way, anti-Semitism and anti-Zionism; such statements have always struck me as profoundly ideological, and I'll deal with them at greater length below.

Taking into account the non-religiosity and relative indifference to (if not outright rejection of) Zionism in this setting, and the distance it maintained from the State of Israel, it is clear that my integration into the Jewish universe arose from the cultural permeation of an almost-destroyed past: the Yiddish that my father Abraham (whose friends called him Aby, and who translated important Yiddish authors into French) and his brother Menahem (Méni) spoke perfectly, my mother not quite as well, and we children not at all, except for my sister Annette, who can get by; the more or less romanticized memories of what Jewish life in Poland had been like; rather mythical references to the Jewish worker's movement, the Bund, an important player in the social democracy of its time, and which articulated, as I've mentioned, proletarian struggle all the while that it affirmed a linguistic identity – because Yiddish was the language of a people.

The culture of this circle of family and friends was able to contain a vaguely nostalgic humor, more or less fanciful anecdotes that did not necessarily reveal any Polish anti-Semitism, only a past that was long gone. As such, my father claimed, with the assistance of multiple hand gestures, that in the village of his ancestors, the dairywoman sold crème fraîche "by the arm": she would dip a hand and forearm into a container full of cream, and then, using her other hand, slide it into the customer's jar. He also said – and again, the story does not reveal a supposed Polish anti-Semitism – that in the same village, or another, the Jewish community, at the end of a long discussion, held a vote to decide whether God existed. I never found out the result of this vote, which may remind people of the French Revolution and of Robespierre having people vote on the Decree of 18 Floréal (May 7, 1794), whose first article proclaims that "the French people recognizes the existence of the Supreme Being and the immortality of the soul."

But the culture of this milieu also, and above all, included the conviction that the Poles (the non-Jewish ones) were all anti-Semites; when I think back, I realize that I never noticed the same palpable hatred toward the Germans, from either the past or the present.

In 1981, when I told my parents that I was going to Poland to study the Solidarność union with my own eyes, they poured cold water on my enthusiasm: "What are you going to do in that country? Even your Lech Wałęsa must be an anti-Semite . . ." The result: in addition to the research I undertook with Alain Touraine, François Dubet, and several Polish friends and colleagues on this movement, which stood at the crossroads of democracy, an open conception of the nation, and a powerful social protest movement, and which filled me with enthusiasm, I threw myself into a personal investigation on Jewish life and anti-Semitism in that country. This response to the challenge given to me by the certainty of my

parents and their friends led to a book.[14] So don't come talk to
me about "axiological neutrality" when my research topics are
at stake!

As I mentioned earlier, in this familial environment, or close
to it, many people worked in the *schmattes*, the making and
selling of clothes, if you like, especially in the neighborhoods of
Les Halles and Strasbourg Saint-Denis, in a place in the middle
of Paris usually referred to at that time as Le Sentier. This
area was known for its strong Ashkenazi presence. So much so
that when, one day in the 1950s, the American uncle of some
friends of my parents, having arrived at Bourget Airport in
France, got into a taxi and uttered two barely comprehensible
words – *les Juifs*, "the Jews" (this was the extent of his French)
– the driver, without a moment's hesitation, drove him to the
Réaumur-Sébastopol metro station, stopped, and told him:
"This is it." My uncle looked around, and when he was able to
read, in a shop window, the name of his nephews, he knew he
had arrived. He wasn't even surprised.

This universe of the *schmattes*, which wasn't always vigilant
when it came to invoices and taxes, as we've seen, had new
life breathed into it thanks to the influx of Jews from North
Africa, not to mention other immigrants. These North African
Jews would later inspire the film *Would I Lie to You?*, which
tells a Sephardic story. Immigrants of the interwar period, like
my grandparents, clashed with the long-established Jews in
France, in Alsace, in Comtat Venaissin, in Aquitaine, and in
the Paris region. These Jews were quite well integrated. Their
descendants, and they themselves, are therefore less affected
by Jewish jokes when these arise from backgrounds that have
only just emerged from poverty and, indeed, destitution, and
when they appeal to a popular culture whose roots lie in the
life of Jewish communities from Central and Eastern Europe;
even though there does exist a specifically Alsatian tradition
of Jewish humor, the jokes and also the social position of their
protagonists aren't the same.

The universe of my grandparents was distinct from that of the descendants of Sephardim from Spain and Portugal, where, from 1492, they were persecuted and expelled, but it was even more distinct from the new arrivals brought by the decolonization of North Africa, or those who came from Egypt. It is mainly recent waves of immigration that nourish the image of an opposition between Ashkenazim, from Europe, and Sephardim, from the periphery of the Mediterranean basin and the Middle East, but also the Iberian Peninsula.

However, we must be very precise here, and avoid distinctions that are too easy. Each of these universes is itself diverse and varied. As such, in my family alone, even though I would sometimes hear nasty statements about Romanian Jews – supposedly the worst, all of them thieves! – or Lithuanian Jews – not much better! – it was always in a joking tone, and without ever having consequences. A nuanced approach to Ashkenazi humor, one that proceeds, for example, from country to country, or even city to city, reveals large differences. "Budapest humor," as Adam Biro explains in his remarkable *Dictionnaire amoureux de l'humour juif,* "was different from that of the shtetlekh,"[15] the inhabitants of Jewish villages in Poland, and he also points out that there was barely any German Jewish humor, because German Jews were already very assimilated. And also because, to take up once more the distinction proposed by Bernard Lazare[16] and popularized by Hannah Arendt,[17] they were "parvenus" rather than "conscious pariahs": social divisions, if we admit that these "pariahs" were generally poor or not very well off, are also a determining factor in Jewish humor, which, to repeat, is first and foremost a humor of the common people. Allow me to add, and Biro invites us to do just this, that we should, in the same way, take note of differences between forms of Sephardic humor from one place to another: to take only one example, Egyptian humor differs from that of people from the Maghreb.

5

The Heyday of Jewish Jokes in France

Here's a dialogue from the film *The Mad Adventures of Rabbi Jacob*, in which an industrialist, Pivert, discovers that his driver, Salomon, is Jewish:

> *"As for me, I'm Jewish."*
> *(Victor Pivert, stunned, after a few moments of silence:)*
> *"You're Jewish? How's that, Salomon, you're Jewish?"*
> *(Salomon confirms with a nod.) "Salomon is Jewish! Oh!"*
> *"And my Uncle Jacob, who's coming in from New York, is a rabbi."*
> *"But he's not Jewish?"*
> *(Salomon, slightly amused:)*
> *"Of course he is."*
> *"But not your family?"*
> *"Yes they are!"*
> *(Victor Pivert, in a resigned tone:)*
> *"Oh my . . . Listen, it doesn't matter, I'll keep you on regardless."*

The venerable old model of the French Republic, which began with the Revolution, began to weaken at the end of the post-war period, in the mid-1970s. It can be defined by a central principle: within the public realm, only individuals who are free and have equal rights can be visible. A famous statement made in December 1789 by the count of Clermont-Tonnerre, a deputy from the nobility, resumed the implications of this for the Jews of France: in order to emancipate them, it is appropriate to refuse them everything "as a nation" (as a community) and to accord them everything "as individuals." Starting from the 1970s, and for about thirty years, the crisis, perhaps best referred to as the destructuring, of this model coincided with an increasing visibility of Jewish identity. For them, this took place in a positive climate, one of confidence; they had the feeling that they were living through good times.

Gérard Oury's 1973 film *The Mad Adventures of Rabbi Jacob* is especially revealing of this climate. This comedy, whose main star is Louis de Funès, features several Jewish characters, but also a rather racist and typically French industrialist, Victor Pivert – played by Funès – who disguises himself as a rabbi to avoid someone who is out to kill him. The adventures of this character are extraordinary, but, from our standpoint, the most interesting element is the fact that this film portrays, without meanness and in a burlesque style, a Jewish universe (baroque though it may be), Jewish characters, and a France that is discovering this Jewishness (a far-fetched one) and accepting its visibility. Gérard Oury's film is certainly not a Jewish joke, but it nicely shows the mutation whereby French Jews appear as figures who have their place in society, and allows people to understand that an enchanted ecumenism with Arabs is possible.

The Mad Adventures of Rabbi Jacob was released on October 18, 1973, while the Yom Kippur War, between the Israeli and Arab (Syria and Egypt) armies, began on October 6, a year after the terrorist attack of September 5 and 6, 1972, which targeted Israeli athletes during the Olympic Games in Munich. Its director received threats, phone calls, and anonymous letters, and a drama unfolded when Danielle Cravenne, wife of the film's publicist, convinced that he supported Israel, which went against her convictions, hijacked a plane to make her indignation known, and was then killed by French gendarmes during a layover at Marseille Airport. This didn't take away from the film's success – it sold more than 7 million tickets – and Louis de Funès explained several times that the film changed him: "This film," he declared upon its release, "did me a lot of good, because I held a few very small anti-Semitic ideas. I must still have a few. It cleansed my soul." The actor's confession reflects the changes taking shape in entire sections of society.

To the sources of Jewish humor in France

Since that time, a not inconsiderable amount of writing has been devoted, in France, to Jewish humor: a search on the database of the French National Library brings up about forty separate works,[1] a list that is in fact not exhaustive, as one would have to add, for example, the writing of Gérard Rabinovitch on Jewish humor, an "art of the spirit," as he calls it,[2] and also the already-cited *Dictionnaire amoureux de l'humour juif* by Adam Biro, not to mention the bibliography at the end of this book.

One of the interesting aspects of this list is that it reveals a peak in the production of this critical literature. One can note that from time to time, in France as in the United States, a rabbi, such as Marc-Alain Ouaknin, publishes a book that has a place in a bibliography such as this one: humor forms part of what representatives of the Jewish religion are able to convey and transmit, and it seems to me that no other religion is willing to take this risk. This is of vital importance, especially if we think about it from the standpoint of the terrible suffering and tragedy that have accompanied this religion from the beginning.

One observes a great deal of publishing activity in the second half of the 1990s, which is certainly the apex of the interest level for the genre of Jewish humor. This phenomenon resembles what was just said about the United States, and took place at the same time, but with significant differences.

There is, first of all, and this is also something I could have discussed earlier, concerning the American experience, a long tradition of humor in Jewish culture in general. Not in the Bible, even if, for Marc-Alain Ouaknin and Dory Rotnemer,[3] laughter played a decisive role in the early days of the Jewish people, since the time when Abraham (at the age of 100) learns that his wife Sarah (aged 90) is pregnant, and he begins laughing. Not with the prophets, aside, perhaps, from a few very rare exceptions evoked by Léon Algazi.[4] On the other hand, the "old rabbis," as Algazi explains, "invented the parable (*aggadah, midrash*), which is the forerunner of the 'good joke,' and the biting or allusive aphorism, of which most Jews who today make clever turns of phrase are the inheritors, even though they may not realize it. The rabbis of the Talmud also delighted in puns. But never for their own sake, or for the vain pleasure of assonance ... In their hands, wordplay always served to catechize, to instruct, and often had deep significance." This is therefore a humor with real density, one that is meant to last, which is also demonstrated by the many pearls of wisdom from the Talmud, as Ami Bouganim notes: if the Sages "put God on their side, it was so that they could be crafty with His word and interpret it as they saw fit. They excluded His voice from their debates – that is, from their religious malice, and the pleasure they derived from having fun with Him."[5] And he continues thus: "Since humor was the sole recourse against the seriousness that threatens to imprison the spirit within pernicious and deadly religious doctrines, the disciples of the sages continuously cultivated it ... Humor is at once the expression of man's sublimeness and his moderateness."[6]

The humor of Jewish jokes is in many regards rooted in the Talmud, and hence in a history that owes a great deal to wandering, exile, and persecution. It allows people to distance themselves from the collective experience of a unique destiny, as well as from the individual experience of this or that difficulty. Its main property is that of inversing or overturning obstacles or misfortune in an imaginary way. It takes stock of problems and tragedies in a lucid but ultimately comforting manner. Talmudic heritage is never so clearly present as in those jokes in which one or several characters reveal an unlimited capacity for splitting hairs and reasoning in complex ways, which is the fruit, as Judith Stora-Sandor puts it nicely, of an "acquired mental habit of being truly incapable of solving even the smallest problems in life without engaging in almost obsessive speculating."[7]

In a more general way, this humor – which, while it is usually far from vulgar, does not exclude vulgarity, as we saw in the joke about the restaurant – reveals positive common traits of the Jews it features: a great capacity for self-derision, logical thinking, incredible but rigorous feats of reasoning, and a sense of the absurd, potentially pushed to the extreme. For a very long time, Ashkenazi Jews, whether religious or not, have loved telling *witz* – this is the German term that Freud uses in the title of the work I've cited above, and Yiddish is very often close to German. We enjoy telling them in family settings, during celebrations, or with friends. Many *witz* originate in Hasidism: it bears repeating that this broad mystical movement born in the eighteenth century was no stranger to a certain humor. And while the founding spirit of Jewish jokes comes to us from the East, from Central Europe and eventually, for France, by way of a detour through the United States, there is also a Sephardic tradition of humor. André Nahum, for instance, speaks of a humor that he qualifies as Judeo-Arab, of which he has recorded many expressions.[8] In a like manner, Muriel Klein deals with the situation of "Noktas," humorous stories that convey a pragmatic vision of the world and often find value in improvisation, among immigrants from the Maghreb.[9]

The apex of the genre of Jewish jokes, which, in France, arrives at the end of the twentieth century, resembles that of the United States, without, however, corresponding to it exactly. These are jokes that Jews themselves take pleasure in telling, or hearing, and today they do so without worrying about expressing themselves in public as Jews, which in France indicates a break from what had been the dominant model, a purely and classically republican model; Anglo-Saxon countries, on the other hand, are much more open to communities expressing themselves as such.

Jews and the Republic

Until the 1970s, French Jews conformed to the ideal resumed by Clermont-Tonnerre's famous statement, which I cited above. The dominant view at the time was one of assimilation, which reduced Jewishness to a strictly private affair, the insistence that Jews should be able to practice their religion. Which they did with relative discretion. This was when Jews in France were referred to as "Israelites," a term that has practically disappeared from our vocabulary.

Support for the Republic took on an extreme form among those whom Pierre Birnbaum has qualified as "Jews of the Republic,"[10] those "state Jews," as he calls them, who are passionate about politics, and throw themselves into the political realm as citizens, not as Jews. So long as this model retained its hegemony, there was no space for Jewish jokes, as we have defined them, to flourish – no public space, in any case. Who, aside from anti-Semites, would tell them, and who would listen to them, when the public sphere was supposed to be composed exclusively of individuals who were free and had equal rights, with no recognition of any particular groups or identities?

The assimilationist republican model was not transformed by the Second World War. Nor was it transformed, and my sister Annette deals with this in one of her books,[11] in the years following the war, at least so long as the consciousness and memory of the destruction of the Jews of Europe was confined, as it were, within appropriate limits, because French society preferred to focus on the Resistance, whether Gaullist or communist, rather than accounts of what was not yet called the Shoah. There was certainly humor and *joie de vivre* among the survivors, not to mention lively forms of collective life and a strong interest in politics, but a broad circulation of Jewish jokes, beyond their home turf, wasn't on the agenda.

Toward the end of the 1950s, however, it became clear, as we can see in hindsight, that a change was about to take place. In 1957, the first annual colloquium of French-speaking Jewish intellectuals was launched, spearheaded by the poet and writer Edmond Fleg, with the hope that its participants would distance themselves from postwar pessimism, and rekindle a Judaism capable of mobilizing Jews who had drifted away from it, such as Vladimir Jankélévitch. It aimed, among other things, as Françoise Schwab explains in her preface to a collection of essays by Jankélévitch, "to foster a conversation among the participants, who were for the most part assimilated or not religious in their daily lives, around specific Talmudic issues."[12] These colloquiums of Jewish intellectuals lasted until the early 2000s. They contributed in important ways to the birth of shifts in ideas, and to the vitality of debates, which flourished in the 1960s and, even more, in the 1970s, and heralded profound transformations among French Jews.[13]

When André Schwarz-Bart's novel *The Last of the Just*[14] was published in 1959, it received a favorable response that contributed to a rising awareness, on previously unimaginable levels, of the genocide of the Jews. This novel, for which Schwarz-Bart was awarded the Prix Goncourt, is a saga, the story of a Jewish family that produces an exceptional person – a "Just Man" – every generation, the last of whom dies in a concentration camp. There is obviously no place for humor in this book, but its enormous impact, in France and abroad, contributed to opening up the space in which Jewish jokes would develop, as it bears witness to a nascent memorial, intellectual, and moral ferment that would be propitious for them.

Up to that point, it had been possible to trace a specifically Jewish humor in various writings, films, and plays. But their Jewishness was discreet, aimed at a public who knew what to look for, people in the know who were liable to understand and even see themselves in humoristic borrowings from Jewish culture. Indeed the very term "Jewishness" dates from this period, owing its use and, it seems, its very existence to the Jewish-Tunisian sociologist Albert Memmi, and his book *Portrait d'un juif* [*Portrait of a Jew*].[15]

I personally reserve a special place for Pierre Dac, to whom the Museum of the Art and History of Judaism dedicated an exhibition in 2023. In the 1950s, our family loved listening to his radio show "Malheur au barbu" ["Woe betide the bearded one"]. Later, in high school, I was part of a small group of friends who passionately read the writings of this humorist. For example, we knew his novel *Du Côté d'ailleurs et réciproquement* by heart. At the time, I would never have discerned the slightest trace of Judaism in his work, nor made the slightest connection with the world of my family and friends. And I was unaware of all the anti-Semitic attacks of which he had been the target, especially by the Vichy propagandist Philippe Henriot, when Dac was an important voice of the French Resistance speaking from London on the BBC during the Second World War. It was to him that I owed a grade that wasn't too humiliating on an oral exam when I was at the Lakanal high school, taking preparatory business school courses. Through a process of drawing lots, I'd been given the subject "A great contemporary

French author," and I had nothing to say until an idea came to me – Pierre Dac! I adored my teacher, Monsieur Sémolué, and I knew he had a sense of humor. When I was called, after an hour of preparation, I discussed the work of this humorist, which I knew perfectly. The teacher asked me for an example of his humor, and I mentioned a "help wanted" ad in *L'Os à moelle*, the magazine that Dac had founded before the war and later relaunched, in which a nightclub announced that it was looking for a watchman who could work days. Monsieur Semolué asked if I found that funny, and I told him to look around the classroom, where students awaiting their turn were cracking up. He decided to give me ten out of twenty: twenty for the packaging and zero for the content. Today, Pierre Dac's Jewishness is obvious, associated with his past as a great resistance fighter as well as his humor, whereas a half-century ago, it was unknown and unperceived.

Other humorists deserve to be mentioned here, such as Francis Blanche, Pierre Dac's partner on the radio and in the classic sketch "Le Sâr Rabindranah Duval," or even comic book stars from the 1960s to 1980s, the writer René Goscinny and the illustrator Marcel Gotlib. Goscinny was always extremely reserved about his Jewishness, but his jokes, from *Les Dingdodossiers* to *Asterix*, are suffused with Jewish humor.[16] In 2014, an exhibition at the Museum of the Art and History of Judaism was devoted to Gotlib and his "Rubriques-à-Brac,"[17] with all their references to Jewish humor, to the absurd, to self-derision, to death, and even, from time to time, to the Shoah (see also his comics *God's Club* or *Superdupont*). Another exhibition feted Goscinny in 2018, providing an occasion for certain lovers of intrigue to make far-fetched hypotheses about the Jewish origins of the village of Asterix: isn't it in fact, they wondered, a copy of or a metaphor for the shtetl?

Gotlib and Goscinny are paradigmatic of an era that was just about to end, in which Jewishness could only be manifested privately. Their humor thus does not present itself as Jewish, even though it is suffused with Jewishness. But Gotlib also belongs to the following period, and, of these two authors, it is he who is most explicitly Jewish. He is a hinge between two eras, whereas his mentor, Goscinny, fades into the background, more connected with the classic republican model. If their relationship to Jewish humor is not the same, this is perhaps also due to the fact that they do not belong to the same generation.

A new sequence

Starting in the 1960s, French Jews developed a new formula, all their own, whereby a strong visibility, both individual and collective, was tied permanently to the Republic. I've always found it astounding that a large number of sensible people, who are interested parties in or friendly toward this Jewish renewal that brings together the practices and values of their own community with an unquestioned attachment to the Republic, completely obscure a significant section of this formula when they speak about politics, namely the one that has to do with community. How can they not see that, if there's one group in France that thinks of itself as a community, it is the Jews – which does not prevent the vast majority of them from being ardent supporters of republican values?

In France, it is possible to send your children to schools that align themselves with the Jewish community, to spend time in and enliven places associated with Jewish culture, to listen to a Jewish radio station (the first, Radio J, was created in 1981), to try to rekindle or to promote Yiddish when possible, to organize the annual dinner of CRIF (the Representative Council of French Jewish Institutions, an umbrella organization), which is an important display of institutionalized Jewish life, without there being the slightest risk of anyone accusing you of separatism. The situation of Islam is very different! It is also possible to belong to a community, the Jewish one, that maintains powerful links, at least symbolic and emotional ones, with another country, Israel, without giving rise to any suspicion of treason – the Dreyfus Affair, from this standpoint, thankfully belongs to the distant past. Muslims, again, are in a very different situation.

My colleague and friend Farhad Khosrokhavar – an expert on Islam in Iran, where he followed the religious revolution from up close, but also in the Arab world and in France – and I have termed this hybrid model "neorepublican."[18] Since the 1970s, French Jews, while continuing to forcefully align themselves with republican values, have become, of their own doing, visible in the public space. They assert themselves in their religious and cultural difference, their relationship with Israel, and their ability to take action to confront anti-Semitism. Until the end of the 1990s, everything they did served to transform the myth of assimilation into the reality of a rather successful integration.

If France's Jewish population was able to truly come to life at the end of the 1960s and the beginning of the 1970s, this is due largely to new dynamics brought by the Sephardim, who left North Africa in the period of decolonization. These new arrivals enlivened a Jewish world that until then had been much more concerned with discretion, and more or less doubled the size of this world – about 230,000 Jews from Algeria, Tunisia, and Morocco arrived in France at this time, and we can add to them the several thousand Jews who came from Egypt in the same period. Since then, the figure of 500,000 is often given when people speak about the Jewish population in France.

One day, I received a slap on the wrist from the psychiatrist and psychoanalyst Alice Cherki for having written in the journal *Traces*, in the 1980s, that Jews from the Maghreb, because they hadn't experienced the Shoah perpetrated by the Nazis, brought with them a certain confidence in life, and a palpable *joie de vivre*. She was not wrong to recall the pogroms and massacres of Jews in this part of the world, like the 140 Jews killed during the riots in Tripoli in 1945. Not to mention the anti-Semitism of French colonists, the "anti-Jewish crisis" of 1895–1900, the calls to repeal the Crémieux Decree, which accorded French citizenship to the "indigenous Israelites" of Algeria starting in 1870, or the election of Drumont as deputy for Algiers in May 1898. We could also consider the brutal and repugnant acts of Pétain in Algeria – the philosopher Jacques Derrida had very strong words about the violence of the politics of Vichy, which stripped his family of French citizenship for two years. But it seems to me, and this is how I responded to Alice Cherki, that none of this is really comparable to the systemic and genocidal destruction experienced by the Jews of Europe.

At the end of the 1960s and beginning of the 1970s, the growing awareness of the nature of the Nazi genocide and the responsibility of the Vichy regime gave French Jews a form of protection and a sense of security: never again should such horrors be allowed to take place. It also allowed people to take stock of the resilience of the Jewish people, which is perhaps what is expressed in the following joke. I take it from George Steiner, who told it on the radio station France Culture during an interview with Laure Adler.

> *One day, God summons a priest, a pastor, and a rabbi, to warn them that in 48 hours a deluge will destroy everything.*
> *The priest prepares to invite all Catholics to pray with him.*
> *The pastor (it's an American joke) prioritizes the idea that everyone must put their finances in order.*
> *The rabbi confirms that nothing will happen for 48 hours, and says: that's not much time, but it should be enough to learn how to swim before it all begins.*

This joke illustrates how rabbis embody the refusal of metaphysics and good sense, but it's also a way of emphasizing the ability of the Jewish people to survive awful tragedies for more than two thousand years.

In a context in which a surge of countercultural movements, but also those with a basis in identity (such as regionalist movements), was accompanied by protests comparable to those seen in the United States (feminist, antinuclear, environmentalist, antiracist), followed by the creation of SOS Racisme and the March for Equality and Against Racism in 1983 (sometimes called the March of the Arabs), French Jews began not only to appear in the public sphere, but also to hold Vichy to account. The trials of Klaus Barbie in 1987, of Paul Touvier in 1994, and of Maurice Papon in 1997–8, by integrating memory, history, and justice, contributed to bringing them a certain sense of security.

Another reason for which they felt confident about the future was their enthusiasm for the existence and success of the State of Israel. In my own family (which, as I've said, was socialist and Bundist), and among my numerous leftist friends (who were fervently pro-Palestinian at the time), as well as among the communists, there had been very little sympathy for the Hebrew state up to then. The image of Israel was basically that of a country where fruit, vegetables, and flowers were grown in the desert, where kibbutzim are concrete realizations of the socialist utopian ideal, and where a population that Hitler wanted to wipe from the earth was coming back to life. But none of this was enough to put an end to the indifference and "a-Zionism" of some, or the combative anti-Zionism of others (who were less numerous but more politicized).

And yet, when the Israeli army emerged victorious in the Six-Day War, the Hebrew David triumphing over the Arab Goliath, many socialist and communist Jews suddenly found themselves supporting the Israeli state, since they were panicked by the specter of another mass destruction, which suddenly seemed possible. In this context, General de Gaulle's famous remarks about the Jewish people – "an elite people, sure of themselves and domineering" – during a press conference in November 1967, aroused keen worries among French Jews, as well as sharp criticisms, even from an intellectual as moderate as Raymond Aron. The illustrator Tim nicely summed up the indignation of many Jews with a drawing in which a Jew who is "sure of himself and domineering" is represented as a deportee, wearing striped pajamas and displaying a yellow star, proudly treading on the barbed wire of the camp in which he is imprisoned. The cartoon was refused by *L'Express*, Tim's employer, and was published as a guest contribution by *Le Monde* on December 3, 1967. This was a time, and not only among Jews, when admiration for the State of Israel was largely prevalent, as was rejection of anti-Semitism, suspicion for which would weigh heavily on de Gaulle – an unjust suspicion, despite the words cited above.

A dynamic diaspora

The terrorist attack during the Olympic Games in Munich in 1972, when Israeli athletes were assassinated by a Palestinian commando group, was viewed as repulsive by a broad political spectrum, from the right to the extreme left, including socialists and communists. Speaking in relative terms, many Jews were members of leftist organizations. One of the most radical of these, La Gauche prolétarienne, even as it was moving toward clandestine acts and terrorism, as was later explained by its leader Alain Geismar,[19] decided, a few months later, in favor of its own dissolution, largely because of the indignation that this attack aroused in the group's leaders. Furthermore, an important figure in the French Communist Party, Roger Garaudy, ended up embracing Holocaust denial after being dismissed from the Party; this was just one step in his slide toward the extreme right.

The Second Vatican Council, which met between 1962 and 1965, sought to put an end to the Catholic doctrine of hatred, rejection, and persecution of Jews. I can still see my father reading Jules Isaac's book *The Teaching of Contempt* [*L'Enseignement du mépris*], and I recall the importance that those in his milieu accorded to this writer, who until then had mostly been known as the co-author of the "Malet and Isaac" history manuals that were used by my entire generation, and others as well. Isaac's influence on the evolution of the Catholic Church was considerable, and much appreciated by progressive Jews. Indeed, Isaac had been influential since the end of the Second World War. For instance, he agreed to write the introductory report for the international conference of the Council of Christians and Jews, which opened on July 30, 1947, in Seelisberg, Switzerland, with the aim of contributing to harmony between Jews and Christians – a project that Pope Puis XII, unlike his successors, declined to support.

Almost everything during these years seemed to herald a rather happy ending to the century for French Jews. Conditions allowed them to feel encouraged to assert themselves without fear, and express themselves in the public realm by displaying a collective identity that bore witness to their resiliency. At the heart of the diaspora, one could see a truly identity-based movement; not satisfied with merely denouncing the recent tragedy of the Shoah, it also showcased its political and social existence, its culture, literature, and religion, a country of reference, and a capacity for action that offset its tendency to isolate itself in a "tearful" history.[20] A great many works bear witness to this vitality; journals and magazines were born, such as *Traces*, which I've just mentioned, and *Pardès*, created by the historian Annie Kriegel. In both cases, my sister Annette was one of the founders. The institution to which I belong, the École des hautes études en sciences sociales, the EHESS, at the instigation of its president, the historian François Furet, decided to develop a program in Jewish studies, beginning with a visiting chair allocated by the Fondation du judaïsme français, and, in 1995, transforming what had been a mere team, or group, into a full-fledged research center. Cultural institutions appeared and developed, including within my family's Ashkenazi universe: my father and a few of his friends decided, in 1962 or 1963, to create a youth movement, the CLEJ, Club laïque de l'enfance juive, which, in the 1970s, 1980s, and beyond, invited young people to summer camps at the Château de Corvol-l'Orgueilleux, in the Nièvre; their success was impressive, and their reputation soon went beyond the one accorded to them by their location.

Support for Israel reached new levels, with, for example, large demonstrations, such as the "Twelve Hours for Israel" in Paris on May 30, 1976, in which tens of thousands of people participated. Its organizer, the lawyer Henri Hajdenberg, who at the time headed the Jewish Renewal [*Renouveau juif*] movement, would later, from 1995 to 2001, become president of the Representative Council of French Jewish Institutions. A commission to study the despoliation of French Jews under the occupation, presided over by Jean Mattéoli, was established by the prime minister, Alain Juppé, in March 1997. It essentially led to a framework for reparations, and, most importantly, to the creation of the Foundation for the Memory of the Shoah, whose funding, which comes from plundered Jewish goods that could not be returned to their rightful owners, is used to support all sorts of projects tied to the main objectives of French Jews: research, memory of the Jewish genocide, teaching, culture, aid for survivors, the fight against anti-Semitism, as well as intercultural dialogue, and the need to remember other genocides.

Another complex phenomenon was at play alongside this new visibility of the Jewish community, because a difference started to emerge in the 1970s and 1980s between younger generations, who would potentially have liked to learn more about the past, and older generations, who haven't always been very forthcoming. Often, Jewish children born after the Second World War experienced, throughout the diaspora, a feeling of being confronted, if not by silence, at least by "an atmosphere," as Muriel Klein has written, "that blends things that go unsaid, snippets that are overheard or hunted down, and sometimes confidences about the past," which has ended up forming "a hollow identity."[21] A neat categorization of periods would perhaps allow us to discern an initial period, immediately after the war, when many survivors would have liked to speak, but when society wasn't ready to hear them; then a phase when they were silent, taciturn; and finally a sort of awakening in the 1980s and 1990s, or indeed later. As such, my uncle, Roger Perelman – and his case is in no way out of the ordinary – waited until the 2000s to discuss his personal experience of the Shoah, both with his family and in public in the *Le Monde*, and then in the form of a book, the second part of which, devoted to Auschwitz and its liberation, comprises some truly important writing.[22]

Following the attack on October 3, 1980, a Friday evening and, what is more, the day of the Jewish holiday Simchat Torah, in front of the synagogue on the rue Copernic in Paris, which left four people dead and almost fifty wounded, an enormous rally brought together almost 200,000 people between the Place de la Nation and the Place de la République. Virtually everyone present believed it was an extreme-right anti-Semitic attack, which resulted in the police following leads that went nowhere, such as that of the FANE, the Fédération d'action nationale et européene, a small group founded in 1964 by dissidents from the Occident movement. Few heeded the words of the historian Annie Kriegel, who immediately, and correctly, raised the possibility that the attack had been carried out by people of Middle Eastern origin. But what I found most striking back then was the fact that many of the slogans in the demonstration were clearly shouted by Jews: "The Jews are in the street," went one of them, which means that the participants spoke as specifically Jewish actors in the fight against anti-Semitism. They were no longer invisible. They expected a lot from the Republic, from the law-based state, and from democracy, but from that point on, they acted as Jews, and not just as citizens. I was also struck on that day by the visibility of Freemasons, many of whom, including, apparently, some who were very highly placed in the organization, wore Masonic dress.

Overnight on May 8–9, 1990, thirty-five Jewish graves were desecrated in the Carpentras cemetery, including one body that was taken out of its casket and is believed to have been impaled. This caused an immense emotional reaction. Jean-Marie Le Pen's Front National, despite denouncing the act, was almost unanimously viewed as guilty, though the accusations against them turned out to be unjust. A demonstration was planned in Paris, to be held next to the Great Synagogue, and the religious authorities sought to ensure that it not be politicized. In the end, under pressure from the French president, it became a march that followed the traditional route of the left, République–Bastille. François Mitterand attended, and became the first sitting president of the Fifth Republic to attend a demonstration.

From the 1970s to the 1990s, the Jewish movement in France was the product of the dynamism of a diaspora that felt things were going rather well, despite the fear of anti-Semitism awoken or amplified by the attack on the rue Copernic. This feeling was clear and explicit. In 1975, for example, Richard Marienstras, an important activist thinker on the left and a university professor who specialized in the work of Shakespeare, published *Être un peuple en diaspora*,[23] exemplary of a larger movement of mostly democratic self-assertion by people with a strong cultural identity. This sense of wellbeing was, of course, relative, since it did not lose sight of the genocide of the Jews, which was still very fresh, or of anti-Semitism, the specter of which was always present. And people beyond the

Jewish world were truly fascinated by it, to such an extent that one writer, Olivier Revault d'Allonnes, spoke of "being a goy in the diaspora"[24] – a goy, in Yiddish, as I remind the reader, means a non-Jew.

I experienced this fascination in my own personal milieu, among the people who at the time were my in-laws: the discovery of a universe that had been unknown, or almost unknown, until then sometimes leads to a keen and sudden love for Jews, because it provides a meaning that had been lacking up to that point. When you've been raised in a world in which all you know about Jews comes from the timeworn Christian prejudice conveyed by religious education, and suddenly you discover the Shoah in all its horror, but also the vitality of Israel and the cultural dynamism of the diaspora, not to mention the participation of many Jews in the revolutionary leftist activity that followed May '68 (where many chanted "We are all German Jews"), it's easy to engage in self-reproach. This also takes the form, among certain people, of philosemitism, many variations of which can turn out to be muddled and indeed troubling. I should note that my in-laws were always marvelous, and could never be classified among those for whom, as Illana Weizman writes, "hatred and pathological amazement issue from the same place."[25]

In the veritable flourishing of this identity-based activity, Jewish humor had a very clear and visible place, often found in political debates and also in literary, artistic, and intellectual life. The energy behind all of this derived precisely from the fact that Jews did not content themselves with evoking the genocide, or with taking Israel as their only reference point. They displayed a real positivity, and did not give in to the "tearful" character of their collective history, or to the externality of an experience whose meaning would always lie elsewhere, in the Middle East.

I spent this period in contact with an Ashkenazi universe, but I have to repeat that the Sephardic world is anything but foreign to this ability to laugh at oneself and make non-Jews laugh, benevolently, at the same time. Examples of this include the success of films such as *The Big Pardon* and *Would I Lie to You?*, both of which I've already mentioned, and of comedians such as Élie Kakou or Michel Boujenah, both Jews of Tunisian origin. It would perhaps be necessary to push the analysis further and take stock of what distinguishes Ashkenazi humor from Sephardic humor, if only in certain of their historical references; the fact remains that, if France differs from the United States in this regard, it is in part because of what Sephardic Jews have brought to the Jewish culture of the former.

Jewish jokes do not, of course, tell us everything about the development of the Jewish world, and even less about that of French society. But they are an expression of this, one that is on the whole benevolent and amusing, and they have forged a place that did not exist before the second half of the twentieth century, at least in the forms that I've evoked above – forms, that is, that are perceptible for non-Jews. They reveal the existence of a population that is resourceful, a relationship with the past for which it has nothing to be ashamed (quite the contrary), and a pride that is expressed every year on April 19, during the ceremony for the anniversary of the heroic Warsaw Ghetto Uprising of 1943. They maintain a link with this past that is over but not completely forgotten. The still-living memory of this past justifiably occupies a place in the public realm. The essayist Alain Finkielkraut, in a book that was a huge success, *The Imaginary Jew* [*Le Juif imaginaire*], summarized what all this meant, or meant for him, which was the opposite of all the humiliation and rejection that arose from anti-Semitism: "I would like to address and meditate upon the opposite case: the case of a child, an adolescent who is not only proud but happy to be Jewish, and who came to question, bit by bit, if there were not some bad faith in living jubilantly as an exception and an exile."[26]

For almost three decades, Jewish jokes accompanied and punctuated the surge toward an identity for French Jews, with confidence and a real capacity to optimistically project themselves into the future, uniting references to past victimhood with everything they brought, culturally and intellectually, to the collective life of the country. This cultural life came to be embodied in institutions. It was thus that the Museum of the Art and History of Judaism opened its doors in 1998, displaying Jewish history in France and the world in all its historical density and cultural diversity.

But things have changed.

6

The American Decline

Anyone who considers, as we have done here, the conditions that turned out to be favorable to Jewish jokes in the United States realizes that it is not far from the Capitol(ine) Hill to the Tarpeian Rock: the apex is at the same time the first step in the decline. Signs of deterioration begin to appear in the 1980s, and then intensified and clearly accelerated at the beginning of the 2000s. Starting from that point, we can distinguish two periods.

Worries and perils

Starting in the 1980s, the relationship between the United States and Israel, and, in particular, between American Jews and Israel, begins to change. Admiration for the young country, which was strong (though not unanimous) from the 1950s to the 1970s, gives way here and there to criticisms that become increasingly virulent, and that relate above all to the Palestinian question. Starting with the first intifada (1987–93), and then with the second in 2000, the image of a combat between David and Goliath, established by the Israeli victory in the Six-Day War in 1967, is reversed: David is now the young Palestinian throwing rocks at the Israeli army. The fallout from this change, or the other aspect of this deterioration, is that the American support for the State of Israel takes on an increasingly organized form, and AIPAC (the American Israel Public Affairs Committee), which begins to gain power in the mid-1970s, becomes one of the most powerful American lobbies. Its interventions give rise to hostile campaigns; in particular, it is accused of dictating foreign policy to the powers that be, and promoting unconditional support for the Israeli government, to the detriment of peace efforts.

Everything concerning the Middle East becomes hypersensitive, and criticism of Israeli politics, which moves further and further to the right, at times borders on an anti-Zionism lacking complexity and nuance, and laden with anti-Semitism. The Durban conference of 2001, "The World Conference against Racism, Racial Discrimination, Xenophobia, and Related Intolerance," quickly gives rise to a scandal, because the anti-Zionism promoted by the organizers is filled with pure and simple anti-Semitism. The representatives from the United States and Israel even decide to leave in protest at the attempts, on the part of the organizers, to equate Zionism and racism. Though anti-Semitism seemed to be on the decline in the Unites States, it finds a renewed space on the left of the political left.

Jews, as we have seen, participated in the struggle of Blacks for civil rights. But this does not mean the relationship between these groups has always been harmonious and lasting. The anti-Semitism of the Black world is certainly not new, but it finds a fresh impetus in the wake of the civil rights movement and the radicalization that is notably embodied by the Black Panthers; in particular, it takes shape in the Nation of Islam, which in 1991 publishes *The Secret Relationship between Blacks and Jews*. This book falsely accuses Jews of having played a leading role in the slave trade. Only the intervention of important Black intellectuals such as Henry Louis Gates Jr. puts an end to the unrest kindled by what this historian refers to as an "anti-Semitic tract."

If American Jews were pioneers in the age of victimhood, they very quickly lost their monopoly. The evolution of debates about minorities put them in a delicate position. They are no longer discriminated against, and their historical sufferings come to be recognized; as such, they can no longer claim to suffer from any mass-scale rejection or domination, or claim the status of victim as assuredly as when America discovered the Shoah in the 1970s and 1980s. The country moved from the discovery of the genocide to its institutionalization, its official recognition, at the very highest levels of state, as symbolized by the creation of the United States Holocaust Memorial Museum in Washington, DC. A misadventure of which my friend Walter Reich was the victim can serve to illustrate the new context. This is what he told me.

When he was director of the Holocaust Museum (a post he had held since 1995), he suddenly learned that Yasser Arafat, the leader of the PLO [Palestine Liberation Front], wanted to visit him during an official trip to the United States. At the request of the White House, Arafat was to receive a VIP welcome. Outraged at having to receive someone he considered a terrorist, with Jewish blood on his hands, Walter Reich refused to see him. Yasser Arafat was seeking to turn this visit into a global media event, which Walter Reich wasn't interested in condoning. He was immediately forced to resign. The icing on the cake: at the very moment my friend was leaving his post, the Clinton/Lewinsky scandal ("Monicagate") broke – the revelation of an affair between the president and a young intern. The media spoke of nothing else, and Yasser Arafat, realizing that his visit to the Museum would go unnoticed and not bring him any media exposure whatsoever, decided to cancel. Walter Reich resigned for nothing.

Beyond this, the terrorist attacks of September 11, 2001 created fertile ground for conspiracy theories, and, here again, the anti-Semitism was obvious, with rumors imputing the attacks to a global Jewish conspiracy.

Many American Jews often feel foreign to, unconcerned by, and even hostile toward movements and pressure in favor of multiculturalism and affirmative action, but some of them are sensitive and receptive to the general evolution of society, to feminism, individualism, the threats posed by the intensification of racism, and the need for antiracist struggles. Others are, above all, sensitive to the risk of the dilution of their identity. And yet others, or perhaps the same ones, have difficulty situating themselves with regard to the transformations that make them uneasy: how, they ask, can we be on the left and in favor of supporting Palestine if this threatens to open the door to an intolerable anti-Semitism? How can we identify ourselves with struggles whose actors foreground gender, race, or ethnic identity if these struggles ignore or even reject us?

The fragmentation of the American Jewish diaspora is also perceptible from a religious standpoint, with some currents that are liberal and progressive (reformed), others that are conservative, and yet others that are orthodox and traditionalist. And even within certain of these currents, the radicalization of support for Israel is not unanimous. In short, there are sharp tensions among American Jews. In what follows, we will see that the problems don't stop there.

The inversion

Starting at the end of the 1990s, we see a perceptible radicalization if we consider not the problem of anti-Semitism but that of racism, as evidenced in Philip Roth's novel *The Human Stain*, published in the United States in 2000: inspired by a real witch hunt of which one of his friends, a professor of sociology at Princeton, was the victim, this book describes the experience of an academic who is forced to take early retirement due to completely fallacious accusations of racism.

And in the 2000s and 2010s, anti-Semitism began to feed cases of twisted logic such as this one.

The American extreme right is anti-Semitic throughout its various currents, which consider Blacks to be inferior and Jews to be evil. The far right's aversion to Jews found very fertile ground in Donald Trump's victorious campaign for the presidency. Hatred turned into deadly violence, for instance with the Pittsburgh synagogue shooting on October 27, 2018, which resulted in eleven deaths. The idea of the "great replacement," developed in 2010 by the French writer Renaud Camus, took on physical form in the Unite the Right Rally in Charlottesville, Virginia, on August 11–12, 2017, in which demonstrators opposed the removal of a statue of the southern general Robert E. Lee; during the rally, white supremacists and other alt-right activists chanted "The Jews are going to replace us."

Hence Pierre Birnbaum's opposition to historian Salo Baron's claim that American exceptionalism allowed and continues to allow Jews in the United States to escape the curse of a "tearful" history, pogroms, massacres, and the genocide of the Shoah.[1] In fact, over the long term, this exceptionalism is at best brief, and at worst an illusion refuted by today's extreme-right violence.

Can Jews, now that they are no longer discriminated against, now that everything concerning the Shoah is well known, recognized, and institutionalized, continue to present themselves as a minority requiring more compassion and understanding for their historical suffering than other groups? Is it not time, as African American activists (among others) claim, to instead think about slavery or the slave trade? Should we not speak more, and better, of other genocides? For those who denounce the various forms of exclusion, domination, and forgetting, there is a temptation to turn away from the Jews, and even to take them to task for having become just another dominant group. In the new discourses of hatred, Jews sometimes cease to be a dominated group and become white, participating in a "whiteness" that oppresses and exploits. More precisely, they are at once described as hyper-white, the quintessence of this whiteness, and sub-white, since they are nonetheless different, given the attributes that continue to be imputed to them, and that take up the stereotypes of the old anti-Semitism. They have no place in white ethno-nationalism, which demonizes them, but they do in those hateful discourses that turn them into whites.

Even outside of these extremes, the climate is increasingly one of intolerance and the systematic intensification of intimidating and paralyzing rationales that go well beyond the "political correctness" of the 1980s, when an attempt was made to respect ethnic or religious minorities, and also women and homosexuals, by avoiding categorizing them in a way that lead to their exclusion. From then on, in North America, statements that would once have been acceptable, some of them humorous, have kindled accusations of racism, anti-Semitism, anti-feminism, homophobia, etc., and can lead to serious problems, even legal ones, for those who make them. For example, and this is not an isolated case, an adjunct professor of literature at the University of Ottawa, Verushka Lieutenant-Duval, used the N-word in a course dealing with queer theory. She mentioned that the gay community in North America had appropriated the word "queer," a bit like certain African-American groups had done with the N-word. This technique of inverting and appropriating stigmas is called "subversive resignification" by its practitioners. Lieutenant-Duval's address was posted on social media, and she was the object of a violent campaign for using the N-word, which, it was claimed, should not be used even in literary or historical contexts, especially by a "white" person, who never has the right to do so. In September 2020, she was suspended by her university administration.

Many jokes can no longer be told, forbidden by a cancel culture that is not very welcoming of humor in general, and that of Jewish jokes in particular.

The struggle, by minorities, for the recognition of their rights doesn't stop with excluding Jews – it can even turn them into enemies. This is particularly the case in universities, where today Jewish instructors are seen as necessarily racist and, as such, qualified as Zionists. At UC Berkeley, an important site of the student movement in the 1960s, and in complete opposition to the aspirations of that period, students attempted, in the early 2020s, to impose a rule that would exclude "Zionists" – Jews – from campus, and foster "Jew-free zones." On February 10, 2022, the *Times of Israel* listed several anti-Semitic incidents at American universities – Vermont, Tufts, George Washington, Rutgers, and Chicago – including harassment of Jewish students as authorities looked on, the indifference of these authorities when anti-Semitic incidents were reported to them, calls to boycott "Zionist courses"; in other words, courses taught by Jewish instructors, and a rampant proliferation of hate speech on social networks. The climate is tense at many establishments of higher learning, and the eight prestigious Ivy League universities are no exception. The outbreak of violence set off by Hamas's terrorist attack in Israel on October 7, 2023 exacerbated and multiplied these incidents, and inflamed many campuses, such as Harvard, New York University, Stanford, etc.

The obsessive and virulent hatred of Jews has also given rise to deadly violence in extreme-right groups, in white supremacist, alt-right, and neo- or post-Nazi circles, and in large segments of the Republican right, where this hatred is more dispersed. At the same time, in a hardening academic and intellectual climate, exacerbated by Hamas's attack, this hatred has mobilized, in the name of anti-Zionism, entire swathes of the other end of the ideologico-political spectrum, among minorities, especially Blacks. It is sometimes extremely explicit, as in the anti-Semitic statements made by Kanye West, a rapper who has become an evangelist in the service of Donald Trump. This hatred sometimes takes strange forms: for instance, according to a belief that is quite widespread, important for a myriad of African American religious groups, Blacks are the true Israelites, one of the "lost tribes" of Israel, and the Jews conspired to steal their religion from them. It must be said that the idea of a tense relationship between Jews and Blacks, even if it is partially true, is insufficient, given how much these groups have also, for a long time, been inventing diverse forms of hybridity. There are, for example, Black Jews and Judeo-Black communities such as the "Black Hebrew Israelites," and various and at times incredible modes of interpenetration of the two identities, which can at times become hateful. As far as I know, there is no place in any of this for the humor of Jewish jokes.

Racists, as a general rule, are never embarrassed by their contradictions; here, this applies to the worst of them, but also to the most ardent activists of an antiracism that can quickly become a race war: the two sides come together in an anti-Semitism that too often leads those who should oppose it to silence, for institutional or political reasons.

On the whole, starting from the 2000s and 2010s, American Jews have had good reason to be more and more worried, and not only for Israel – for themselves as well. They have experienced a real feeling of insecurity and potential abandonment in the face of threats that have converged even when those making them have little to do with each other: the racist alt-right and certain African American groups that come together in the hatred aimed at Jews. In addition, Jews are no longer considered as actors contributing in an exceptional way to cultural renewal; they no longer create (or do so far less than before) new reference points, interesting ways of thinking, or stimulating intellectual arguments; Israel's move to the far right deprives them of arguments allowing them to display a newfound pride, even if it is true that a democratic mobilization to counter these developments is increasingly evident among members of the American diaspora. This is not a time for smiling or laughing, or for the Jewish jokes that it was once possible to share with others, in a mode of empathy, confidence, kindness, and a certain *joie de vivre*. The war started by Hamas in October 2023 has only made things worse.

7

In France, a Changed Situation

Developments that are in many ways comparable can be observed in France, in the same time frame, following the same two phases as in the United States, though once again there are important differences at play.

The rise of fear

These changes are primarily linked to transformations specific to recent immigration, that of the postwar period, which is essentially from North Africa, and to the way this new population relates to the Israeli-Palestinian conflict.

For three decades after the war, until 1973 or 1974, migrants from the Maghreb who arrived in France were single men responding to the demands of industry, and sometimes also those of farming. They were there to work, and lived apart from the rest of the community. They had no children in need of schooling, and lived in housing estates built specially for them, or in short-term lodgings. They didn't vote and they weren't citizens. They saved their money with the objective of returning to their own country.

Starting from the middle of the 1970s, this immigration for the purpose of work became one aimed at settlement, at the very moment the economy was entering a crisis, unemployment was rising, and new forms of work organization were breaking with Taylorism and the mass use of unqualified labor. Family reunification policies, which were guaranteed by European directives introduced into French law in 1974, contributed to this transformation. The image of the immigrant ceased to be that of the male worker who thought only of returning home, and became that of the unemployed worker accompanied by children, with access to citizenship. Racism correspondingly adjusted, moving from emphasizing physical characteristics that would justify considering migrants to be inferior, to noting cultural differences, which made them constitutionally incapable of integrating into the nation.

From the end of the 1970s, the theme of broad insecurity invaded public discourse. It was often blamed on migrants, their children, and the suburbs [*banlieues*], where many of these families now lived. Ten years later, in October 1989, the first "veil affair" aroused impassioned exchanges: when three young Moroccan girls refused to remove their Islamic veil within the walls of a public school in Creil, they ensured that Islam would go to the very heart of public debates, and remain there for a long time, along with the theme of *laïcité*, the secular nature of French state institutions, which until that point had ceased to be an issue.

Over the course of about ten years, these developments, and other related themes, had a significant impact on the Jewish question in a significant manner. The stage was set for this to happen: the crisis in immigrant neighborhoods, insecurity, delinquency, riots and related urban violence, and the questioning of the republican model of integration, with Islam becoming the country's second-largest religion. One must also take into account, however, racism and discrimination, and the rise of the Front National, which, by the early 1980s, had ceased to be a small and insignificant group.

The rise in awareness of the reality of the new anti-Semitic threats comes from lived experience, notably that of Jewish families who observe that their children, in public school, are the victims of attacks and insults, and are not sufficiently protected by school administrations. Parents end up removing their children from these schools and opting for private education. Or leaving the neighborhood in which they see themselves as threatened, along with their children, to find a place where they feel protected – which contributes to communities being segregated from one another, as the sociologist Erik Cohen observed very early.[1]

Another sociologist, Didier Lapeyronnie, in a now-classic study,[2] took stock of the real meaning that anti-Semitism assumes for the inhabitants of poor neighborhoods on the outskirts of cities: it constitutes, he says, the empty language of those who are deprived of language and are shut away in ghettos. Jérôme Fourquet and Sylvain Manternach, in a book for which I wrote the preface,[3] show how, as a result, the Jewish world is turning to the right politically, and many Jews are migrating to Israel, undertaking the *aliyah*. This is not the time, as it was before, for laughing and poking fun at yourself in shared good humor. And if there is humor, it is mainly within closed groups, likely virtual (shared on social networks), and increasingly caustic.

Jewish organizations compile lists of attacks against Jewish institutions and their property (synagogues, community centers, schools, cemeteries), and against people (assaults, threats, etc.). Their statistical data, combined with data from public sources, can certainly be criticized, as they take into account neither the reticence, on the part of police and judicial authorities, to register complaints, nor the fact that the victims do not make themselves known to them; as such, they underestimate the number of attacks. On the other hand, determining what is and isn't anti-Semitic is not always obvious: a Jew can be assaulted, for example, without it being because he is a Jew; from this standpoint, the risk becomes one of overestimating the number of attacks. Nonetheless, the numbers are clear enough to speak volumes, which politicians on the right perceive faster and better than those on the left – and at the turn of the century (1997–2003), power was divided between right and left, with a right-wing president, Jacques Chirac, and a left-wing prime minister, Lionel Jospin.

In a context in which Islam and immigration, which are often associated in public opinion, are seen as worrisome, whether we're dealing with the headscarf affair of 1989 or terrorist attacks in France (such as in 1995) or the United States (with 9/11), it appears that there is an anti-Semitism expressed by people who descend from Arab-Muslim worlds. This phenomenon fuels nagging concerns for many Jews, who find support in it, as is demonstrated by a successful collection of essays edited by Georges Bensoussan (using the pseudonym Emmanuel Brenner), *Les Territoires perdus de la République*,[4] for both their hyper-republican ideology and, especially, their worries – their "malaise," their "disarray," as many newspapers and magazines wrote of the book, sometimes in cover stories, beginning in 1999.

Are we dealing here with a projection, on French soil, of Middle Eastern tensions? The answer is probably a partial yes, because whenever these tensions increase, we see a rise in anti-Semitic violence. Is the left at fault, given that it really was slower than the right to become aware of the seriousness of this phenomenon? This, in any case, is the opinion of intellectuals and politicians on the right, and also of many Jews, who come to adopt the vocabulary of right-wing and far-right intellectuals, speaking, for instance, following Pierre-André Taguieff, of a "new Judeophobia," a term that is currently enjoying success; these same people call for a ban on the term "Islamophobia," as if it were legitimate to consider a phobia toward everything that is Jewish, but not toward anything to do with Islam. Ideologues are never embarrassed by their own contradictions.

It is true that a combination is at work, that of an anti-Zionism that aligns itself, first, with postcolonial ideas and movements that equate Israel with colonization and Zionism with apartheid; second, with an anti-capitalism that associates Jews with money; and third, with the cause of Palestine, which is very appealing to the left. It is also true that the anti-Israel demonstrations and support for the Palestinians, in which ecologists and those on the extreme left participate, often include anti-Semitic elements, and even lead to violence. This was the case in the attack on a synagogue during a demonstration in July 2014 in Paris. This type of amalgam is mostly the work of a slide toward the extreme, one that goes beyond the parliamentary or institutional left. The embodiment of this slide in the media is the comedian Dieudonné, whose anti-Semitic excesses, in his shows and more generally in his language, reached new heights in the early 2010s.

In the 2000s, opinion polls showed the persistence of a right-wing anti-Semitism, one that was classic in its stereotypes, and in a long-term decline: Jews, according to these stereotypes, have "too much power" or are not "French like the rest of us." There is also the politically and ideologically explicit anti-Semitism, with the rise of the far-right Front National, founded and led by the notorious Jean-Marie Le Pen. This movement found an audience (albeit not enormous) among certain people from North Africa: the *pieds-noirs*, people of European descent born in Algeria during French rule, who sometimes hold feelings of hatred toward Jews who arrived in France as a result of the same decolonization. One of my students, Clarisse Buono, shows, in her dissertation,[5] how the distance separating these two groups is due to a complex history, one that was not always kind to North African Jews. She discusses the case of the singer Enrico Macias, who, when his song "Les Filles de mon pays" was released, was perceived as a repatriated *pied-noir*, only to become far better known, with the passing of time, as a Jew who was active in French politics and supported Israel.

On the other hand, a phenomenon that derives from conspiracy theories goes, perhaps, in the opposite direction. Since the end of the 1970s, a persistent strand of Holocaust denial successfully sought to deny the existence of the gas chambers, even though an important conference, organized by Raymond Aron and François Furet in 1982, did much to challenge this negationism.[6] It was at this time that I discovered the work of Jean-Claude Pressac, a pharmacist who was much better at dismantling Robert Faurisson's denial of the existence of gas chambers than many historians and philosophers. At first he was fascinated by Faurisson's ideas, but he took the approach of an engineer or architect, studying the plans of the crematoriums, the way they worked, the materials that had been purchased for their construction – in short, concrete proof rather than testimony. The evidence he found led him to break with Faurisson. His presentation during the conference, even if it wasn't as elegant and deep as those of the important researchers who spoke, nonetheless marked a turning point by shattering negationist currents from within. Today, Holocaust denial has largely receded, though many other conspiracy theories blaming Jews continue to prosper. We saw this, for example, in the rumors (discussed above) concerning the role supposedly played by Jews in the 9/11 attacks, or during demonstrations against the "vaccine pass" in the summer of 2021, when they were accused, here and there, of taking advantage of, and profiting from, the pandemic.

At the same time, the elements that have led to the cultural vitality of Jews since the Second World War, namely *Yiddishkeit* and pre-war memory, are fading away. The more recent minority immigrant groups, notably those from the Maghreb, are contributing in increasingly significant ways to renewed cultural dynamics, driven by artists, writers, and intellectuals, even as the former Jewish revival is losing its edge.

In 2003, conscious of these tendencies, and in order to take stock of them, I launched a large field study, which brought together a dozen French researchers. We investigated various locations and environments, and the results were published in 2005.[7] This publication unexpectedly led me to my being personally confronted on an important issue.

The very day the book went on sale in bookstores, the newspaper *Libération* extensively reported on it, in the form of an interview. During this interview, I noted in passing that the positions taken by CRIF and other institutional representatives of French Jews in favor of Israel ended up strengthening the equation "diaspora Jews = Israel," regardless of what the leaders of these institutions thought. And at a time when the politics of these leaders was endangering peace, this could only encourage a form of hatred that conflated French Jews with the politics of the Hebrew state, putting the latter's very existence into question.

So I arrive at my office on April 19, 2005, carrying the newspaper, feeling quite proud. The telephone keeps ringing. It's the president of CRIF, Roger Cukierman. He hasn't read my book, of course, and all he's retained of the pages devoted to it by *Libération* is my remark about the unconditional support of Israeli politics by French Jewish institutions. His words are violent and quite serious: I shouldn't have said that. He demands that I retract my words in one or another press outlet. I answer that if he can give me a meaningful example, just one, of critical distance, in which CRIF didn't blindly follow the Israeli government in its politics, I would publicly walk back my words. We hung up; it was very tense. He calls back an hour later, vaguely ashamed for the brutal way he'd spoken to me earlier, this time to invite me to breakfast at La Coupole in the next few days. We did end up meeting, and the tone was more relaxed.

But a little while later, when I really did take a public position in favor of Edgar Morin, an internationally renowned sociologist who has never concealed his Jewish identity, and who was targeted by an extraordinary media campaign for anti-Semitism – he had signed a petition in favor of Palestine, one that was very severe toward Israel – I noticed that my book had been given a scathing and dishonest, not to mention mediocre, review on CRIF's website. I also learned that other Jewish organizations had made forceful suggestions to boycott me, and a lecture that a lodge of the B'nai Brith (Jewish Freemasons) had asked me to give was canceled at the last minute. This episode would be repeated fifteen years later, when the Strasbourg CRIF, after joining in with another organization that had invited me to give a lecture in that city, conspicuously withdrew from the project.

The leadership of CRIF in 2006 was very different from how it had been when the lawyer Théo Klein – a great man – was at the helm, and later, Henri Hajdenberg, another remarkable lawyer who, after meeting Yasser Arafat, explicitly refused, in 1999, to blindly follow Israel, and declared, in a wonderful spirit of responsibility and openness: "We have to increase our contacts with the Arab world, its leaders, those who drive its opinion, and others besides. Arab society has a poor knowledge of the Jewish world, and the reverse is also true. We don't have to take the place of Israeli leaders, but we should seek to share the sensibilities of Israelis and diaspora Jews, and also to listen to the analyses of Arab leaders."[8]

In 2005, the climate that prevailed in the main French Jewish institution exercised strong pressure on the diaspora, which was expected to support Israel at every opportunity, even at the cost of subordinating itself; statements that were even remotely divergent were excluded. It became forbidden to criticize Israel, and even to seriously report on what was happening there, even though opposition media outlets such as *Haaretz* were doing just this. Torrents of mud were slung at the political scientist Pascal Boniface for having engaged in this sort of criticism; these attacks were revolting, as I explained in my preface for his book *L'Antisémite*.[9] In the same way, the correspondent for the France 2 television network in Jerusalem, Charles Enderlin, paid dearly for his reporting on the death of a Palestinian child during an armed confrontation on September 23, 2000: even though a document established the responsibility of the Israeli army, a campaign was unleashed against him that would last years, during which the businessman Philippe Karsenty, the journalist Luc Rosenzweig, the essayist Alain Finkielkraut, and the CRIF, among others, falsely accused him of deception and of spreading pro-Palestinian propaganda. Pierre-André Taguieff, an intellectual known for his work on racism, spoke, without any fear of being ridiculed, of nothing less than "the images of the supposed murder of a young Palestinian by the Israeli army, reactivating the stereotype of the 'Jewish child-killer'": this specialist in conspiracy theories had himself fallen prey to conspiracies.

Charles Enderlin discussed all of this, notably in his book *Un Enfant est mort*,[10] and then in another work for which I again wrote the preface, in which he developed a series of lectures he'd been asked to give by the Fondation Maison des sciences de l'homme, *De Notre Correspondant à Jérusalem: Le journalisme comme identité*.[11] Philippe Karsenty, by far the most active campaigner against Enderlin, would end up being convicted for defamation by a court of appeal.

Since 1993, and especially since the assassination of Yitzhak Rabin in 1995, Israeli politics has almost always followed a right-wing path. This orientation, when it appeals for the automatic support of diaspora Jews, works by counting on the idea that they will also move rightwards, and by showcasing those who are the most right-wing among them. This, in return, can only serve to radicalize those who count themselves as victims of current Israeli politics, whether in nationalist terms that are favorable to the Palestinians, or in religious, Muslim, and, indeed, Islamist terms.

From then on, in public opinion, it has been easy to associate support for Israel with the hatred of Arabs, migrants, or Muslims, and, symmetrically, it has become easy to express hatred for Jews, who are perceived as always being allied with the politics of the Israeli government, in the form of anti-Zionism. The unnuanced equation "anti-Zionism = anti-Semitism" is a construction that mirrors, in an inverted form, how the diaspora is expected to fall into line.

It is true, however, that Jewish institutions are making efforts not to cut themselves off from other minorities, and are beginning to look at genocides other than the one carried out by the Nazis: Armenia, ex-Yugoslavia, Rwanda and surrounding countries, and other examples of historical suffering, starting with the slave trade. I got along well with the president of CRIF, Richard Prasquier, elected in 2007; only later did I learn, sadly, that he had been among the most ardent adversaries of Charles Enderlin. Since I was a close associate of CRAN (the Representative Council of Black Associations in France) and its president Patrick Lozès, I contributed to the dynamics of rapprochement by sparking interest in a meeting between the two presidents, Prasquier and Lozès, which led to a conference called "The Face: Encountering the Other," co-organized by CRAN, CRIF, and the Collège des Bernardins, a Catholic institution, which also hosted the event. As president of the scientific council of CRAN, I was always invited, back then, to the CRIF annual dinner – as a Black, and not as a Jew. But finally, Roger Cukierman, who had been so unfriendly toward me, developed a constructive relationship with CRAN during his third term as the head of CRIF (2013–16).

All of this is evidence of the real efforts, on the part of the Jewish world, to develop a closer relationship with the Black world. But this should not mask the existence of very different tendencies, illustrated, for instance, by the declarations of

Alain Finkielkraut to *Haaretz* on November 19, 2005: "People say that the French national [soccer] team is admired by everyone because it features blacks, whites, and Arabs. In reality, the national team is now black, black, and black, which makes it the laughing stock of Europe." This statement provoked a firestorm of controversy in France.

Inversion, in France as in America

More recent transformations, perceptible since the 2010s, have not merely prolonged the developments I have just discussed – they have also greatly transformed them, bringing about many fronts on which the hatred of Jews is expressed.

This includes straightforwardly base crimes, such as the murder of Ilan Halimi, who was kidnapped, held prisoner, and tortured in January 2006 before being left for dead by Youssouf Fofana's "gang of barbarians." Fofana, after his arrest and conviction, claimed, in prison, to be a follower of Islam, even after committing acts that have nothing to do with religion. Just as religion apparently had nothing to do with the assassination of Mireille Knoll twelve years later, in March 2018.

The evolution also includes Islamism, or the racial and religious hatred that is the counterpart of a no less radical anti-Zionism. As the psychiatrist Marc Sageman, a former CIA officer, has shown with regard to the 9/11 terrorist attacks,[12] one of the driving forces behind Islamism is an obsessive anti-Semitism, whereby people seek to kill Jews simply because they are Jews. This was the case for Mohammed Merah in Toulouse, France, in March 2012, and for Amedy Coulibaly in Paris in January 2015, when he took hostages in a kosher mini-market near the Porte de Vincennes.

This terrorism and these crimes mark an important step in the development of the hatred of Jews, for whom they obviously add to a sense of fear and insecurity. And this is only the visible or spectacular tip of an iceberg situated at the crossroads of Middle Eastern conflicts and separatist tendencies at the very heart of French society. This differentiates them from the previous period, when events such as the anti-Semitic attack on the rue Copernic in 1980 or that of the rue des Rosiers in 1982 were perpetrated by terrorists from abroad, and when the horrific crimes of the Jewish cemetery of Carpentras in 1990 were perpetrated by a handful of young neo-Nazis, as we learned in 1996.

Anti-Semitism also occurs in new forms of mobilization that are unrelated to Islamism. On the one hand, in the Gilets Jaunes movement, in whose Saturday demonstrations, notably the one that took place on December 22, 2018, in Paris, one hears expressions of hatred toward Jews – though it must be said that these are limited. On the other hand, in the conspiracy theories that made gains with the Covid-19 virus, and above all in the demonstrations against the vaccine and the vaccine pass that took place in summer 2021, as I've mentioned, and which led to a public surfacing of this hatred. When protesters in various demonstrations hold signs on which the word "QUI" ["who"] is written, everyone understands that they're targeting certain Jews, and Jews in general.

The same goes for the mural by the graffiti artist Lekto on a wall in Avignon, which shows the essayist and former counselor to François Mitterand, Jacques Attali, manipulating Emmanuel Macron with puppet strings – a Jew manipulating a president who in the past worked as a banker for Rothschild and Co. The broadcasting of this mural by media outlets in June 2022 led to a huge outcry, and it was erased after a few days, following the intervention of the prefect of the Vaucluse.

Even if all this is limited in scope, it is no less true that the phenomenon has attained public and political visibility. At the same time, the main political force of the far right, the Rassemblement National, the new name for the Front National since 2018, no longer comes across as a party with an anti-Semitic leader at the helm. The distance taken by Marine Le Pen from all expressions of hostility toward Jews is at the heart of her strategy of de-demonization. The attempt by Éric Zemmour, a candidate for president in 2022 and himself a Jew, to outflank the RN on the right by taking very radical positions was also an attempt to win the votes of Jews who were motivated by a fear of Islam. The war against Israel started by Hamas in 2023 confirmed the RN in its decision to position itself as a resolute ally of Israel, and an actor vigorously engaged in the struggle against anti-Semitism.

In addition, the growing influence of social networks, which has become decisive in just a few years, encourages the circulation of hatred and threats, and generates new accusations against Jews, who, according to these hateful remarks, are seeking rules, laws, and means of control that benefit only them, even though they already benefit from a "double standard." Why, ask young anti-Semites, is it allowed to publish blasphemous images of the prophet Mohammed in France, but forbidden to doubt the existence of the gas chambers?

As we have seen, anti-Semitism inspires radical Islam. But it inspires others as well, and contributes to the spread of a conviction that can be found in the vocabulary of a new semantic system: the French Republic is the target of a broad range of threats. This idea of a general danger aimed at the Republic sometimes itself becomes extremist, unnuanced, liable to conflate radical Islam with the whole of Islam – to conflate terrorists and simple Muslims. Viewed from this perspective, the hatred of Jews is just one aspect of a much larger process, and those who think in this way aim their criticism and denunciations not only at Islam, but also at a blind or naive left that is viewed as supporting Islam. This mobilization against anti-Semitism, and for the Republic under threat, thus takes issue not only with "Islamo-leftism," but at the same time with the following: "Wokeism," seen to be ravaging universities by foregrounding ethnic, racial, and gender identities that have become intolerant; "cancel culture," which ostracizes the individuals it targets while denying history and destroying culture; and postcolonial or decolonial studies. In several of my writings, I have analyzed these "republicanist" incantations, which blow supposedly "wokeist" episodes out of all proportion; I'm not saying these episodes aren't important, but republicanists abusively generalize them based on a few isolated occurrences. In my book *Alors Monsieur Macron, heureux?*, I reproached President Macron for having allowed at least two of his ministers, Jean-Michel Blanquer and Frédérique Vidal, to become participants in these incantations.[13] Those who proceed in this way throw the baby out with the bathwater, casting antiracist action, cultural contestation, and social movements in a poor light in the name of contesting their anti-Semitism and various other excesses; these excesses exist, as is often the case with collective mobilizations, on their periphery, not at their heart.

These "republicanist" claims must be clearly distinguished from the RN's extremism. Both are in search of a principle of unity that would assure the harmony of the social body, and in France such searches always refer to the nation and the Republic, indeed to both at the same time. But those who appeal more to the Republic than to the nation in order to assure the unity of society, and who are convinced that there are grave threats targeting this society, generally aim to protect Jews, and not to take issue with them: hasn't Islamism killed Jews? We can see this republicanist orientation in the positions of right-wing intellectuals such as Pierre-André Taguieff or Alain Finkielkraut, and in statements by politicians such as Manuel Valls or Jean-Michel Blanquer, as well as in articles written by, or petitions that include, Jewish figures. This difference may fade away with the RN's clearly displayed rejection of all anti-Semitism, and with its explicit support of Israel.

"Republicanists" not only pervert and destroy public debate by undermining anyone who doesn't share their opinions; they also tie themselves in intellectual knots. The arguments of certain of them turn into *ad hominem* attacks, as I have personally experienced in two hurtful articles. The first appeared on the site of *Marianne* on May 3, 2021 (I responded on May 7 in an article entitled "Michel Wieviorka répond à ses détracteurs: c'est le degré zéro de la vie intellectuelle" ["Michel Wieviorka responds to his critics: 'This is the basest form of intellectual life'"]). The second was published around the same time in *Droit de vivre, DDV*, the magazine of LICRA, the International League against Racism and Anti-Semitism. It was quickly withdrawn after I pointed out its unconscious anti-Semitism. Poor LICRA, whose magazine, which they would like to think is important, begins by including an article that reads like an anti-Semitic handbook for hate, including a comparison between myself and a bat, like in the 1930s in the cartoons of the *Stürmer*. The article disappeared from the magazine without the slightest display of regret, the slightest apology, allowing its editors at the same time to avoid the response they would have had to accord me! And during all this time, the writer of this article, Isabelle de Mecquenem, who holds a degree in philosophy – I kid you not – and compares me to a bat, continues to play a variety of roles in the initiatives put into place by the Macron administration to promote secularism.

The historian of psychoanalysis Élisabeth Roudinesco, giving an account of a conference at the Sorbonne on January 6, 2022, in which certain of these "republicanists" reached true summits of stupidity and resentment, put these ideologues, who are as mediocre as they are aggressive, in their place.[14] She was also the first person to publicly draw attention to the unconscious anti-Semitism of Isabelle de Mecquenem.

Overall, "republicanism," whether on the part of Jews or of non-Jews, and which is most often positioned on the right or extreme right, is associated with an obsessive fear of Islam; indeed, it seems that, for republicanists, the only good Jew is the one who is involved in the fight against this religion. All of this occupies a not insignificant place in public debate, and, where French Jews are concerned, contributes to building a space that is no longer related to the hopes and joys of the previous epoch. A space in which suspicion and hatred destroy empathy and kindness, but also dialogue, and in which humor, when it exists, can no longer contribute to bringing together intellectual and political communities, or to bringing them into contact with other communities. This climate no longer allows for the building of bridges, not to mention a sense of connection, understanding, and compassion. Invective, the negation of otherness, and frameworks of rupture and, indeed, violence all win the day. Jewish history, and the history of the Jews, now continues in the absence of Jewish jokes.

Analyzing these developments, far from taking us away from the topic of this book, explains why humor finds it much harder today than in the past to locate conditions that are favorable to its spread. It's true that people continue to tell Jewish jokes, and, indeed, social networks ensure that they circulate widely. But in doing so, they come to be conflated with other jokes that border on anti-Semitism, or authorize it: telling jokes virtually means they function differently, and don't have the same effect as when they're told in plays, films, or more traditional media, not to mention one-on-one meetings and encounters.

As such, there are many similarities between developments in France and the United States. But let's not draw the conclusion, as people often do in French politics, that this is yet another manifestation of the logic of importation, whereby the French borrow problems, categories of thought, and debates from the Americans. Obviously there are exchanges from one shore of the Atlantic to the other, and which go in both directions: the American alt-right, for example, is very fond of Renaud Camus's concept of "great replacement." It's not only the Americans who export ideas!

But the national histories, social structures, and political cultures of the two countries differ considerably: the question of Islam, in France, is not the same as the Black question in the United States; the French republican model is culturally specific and is not the same as that of the United States, even if the question of identity is coming increasingly to the fore in both countries. France was a great colonial power, which is not the case for the United States, whose global hegemony arose in large part other than by way of colonization, and where the colonial question mostly takes the form of the Black question, linked to the slave trade, slavery, and racism.

But if we want to understand the evolution of the impact of Jewish jokes, we can nonetheless invoke two common and decisive aspects, one having to do with the past, namely the genocide perpetrated by the Nazis, and the other having to do with geopolitics, and which goes back to Israel. Both invite us to think globally, both in time and space, and not to confine ourselves to analyzing each national experience independently of all others, or even of limiting ourselves to their comparison.

There is first of all the weight of the Shoah, at the heart of the age of victimhood, which is also the era of memory and the witness. This weight, which recalls the historical suffering of the Jews of Europe, and their destruction during the Second World War, affects the two countries in different ways, but also with important similarities. In both cases, it seems to me that the Shoah is becoming less and less important, at least when compared to the recent past, because the genocide belongs to the more and more distant past when compared with other tragedies on which people focus today. And also because talking about the Shoah does not convey the positive aspects of a culture; it does not spur people on to take action beyond recognizing its horrors, its evil, and its destruction. The empathy authorized by Jewish jokes requires elements other than those associated with victimhood; it demands that one go beyond a solely "tearful" relationship with collective life, ideas, and new or different ways of seeing the world, without losing this reference to the tragedy experienced by the Jews – the

Shoah, which today is losing its relative importance. What was for many the very moving discovery, in the 1970s, of Nazi barbarity has today lost much of the force that comes with novelty.

Then there is the question of Israel and its relationship with the diaspora. The United States, with its 5 million Jews, and France, with 500,000, are the two main countries in terms of a Jewish presence, but behind Israel, which, in 2022, had a population of 9.6 million people, 75 percent of whom are Jewish.

The time has come to consider the existence of this state and the functioning of its society in the light of Jewish jokes, or rather, as we will see, in the light of their near absence in Israel. But before looking at this, we indicate that what has just been said about France and the United States, regarding a phase of openness (broadly speaking, the last thirty years of the twentieth century), followed by a period of closure, in which we live today, is confirmed when we consider other countries that include Jewish populations, even though they are much smaller. The case of Poland is a good illustration.

Before the war, that country had a Jewish population of almost 3.3 million. Today, only a few thousand remain. Strong nationalism and hegemonic Catholicism fed, for a long time, an anti-Judaism, which certainly was not weakened by postwar communism. But in the context of the crisis and then the end of "real" communism, beginning at the end of the 1970s, we saw a bright spell, the development of a new climate made up of more understanding and listening. The "Round Table" of 1989 was a decisive step for the country's entrance into democracy, and also for the way it manages its past. In the 1990s, several opinion polls showed a meaningful drop in indicators of anti-Semitism. At the end of this phase of openness, the decision was made, among other initiatives regarding Jewish culture and the country's Jewish past, to create the Museum of the History of Polish Jews, which was inaugurated in Warsaw on April 19, 2013 on the site of the former ghetto, in commemoration of the seventieth anniversary of the Warsaw Ghetto Uprising.

A new historiography developed in Poland, which established, on the basis of proven facts, how non-Jewish Poles behaved toward Jews during the war, and then under the Nazi and Soviet occupations – and which also showed how they participated in the Shoah. But today, the works of Jan Gross, Jan Grabowski, Barbara Engelking, and other historians dealing with this issue are the object of violent far-right campaigns, authorized and indeed orchestrated by a Polish government that was itself right-wing and illiberal until the parliamentary elections of 2023. Their presentations, in conferences both within and outside Poland, are violently interrupted, and they are the targets of incessant attacks that accuse them of sullying the nation's memory, betraying the country, and promoting a biased and false vision of the past, making Poles bear responsibility for the genocide that was the work of the Germans, even though their historical work is careful, rigorous, and based on facts. The prospect of eventual demands of restitution for possessions plundered during the war and then the communist period is a burning issue: aren't Jews in fact the "Hyenas of the Holocaust" – an expression that recalls the accusations of "Shoah business" that flourished in the United States with the publication of Norman G. Finkelstein's book *The Holocaust Industry*?[15] Old accusations of ritual murders and deicide resurfaced, and opinion polls showed a clear anti-Semitic reversal compared to the preceding period. A 2018 law, unanimously approved by the Polish parliament, forbids people from speaking of "Polish death camps," decreeing that anyone who "claims, publicly and contrary to the facts, that the Polish Nation or the Republic of Poland is responsible for Nazi crimes committed by the Third Reich . . . or for other felonies that constitute crimes against peace, crimes against humanity or war crimes . . . shall be liable to a fine or imprisonment for up to three years."[16] In short, the law forbids historical investigation. Such extreme patriotism has profound effects, especially in teaching. This anti-Semitism may become less active as a result of the legislative elections of October 15, 2023, which put an end to eight years of rule by the Law and Justice Party (PiS), opening the door to a center-left coalition.

The fact remains that in Poland, just like in France and the United States (even if slightly later and in ways that are all its own), intolerance, hatred, and stigmatization have been rekindled toward Jews since the mid-2010s, after an initial phase of openness, to the detriment of the work of historians, and, more broadly, truth and democracy.

8

What About Israel?

My father once went to Israel, and he came back happy. He was able to speak Yiddish there on several occasions. One particular episode really made him laugh. He got into a taxi, and the driver, who spoke Yiddish and was extremely talkative, made the following complaint:

> *"I work 24 hours a day, seven days a week, 52 weeks a year, but life has become too expensive. I got by up to now, but I'm going to end up not making ends meet!"*
> *"What will you do?" my father asked.*
> *"Easy. I'll get up an hour earlier every morning."*

At first glance, there's nothing especially Jewish or Israeli about this exchange: it could take place in any city in the world. And up until thirty or forty years ago, you could still find cabbies in New York who spoke Yiddish. Does this mean that Jewish humor is dissolving into a universalism? In fact, not completely: this joke remains Jewish because of how the driver plays with the absurd in order to bring it off. But we're at the borders of the Jewish joke as I've defined it, because this Jewishness has an extremely tenuous relationship with the absurd, perceptible only to those who are already very steeped in the humor it conveys.

Jewish jokes are rarely set in Israel, and that country seems to produce very few of them. They don't really correspond to its culture. This is something that demands to be looked into, in addition to what is taking place at the heart of the Hebrew state, and the relationship between the two spaces of Jewish life: the State of Israel and the diaspora.

A democracy becoming illiberal?

Whether we're talking about France, America, or other countries, the relationship between the diaspora and Israel is complex, diverse, and liable, as we have seen, to change with time, even for the same person. There are geopolitical aspects to this for diaspora Jews, for the relationship is made of up interactions between their belonging, as citizens, to one country – the inside, whether American or French – and their ties to another – the outside, namely Israel. And even if we don't take Israel into account, the relationship weighs heavily on representations and debates within France or America. As such, everything that touches upon Israel can be seen in the relations between Jews and Blacks in the United States, and with the descendants of migrants from the Arab-Muslim world in France – which does not exclude the possibility that it might be seen in relations between American Jews and the Arabs and Muslims of the United States, or between Jews and Blacks in France.

For a good third of a century, after its creation in 1948, Israel was quite well perceived overall in both countries. But since the beginning of the 1980s, and more precisely since the military operation in Lebanon in 1982, the poorly named "Operation Peace for Galilee," Israeli politics, disastrous for the image of the Hebrew state, led to a radicalization of positions, inciting Jews to take sides with regard to this politics, and not by affirming themselves as part of a diaspora, or with reference to an autonomous diaspora. The expectation of Israeli governments in recent years is that the Jews form a single people, and that the diasporic element of this people must therefore fall into line with Israel.

This generates tensions and ruptures, all the more so given that this politics has in no way solved the Palestinian question, and allows us to see fewer and fewer real possibilities for a just and lasting resolution. The prospect of a real peace and the construction of two states, Israeli and Palestinian, have grown more remote since the failure of the Oslo Accords, which were signed on September 13, 1993, in Washington, and the assassination of Yitzhak Rabin, who embodied these Accords, on November 4, 1995. The situation took a dramatic turn with the war between Hamas and Israel that began in October 2023 and continues to rage.

Today, Israel is among the democracies that are poised to become illiberal. Let's quickly take stock of the situation, which is worrying and upsetting for many diaspora Jews. In Israel, a nationalism associated with religion is in power, both of these in their most extreme forms, often racist, homophobic, and misogynist. This tends toward an annihilation of the law-based state. Under the guidance of Benjamin Netanyahu, against whom valid accusations of corruption have been leveled, the country has strayed considerably from its founding principles. Legislation in the service of authoritarianism has weakened all opposition from the left, and reduced the rights of Israeli Arabs; the independence of the judiciary has been challenged, and the supreme court risks losing all importance. The religious Zionists have the wind at their backs in their reasoning on the occupation of the Palestinian territories, which they take to be their divine inheritance, to the point that the prospect of a theocratic state cannot be excluded.

The image of the Hebrew state has deteriorated more than ever, including among diaspora Jews, whose support of Israel had previously been assured: "The ideal of democracy in a Jewish state is in jeopardy," as a *New York Times* editorial put it.[1] And since October 2023, the situation has become critical, since it is now a question not only of Israel's politics, but of its survival, on the one hand, and, on the other, of a war that has resulted in tens of thousands of civilian deaths.

But we must complete this picture by pointing out the forces of progress that both demonstrate and resist, above all in Israel, the government's slide toward illiberalism. These protests, which have brought out tens of thousands of people, are evidence of a real and determined opposition: the government's projects have collided with a dynamic force going in the opposite direction. The protests include democrats, of course, among them soldiers and reservists, but also important economic actors, in particular high-tech entrepreneurs, concerned for the country's financial perspectives. Like Netanyahu's politics, this democratic outcry has also had repercussions in other countries, especially the United States, where opposition is strong. It is less so in France, but it does exist. For example, I am among the signatories of a declaration in support of the democratic movements in Israel.[2] These movements have caused the government to hesitate: it deferred (though it later relaunched) its project to make the supreme court subservient to its own decisions. All of this weighs heavily not only on the internal life of the country, but also on its regional politics, and, in a worrying development for Israel, on its relationship with the United States. The war, since October 2023, has inaugurated a new period, and no one can predict how it will turn out. Former disagreements have been shelved for the time being because of the need for unity in defending the country, but the new reality has brought about the specter of a generalized civil war, and generated serious international tensions that are liable to call into question the Abraham Accords (peace treaties signed in 2020 by Israel, the UAE, Bahrain, Sudan, and Morocco), and to affect the image and diplomacy of Israel in many countries. The issue of the hostages taken by Hamas has given rise to an important mobilization on the part of Israeli citizens, which call into question not so much democracy as the way the government has conducted the war.

It has become difficult in the diaspora to put forward an unconditional identification with the Israeli government, and, at the same time, those who promote the unnuanced equation "anti-Zionism = anti-Semitism" have exposed themselves to lively criticism and opposition: what do those who demonstrate unshakeable support for the current Israeli government make of democracy, the law-based state, the rejection of corruption, and the recognition of the Palestinians? Do they not support an authoritarianism or an extremism that are combined with ultra-nationalism and ultra-orthodoxy, as the political scientist Samy Cohen puts it?[3] The issue has become even more serious since October 2023: in the United States, France, and other countries, opinions have hardened, and the issue of Palestine has been raised once again. Between unconditional support for Israel and pro-Palestinian positions that exonerate Hamas for its terrorism, the space is limited for those who seek to promote negotiation and, indeed, compromise, and to move toward a lasting and just peace between the two peoples.

Stormy and painful identifications

The current situation impoverishes terms of debate and hardens positions. Many diaspora Jews feel wounded by developments in Israel, including its military response to Hamas, and, since September 2024, to Hezbollah, but there is strong pressure on the part of others to approve these actions, and thus to imply, more forcefully than ever, that the only option is to agree that anti-Semitism and anti-Zionism are the same thing. The gulf has widened between those who call for the support of Israel, even at the cost of endorsing the illiberal drift of its government and its brutal actions in Gaza and Lebanon, and those who cannot accept this (or can do so no longer). Between these two extreme positions, it is difficult to resist the division and to maintain and defend positions that clearly distinguish the country from its government. It is not easy to support democracy and the rejection of illiberalism, and also the demand for moderation in the military conduct of the war, while at the same time combating the hatred of Israel. The way the diaspora is associated with the Hebrew state has become a problem for many Jews, as has one of the aspects of this association, namely Zionism.

In addition to proposing simplistic and dichotomized under-standings of the current situation, remarks about Zionism are often forgetful of history and other things besides. Before the birth of Israel, many political and religious voices in the dias-pora rejected Zionism – I know something about this, because the Bund, so dear to my parents and their friends, was among those that tended in this direction; it was created in 1897, par-tially in opposition to the First Zionist Congress, held the same year in Basel. In addition, after 1948, many anti-Semites were essentially in favor of the creation of Israel – politicians such as Pierre Boutang and Jean Madiran, the lawyer Jean-Louis Tixier-Vignancour, the general Lecomte, and also religious figures; today we still see this, with the support of Israel on the part of important representatives from American evangelical churches. One can be anti-Semitic and Zionist at the same time.

Israel's drift toward illiberalism, and the damage being caused to civilian populations by its retaliatory attacks on Hamas, are preoccupying for Jews in France as well as in the United States. One consequence – no doubt minor, but a sign of the times that is of great interest for our purposes – is that these obviously contribute to the depletion of the genre of Jewish jokes, in the way we have thought about it here – funny stories that can be told and heard by non-Jews without stoking anti-Semitism. Who would want to kindly poke fun at Jews given all that is currently taking place? Who, today, can look past the military and political events taking place in Israel, and appeal for goodwill and understanding by way of humor? Don't Jewish jokes risk become inaudible – unless they are interpreted in a way different from how they were originally meant, thereby approaching anti-Semitism?

This is a genuine question for the Jewish diaspora in the United States and France. It confronts us with an observation that I should perhaps have dealt with earlier, because it has been true of the Hebrew state since its birth: for even though the space for Jewish jokes and the conditions favorable to them owe much to how people in these two countries, both Jews and non-Jews, think about Israel – its existence, its political life, its struggles – it is nonetheless true, incredibly, that Israel – its inhabitants and its cultural, social, and religious figures – are generally absent from the content of these jokes. Of course, many jokes are told in Israel; in his book on Jewish humor, cited above, Joseph Klatzmann devoted about twenty pages to Israeli humor; and even after October 7, 2023, humor continues to exist, though it has become dark, sarcastic, and polemical, and is used above all to consolidate the Jewish world in the face of violence, war, and criticism that is often laced with anti-Semitism. But self-derision is not the main characteristic of this humor, which frequently takes aim at a particular group of Jews, Moroccans or Iranians, for instance, a little like Belgian jokes in France in the 1980s and 1990s. Those who tell these jokes never need to ask themselves if a non-Jewish audience will appreciate them, because they are destined only for Israeli Jews. It is difficult to imagine an important audience among the country's Arabs, who are a minority.

Israel and Israelis are seldom part of the diasporic universe of Jewish jokes, and then only incidentally. Jewish jokes, the way this book understands them, must of necessity be heard and understood by non-Jews. They only really count in and for the diaspora, because they are founded on the assumption of empathy between Jews and non-Jews, and a coexistence that is, if nor harmonious, at least tolerant and above all democratic. And if one considers, as I do, that they say, or used to say, something about Jewishness, then one must admit that they highlight the existence of a gulf that risks opening up in the heart of the Jewish people, between Israel and those who do not live there.

This gulf obviously does not prevent questions being asked about the system that Israel and the diaspora might constitute. Already in 1965, Georges Friedmann questioned the meaning of the idea of a Jewish people since the Israeli experience might seem to call into question what it had been up to that point.[4] This sociologist, who played a decisive role in the reconstruction of the social sciences in France after the Second World War, whose research concerned labor, and who helped important figures of the following generation, such as Alain Touraine, Edgar Morin, and Michel Crozier, to get started, liked to travel to Israel – he felt good there. This did not prevent him from thinking that this country heralded the birth of a new nation, rather than the continuation of the existence of a Jewish people in an association between the diaspora and the young state: "The 'Jewish people'," he wrote, "is disappearing and giving place to the Israeli nation."[5]

From a different standpoint, and around the same time, Vladimir Jankélévitch insisted on the idea of a tension "between this country, which is both like and unlike other countries, and the unprecedented fact of a dissemination that remains on its outside, and that will no doubt never be completely absorbed by it . . . This situation of tension . . . is the source of a fertile debate."[6]

The problem is that, today, Israel is no longer a country "unlike other countries." In many respects, it could become a country that is worse than others, if its rightward and theocratic drift continues, and the war with Hamas and Hezbollah does not lead to a lasting resolution. In this case, diasporic Jews will have to make a choice, following the triptych proposed by Albert O. Hirschman in his classic work *Exit, Voice, and Loyalty*:[7] take their distance with respect to it, protest it, or promote an unconditional identification with it. It has become difficult, costly, and painful for Jews who identify with Israel's founding values and promises to love it like Georges Friedmann did, but it is also not possible for them to break with it and forget that it is a Jewish state, especially after the war that began in 2023, and the wave of anti-Semitism that this has exacerbated all over the world. For the diaspora, the relationship with Israel is laden with various concerns; it is also contradictory, unless one settles the matter by either becoming an orphan with regard to a part of one's Jewishness, or validating, in an unnuanced way and without critical distance, Israel's theocratic, extreme-right orientation. Up to now, the situation was tenable, falling within what Jankélévitch called an "invigorating polarity that electrifies Jewish consciousness."[8] But the tension can only remain bearable, electrifying the Jewish consciousness, if the downward slide stops, and the democratic opposition to the current government, both in Israel and among the diaspora, obtains tangible results. And if a different form of politics regarding the Palestinians opens up the prospect of a lasting solution to the conflict.

We can now return to the relative (temporary?) decline of Jewish jokes. It owes a great deal not only to the developments in those societies in which the diaspora lives, but also to the contemporary path of the Hebrew state. In this sense, it is a global phenomenon.

For such jokes to prosper in the past, as I think I've shown, they had to make sense on both the international and national levels. They thus found a place in specific historical contexts, where ample space was made available to them in the 1970s to 2000s. They were enjoyable then because Jews were perceived, in these contexts, and often perceived themselves as well, as belonging to culturally diverse societies, in contact with other groups, existing on a basis of civic and political equality with at least some of these groups in the United States and France. But in Israel, the only significant non-Jewish group is made up of Palestinian Arabs, and it is difficult to imagine them enjoying Jewish jokes. Especially now, when we find hatred and violence flourishing on a huge scale.

Conclusion: The Last Jewish Joke

In 2005, as was the case every year between 2002 and 2020, I presided over Les Entretiens d'Auxerre, an annual two-day conference, the theme of which, on this occasion, was "Dealing with life, dealing with death." Among the participants were Henri Atlan, Jean-Claude Ameisen, Régis Aubry, Philippe Bataille, Philippe Lazar, Gaëtan Gorce, and Dominique Bromberger. We talked about the end of life, religion, and ethics.

Life and death

At one point during the conference, during a meal between two sessions, one of us – I think it was Henri Atlan, a very learned man, just as comfortable talking about Spinoza as about biology, as knowledgeable about the Talmud and about the complexity and organization of the living being – looked back on the exchanges we'd had during the session, and told the following joke.

> *A priest, a pastor, and a rabbi ask themselves when life begins.*

"For us Catholics," declares the priest, "it's very simple. Life begins at conception, when a spermatozoon encounters an ovum."

"For us Protestants," says the pastor, "it's different. Life begins when an embryo begins to form, in other words sixteen or thirty-two cells."

"For us Jews," replies the rabbi, "it's something else entirely. Life begins when the dog is dead and the kids are gone."

The rabbi, in this joke, is on the side of real life, rather than that of ethical, scientific, or metaphysical speculation, where the other protagonists are situated. It is not so much a religious figure who expresses himself here, but a Jew, which reminds us that this term refers to a people, a nation, and/or a religion, which is not the case with Catholics or Protestants. When he speaks as someone who belongs to a tradition, a people, or a nation, as he does here, the rabbi represents a sort of concrete truth, which has universal value – you obviously don't have to be Jewish to understand the conception of life he puts forth.

The joke about the beginning of life might make one think that the humor it conveys is evidence of a double dissolution of Judaism or Jewishness: the religious and the sacred seem to vanish, even though in principle they are borne by the rabbi, and the Jewish community is just as diluted, whether it is thought of as a people, a nation, or a minority group, because what the joke says about life, the dog, and the kids can be true for everyone, whether Jewish or non-Jewish. You have to look elsewhere if you're searching for something irreducibly Jewish, and if you're concerned by the possibility of this double dissolution, a possibility that haunts me. This is not the case for someone who defines himself by way of religion, or through a strong connection with the state of Israel.

And since we're talking about the end of life, allow me to evoke, in a bittersweet way, at once sad and happy, the memory of a friend of my parents, Perelmutter, a man who was always cheerful, warm, and who, I think, worked in the *schmattes*, or it could have been leatherworking. He had a favorite expression, which he used every time he drank tea on Sunday afternoon among family and friends: "This tea saved my life."

So one Sunday, he gets home, a little tired, he'd been working, and his wife serves him a *glus tei*, a "glass of tea," as usual. He drinks it, declares "This tea saved my life," and drops dead. This type of death, as a rabbi told me one day, is the "kiss of God." I've heard this story a good dozen times, always with a kind of tenderness for those who knew old Perelmutter, who was so jovial – which is also a way of keeping tragedy at bay.

In the exhaustible family of jokes that feature a rabbi and other religious leaders, one dimension deserves to be emphasized: the representatives of the great classic religions – until the 2000s, Islam didn't have as much of a place in France – have discussions, get along well, exchange thoughts, speak, listen, understand each other. And even if it doesn't take much to understand what distinguishes the rabbi and what gives the joke its flavor, there is still an understanding and a closeness between all of them. This is recent. The past relationship between Catholics and Protestants is marked by religious wars, persecution, and massacres, like that of St. Bartholomew's Day; and where Jews are concerned, although it is true that Jewish courtiers were sometimes accepted by Christian authorities, and there were relatively congenial historic periods – golden ages of sorts, which we must nonetheless not mythologize – for centuries, the hatred of Jews was inseparable from Christianity, until the Second Vatican Council of the 1960s. Whereas, in this joke, a priest, a pastor, and a rabbi take pleasure in exchanging ideas about an important religious, ethical, or moral issue. Times really have changed.

For several years now, I've been interested, in my private life as a citizen and as a sociologist, in the end of life and old age. Even before reading the journalist Victor Castanet's bestselling book *Les Fossoyeurs. Révélations sur le système qui maltraite nos aînés* [Gravediggers. Unmasking the system that mistreats our elders],[1] I was aware of the poor and sometimes even horrific treatment that can be found in retirement homes: I saw how my own mother, in an establishment in Paris that was certainly not the worst, was cut off from almost everything when she contracted the Covid-19 virus, especially during lockdown. Visits to her room, by a nurse or caregiver, became increasingly rare; someone wearing a mask would stop by once in a while to leave or collect a tray or some medicine, leaving after only a few seconds.

This was when I became a member of an association whose focus was old age, and for which my friend Véronique Fournier, a cardiologist and pioneer of clinical ethics, asked me to speak out as a sociologist: within the first few minutes of the first meeting I attended in June 2021, I was made to understand that what I said meant something to this group, because I spoke from the perspective of a researcher, but above all because I was a part of this mobilization of "old people" in a concrete way.

We did some great things, and we continue to do so. In particular, I was there for the birth of the CNaV, the Self-Proclaimed National Council for Aging, which has been written about in the national press. Ariane Mnouchkine hosted its first demonstrations in her Théâtre du Soleil in the Cartoucherie in Vincennes.

To say it once again, the demand for "axiological neutrality" that annoys me so much, and that a few phonies and pedants so delight in, really doesn't get you very far if you want to understand why and how my research activity has come about – in particular, the MGEN, the Mutual Insurance Firm for National Education, supports my research on the end of life.

In November 2022, I asked for and received permission to observe, as a sociologist, the work (based in deliberative democracy) being done by the Convention citoyenne sur la fin de vie [Citizen Convention for the End of Life], of which the French president was in favor.

It is attached to the CESE, the Economic, Social, and Environmental Council, which runs it. Around 180 citizens, randomly chosen, reflect on current policies around end-of-life care and the possibilities for improving it, including from a juridical standpoint. The discussions are complex, structured, at least at the beginning, by the opposition between two points of view: one that is hostile to everything that concerns assisted suicide and euthanasia and only wants to discuss hospice care, and another that seeks to modify the Claeys-Leonetti Law so as to allow active assistance for ending life. Religion occupies an important place in these debates, and on Friday, December 16, 2022, at 2:30 p.m., the Convention was set to hear the testimony of six of its representatives, and not the least important: Antony Boussemart (co-president of the Buddhist Union of France), Haïm Korsia (Chief Rabbi of France), Laurent Ulrich (Archbishop of Paris), Chems-eddine Hafiz (Rector of the Grand Mosque of Paris), Christian Krieger (President of the Protestant Federation of France), and Marc Alric (Romanian Orthodox Bishop of Neamt).

At 2 p.m., I was in the great hall of the CESE when they all arrived at about the same time. I happen to know the Chief Rabbi a little, as well as the Rector. They were almost all there, together; I greeted them and spent a moment with them.

We had a pleasant conversation. It seems that they all get along very well, and are in general agreement on end-of-life care: yes to hospice care, no to assisted suicide and euthanasia. As the climate was relaxed, I asked the Chief Rabbi if I could tell Henri Atlan's joke about the beginning of life, which he in fact knew. Yes, he said, and I'd barely finished when the pastor (if I'm not mistaken) noted that the rabbi's answer in this joke should have included the mother-in-law along with the dog and the kids – and it did, in the version he'd heard. Then Chief Rabbi Korsia told another joke, which I reproduce here with in my own words; I may have twisted his words, but not much – Jewish jokes are meant to be spoken, and every person who tells them gives his own personal touch.

The last Jewish joke

This takes places in a faraway city. In a seedy location, four people are playing cards for money: a priest, a pastor, an imam, and a rabbi. An odor is wafting about, and what they're smoking is surely not tobacco, or not only. Suddenly, the police burst in.

"Men, you're a disgrace to our city," says the chief of police. "You should embody the highest values, and I find you playing cards, smoking, who knows what else . . . And what's more, you're playing for money!"

The clergymen vigorously deny that they're gambling, but the police chief doesn't believe them. He says to the priest:

"Swear to me on the Holy Bible that you're not playing for money."

"Yes, I swear," says the priest after trying to dodge the question and finding himself cornered.

"You too, swear," the chief orders the pastor.

"Embarrassed, squirming and wriggling, but not finding a way out, the pastor declares:

"Yes, I swear."

"Your turn – swear," the chief of police commands the imam. He finally complies after a few vain contortions.

"It's your turn – swear," the police chief finally says to the rabbi.

"Seriously," he responds, "you don't really think I'm gambling all alone?"

By then it was 2:30 p.m. The time had come for the representatives of these great religions to move to the amphitheater of the CESE to present their position on end-of-life care and respond to the citizens' questions.

And so these religious dignitaries, among the highest in the country, in what was perhaps a sign of their patience and tolerance toward me, and seemingly without batting an eyelid, agreed to listen to a sociologist, and then agreed, above all one of them, to listen to a rather secular joke, which certain audiences might find antireligious or at least disrespectful. We have moved far from the times and the places in which the sacred, and the distance it requires, were the rule.

The one who takes things furthest in the joke about the cards is the rabbi: he participates in the debauchery just like the others, but he also avoids perjuring himself, by using his intelligence. There is something troubling about this.

Since the 1970s, we have entered into the age of victimhood, in which Jews are the foremost paradigmatic figures, but in this joke, the Jew is the one who deals with the situation more skillfully than the others. This echoes jokes that aren't really Jewish, but that demonstrate anti-Semitism or reveal it in a critical manner, for example by illustrating stereotypes relating to the supposed ability of Jews to get out of tricky situations in ways that are intelligent and, to a greater or lesser degree, selfish. Here is one, for example, that circulated in the age of the decline of "real" communism, and that was told to me in Poland, at the beginning of the 1980s, when Solidarność prefigured, in its struggle, the end of the regime and of the Soviet system more generally.

What follows takes place in a context in which stores are empty, and in which you have to line up for hours to buy the slightest bit of food. The people in the neighborhood have just been advised that a delivery of meat will arrive at the central butcher shop, and they are invited to make their way there. They arrive in their hundreds, starting in the early morning, to wait. After several hours, a loudspeaker announces a delay, and specifies that there will not be enough meat for everyone. The Jews are asked to return to their homes. Night falls.

The next morning, before the line has even moved, the loud-speaker announces that the delivery of meat won't be arriving after all. The people who were waiting patiently are asked to return to their homes. Suddenly everyone, whether annoyed or dejected, begins to say the same thing: once again, the Jews got off better than we did.

This joke is somewhat unique because it presents the Jews as passive. It's not a joke that is hostile toward them, but one that illustrates, in a funny way, the mechanisms of hatred and bad faith. It is above all anti-communist, and thus belongs to a genre different from Jewish jokes, because it is only funny for an audience that is hostile to those in power – a communist party or its ideology. It reports a widespread anti-Semitism, one shared by the entire crowd, while at the same time it fore-grounds a government that is loathed.

But let's return to the joke about the card game. The response by the rabbi to the policeman is worthy of further examination. It doesn't so much display humor as it does wit, a capacity to confront a delicate situation with intelligence, which makes it quite pleasant. But it also has a slightly unpleas-ant side, because in the end it allows the others to lie while God is watching. The rabbi is more intelligent, thus conforming to a stereotype often applied to the Jews, but this allows him merely to take advantage of his superiority all alone, without any generosity.

This is why this joke is different from the others I've told up to now. It can make people uncomfortable because to some degree it approaches ideas that associate Jews with deviousness and indeed evil, without sufficiently enacting any distancing or diversion. The other religious representatives are distressed because they perjure themselves, but the rabbi avoids this, even though he participated in the card game just like them. The Jew is no longer a victim; he gets out of the situation, at least with less damage than the others. He doesn't exhibit any solidarity; he's not like the others; he's at once cunning and malevolent and defends only his own interests.

We're in a troubling gray area here in which the Jewish joke begins to cut itself off from a certain universalism, which is not flattering for the Jewish community. On this occasion, humor ceases to explode stereotypes, as it did in the case of the comic Popeck, who pushed the greed of his character so far that it became absurd and unreal. This is why I'm calling this joke about the interruption of the card game by the police the last Jewish joke, the one that ends an age. Because this joke truly belongs to its time, if only for the presence of the imam, which tells us that we must now take Islam and its institutional representation into account, which wasn't the case in France thirty or forty years ago. Most importantly, with this joke, the very element that gave the genre its flavor begins to be lost: a way of staging things that appealed to empathy for those it gently and even tenderly poked fun at; a humor that poked fun at itself even as it displayed a level of intelligence.

Jokes, whether Jewish or otherwise, make us laugh. They instantly bring together all sorts of feelings, memory traces, and opinions, without generating explicit reflections on everything they've awakened. This is why they can be linked, as in Freud's work, to the unconscious, to everything that isn't said and isn't formulated, or is formulated in other ways. This aspect of jokes is perhaps also what is referred to by Henri Bergson's famous definition of laughter: "Something mechanical encrusted on the living."

The most defining characteristic of Jewish jokes is that they are favorable, and not hostile, to Jews. They are made for them, and generally by them, or for those who appreciate them or at lease do not reject them. They allow those who tell them to be in step with those who listen to them, by proposing an imaginary passage to these listeners from sadness to happiness, from a difficulty, whether large or small, to its resolution.

When they lack this, they are, to use Freud's term, *tendentious*: they encounter "people who do not want to listen to them,"[2] or who find in them the validation of their prejudices and other stereotypes; they put themselves in the service of hostile or obscene tendencies, and move outside the definition of them that we have proposed.

As soon as they cease to deal with characters or a universe that are not detestable, or distance themselves from the evocation of warm, open, and unifying relationships that are sensitive to reality; as soon as they lose contact with positive representations that Jews can have of themselves, cease to put across the love of the other, weigh themselves down with irony, and stray from kindness or at least indulgence; and as soon as they cease to poke fun at anti-Semitic stereotypes to the point of making them unworkable or impossible, they step outside the register of Jewish jokes as I understand them. And they thereby risk bringing those who tell or listen to them down a slippery slope that leads to hatred.

Jewish jokes generally include a strong dose of self-derision: their humor is aimed at the self, themselves, their own people; but if others cannot understand them and share them, they cease to conform to the definition that I've proposed. They go from being Jewish jokes to anti-Semitic jokes, of which there is no lack.

In general, jokes flatter one group of humans by targeting another: the self only posits itself through opposition, as Hegel said. What is exceptional about Jewish jokes is that they are an example of people laughing at themselves to reinforce themselves, or at least so as to not lose contact with their group; they do this to posit themselves, but also to be in step with others, to live alongside them in full awareness of their differences, and in relative good humor.

Jewish jokes can still bear witness to a belonging to the Jewish world, or appeal to this belonging. In extreme cases, they can stage or bring to life what remains Jewish even in the refusal of religion, and even when the relationship to Israel is very strained. They thus play a decisive role in a Jewishness that they seek not to break with. They can also include an accent, as well as gestures, body language, and mimicry, which, as Freddy Raphaël notes regarding the specific case of Alsace and Lorraine, "expand the possibilities of language, [ensuring] the intertwining of Hebrew turns of phrase with the expressions that give Alsatian Yiddish its musicality";[3] they thus belong no less to the expression of a real and living community than to that of a more or less residual memory.

Starting in the 1970s, with the discovery of the annihilation of European Jews by the Nazis, the awareness of which spread to the whole of society, French and American Jews were able to put forth an unprecedented and tragic experience of suffering, which generated feelings of understanding and a certain benevolence toward them, as well as a greater acceptance of them. Jewish humor, and an intellectual originality largely inherited from Yiddish culture, was experienced as a vector of innovation and stimulation for society as a whole, giving rise to an interest, also benevolent, for this cultural inventiveness that had in some way survived the destruction of Jewish communities in Europe. In France, the arrival of Sephardic Jews from North Africa, due to decolonization, brought a second wind to this trend. Finally, the positive and at times even heroic image of Israel, its politics, and its geopolitics gave diaspora Jews a shared foundation, which they found reassuring and rewarding for almost a half century.

The third of a century that ended with the year 2000 was thus a singular historical moment, one that I experienced, in which three unprecedented phenomena converged for the Jews of France, America, and certainly elsewhere (such as Poland, as I've discussed) to constitute favorable conditions for the expansion of Jewish jokes. This convergence set out a space in which they could be welcomed by a well-disposed audience of both Jews and non-Jews.

Then, each of these three dimensions started to weaken, even before the arrival of the twenty-first century. The memory of the Shoah became institutionalized, established in teaching and various sites of commemoration, which strengthened it but also took away from the shocking effect it had in the 1970s and 1980s. Cultural and intellection innovation petered out, losing its momentum. And what we now see of Israel no longer allows it to embody promises of democracy, justice, and progress as it did in the early years of its existence. What once converged has now broken apart, and the space created by these three dimensions has shrunk at an incredibly fast rate. In a certain way, Jewish jokes helped us to reflect on Jewish history – the birth, heyday, and decline of a period of history that was very happy for Jews. And vice versa. Not everything in their humor is unconscious.

This observation can have considerable implications for the very definition of Jewish identity today – an issue that has been delicate for a long time, as evidenced by the fifty or so responses to the letter that David Ben-Gurion, then Israeli prime minister, sent in 1958 to several important Jewish figures, in Israel and the diaspora, asking them: "Who Is a Jew?"[4] Richard Marienstras, in a book I've already cited, *Être un peuple en diaspora*, came up with a response, avoiding the issue by way of humor: Jewish identity, he wrote, lies in the fact that Jews spend all their time thinking about their identity.

In 1946, with the war over, Jean-Paul Sartre published *Anti-Semite and Jew*.[5] Let us look here at this famous text, and especially the main idea (acknowledging that things are more complex than this), namely that the Jew is anyone considered as such by non-Jews. For Sartre, who deals primarily with anti-Semitism and anti-Semites, it is the gaze of the other that creates the Jew – not history, not religion, not language or culture, and not a territory of reference (Israel). The historical moment that was the heyday of Jewish jokes is a problem for Sartre's approach, though perhaps only temporarily: when the genocide and indeed the shock of its discovery lose their primacy as references, when interest in the intellectual heritage and cultural vitality of *Yiddishkeit* begins to wane, when Israel ceases to be viewed in a positive light, and when the capacity for bringing to life a Jewishness that also interests non-Jews is absent, these jokes can only appear as vestiges from the past, and hence, potentially, as belonging to the history of ruins.

The current situation, which is less conducive to highlighting historical Jewish suffering and the Shoah, less favorable to a shared (even if tense) relationship with non-Jews and with Israel, and less dynamic culturally, currently leaves diaspora Jews with only difficult choices: a rather firm and potentially radical religious identity, theocratic with regard to Israel; unnuanced support of Israel government policies, regardless of how extreme they may be; political support for the democratic movement currently resisting the movement toward illiberalism, whether in Israel, the United States, or France; or the adoption of the definition proposed by Sartre, whereby they are Jews solely as a result of anti-Semitism.

But even if this last choice still makes sense, there's a good chance that it could be the final step, or final (and potentially insurmountable) obstacle, before a pure and simple forgetting – assimilation, not integration. But – and to return to the words of Jankélévitch – even in the face of the looming threat that Jewish identity may simply dissolve, doesn't there remain a "je ne sais quoi," something "impalpable," an "ambivalence" arising from the desire to simultaneously erase and retain differences? This "je ne sais quoi" is what we eventually find in Jewish jokes. Can one not, as Adam Biro writes, be "a Jew by humor"?[6] Isn't the humor of Jewish jokes that which is most able to resist, allowing one to convey something that is not entirely lost or forgotten, that remains "electric," and cannot be reduced solely to the gaze of the Other? Perhaps, provided that one avoid two dangerous tendencies. On the one hand, that of a dissolution into universalism, in which these jokes are no longer "Jewish" except indirectly and for an informed audience, as with the remarks of the taxi driver that so amused my father. On the other hand, that of a slide toward a disturbing zone in which anti-Semitism can forge a path, such as in the joke about the card game. This book thus ends with a question, which might make things even more perplexing. Like in the following joke:

> *A goy and a Jew are having a conversation in a train.*
> *"Why," asks the goy, "do you Jews respond to every question with another question?"*
> *"Why not?"*

Notes

I: The American Invention of Jewish Jokes

1 Odile Jacob, 2005.

2 In her 1973 novel *The Fear of Flying*.

3 See Sigmund Freud, *Jokes and Their Relation to the Unconscious*, trans. James Strachey (W. W. Norton, 1960).

4 See his "Culture and Symptoms: An Analysis of Patients Presenting Complaints," *American Sociological Review*, 31 (1966), pp. 615–630.

5 *L'Humour juif dans la littérature de Job à Woody Allen* (PUF, 1984), p. 262.

6 *Les Juifs américains du XVIIᵉ siècle à nos jours* (Calmann-Lévy, 1972), p. 237.

7 *Histoire des relations entre Juifs et Noirs. De la Bible à Black Lives Matter* (Albin Michel, 2023).

8 *La Concurrence des victimes* (La Découverte, 1997).

9 *The Originals* podcast, *Los Angeles Magazine*, episode 6, 2020.

10 "The Yiddishisation of American Humor," *Esquire*, October 1965, pp. 114–15.

11 In his *Dictionnaire amoureux de l'humour juif* (Plon, 2022), p. 150.

12 *Mel Brooks: Disobedient Jew* (Yale University Press, 2023).

13 See Cathy Lynn Grossman, "Survey: Being Jewish Means Being Funny, and That's No Joke," *USA Today*, October 1, 2013.

14 *Jewish Comedy: A Serious History* (W. W. Norton, 2017).

15 *Jewish Humor: What the Best Jewish Jokes Say About the Jews* (William Morrow Paperbacks, 1998).

16 *The Big Book of Jewish Humor*, republished by William Morrow Paperbacks in 2006 for the 25th anniversary of its initial release in 1981.

17 February 12, 2009.

18 *Histoire des Américains juifs* (André Versaille, 2008).

II: Prolegomena

1 *L'Humour juif* (PUF, 1998).

2 La Découverte, 1993.

3 *Le Shtetl, la bourgade juive de Pologne. De la tradition à la modernité* (Payot, 1986).

4 Harvard University Press, 1973.

5 See Freud, *Jokes and Their Relation to the Unconscious*, especially the second chapter, "The Technique of Jokes."

6 *Gefilte fish*: stuffed carp, a specialty of Central European Jews that has today become a high-end dish.

7 *L'Humour juif dans la littérature de Job à Woody Allen* (PUF, 1984), p. 55.

8 Ibid., p. 60.

9 Ibid., p. 61.

10 Wolf Wieviorka, *Est et Ouest. Déracinés* (Bibliothèque Medem, 2004; Points Seuil, 2023).

11 *Zibele* are small onions.

12 See Dreyfus's book *Hannah Arendt et la question juive: pour une relecture* (PUF, 2023).

III: In France, in the 1960s and 1970s

1 *Rire pour réparer le monde: l'humour des juifs d'Alsace et de Lorraine* (La Nuée bleue, 2021), p. 11.

2 Trans. Deborah Cowell (Liverpool University Press, 2009).

3 Aron Jean-Marie Lustiger (1926–2007) was a French Catholic cardinal who was born into an Ashkenazi Jewish family. – Trans.

4 Jean-Marie Lustiger, *Le Choix de Dieu: entretiens avec Jean-Louis Missika et Dominique Wolton* (Éditions de Fallois, 1987).

IV: What Counts as a Jewish Joke and What Doesn't

1 In "De l'essence du rire et généralement dans les arts plastiques," quoted by Daniel Grojnowski, *Les Rires d'hier et d'aujourd'hui* (Presses universitaires de Rennes, 2022), p. 46.

2 Ibid., p. 11.

3 Ibid., p. 10.

4 Darty is one of Europe's largest retailers of electronic goods. – Trans.

5 *Rire. Une anthropologie du rieur* (Métailié, 2018).

6 *Laughter: An Essay on the Meaning of the Comic*, trans. Cloudesley Brereton and Fred Rothwell (Macmillan, 1911).

7 Freud, *Jokes and Their Relation to the Unconscious*.

8 Freud, "Humor," *International Journal of Psychoanalysis* 9 (1928), pp. 1–6.

9 For more on this lovely chapter of political and social history, see the book written by a close friend of my parents, Henri Minczeles, *Histoire générale du Bund: Un mouvement révolutionnaire juif* (Austral, 1995; Denoël, 1999; L'Échappée, 2022).

10 The term "Islamo-gauchisme" has been used in France to refer to what some see as a recent convergence between Islamism and leftism, especially in universities. – Trans.

11 La Boîte à Pandore, 2021.

12 Stanford University Press, 1996.

13 Le Seuil, 2022.

14 *Les Juifs, la Pologne et Solidarność* (Denoël, 1984).

15 (Plon, 2022), p. 41.

16 *Le Fumier de Job* (Didier, 1928).

17 See especially *The Jew as Pariah* (Grove Press, 1978).

V: The Heyday of Jewish Jokes in France

1 David Kurc and Jacqueline Kurc, *L'Humour yiddish* (Eyrolles, 2019); Alter Druyanov, *Le Rire de Chelm* (Matanel/Berg international, 2017); Victor Malka, *Le Dico de l'humour juif* (Points, 2017); Franck Médioni, *L'Humour juif expliqué à ma mère* (Chiflet & Cie, 2017); Daniel Lifschitz, *Ri-rabbin qui rira le dernier* (Salvator, 2017); Teh 'im na'na' [Tel-'Abiyb]: Biymat Qedem, hwṣa'at spariym (2014); Marc-Alain Ouaknin, *La Bible de l'humour juif* (Michel Lafon, 2012); Frédéric Pouhier, Sylvie Jouffa, and François Jouffa, *L'Officiel de l'humour juif* (First éditions, 2012); *La Vérité si je mens* (Chiflet & Cie, 2012); Josy Eisenberg, *Ma Plus Belle Histoire d'humour* (D. Reinharc, 2011); Richard Zéboulon, *Le Zéboulon, petite anthologie de l'humour juif, Opus 1 et 2* (Le Bord de l'eau, 2005, 2006); *Mots d'esprit de l'humour juif* (Le Seuil, 2006); Seper hahwmwr hayhwdiy hagadwl, 'Wr Yhwdah, Kineret, 5764 (2004); Krzysztof Zmuda, *Anegdoty Żydowskie* (Ad Oculos, 2003); Marc-Alain Ouaknin and Dory Rotnemer, *Tout l'humour juif,* (Assouline, 2001); Gilles Achache, *J'aurais tant voulu qu'il soit docteur!* (Calmann-Lévy, 2000); Élie Kakou, *La vérité, j'te la raconte!* (J'ai lu, 1999); Erika Birgit von Kretzer (dir.), *Zwischen Himmel und Erde* (Gütersloher Verlagshaus, 1999); Dory Rotnemer, *La Nouvelle Bible de l'humour juif,* vol. 1 (Éditions du Rocher/Bibliophane, 1999); Marc-Alain Ouaknin and Dory Rotnemer, *La Bible de l'humour juif,* 2 vols. (vol. 1, Ramsay, 1995; vol. 2, J'ai lu, 1998); Paul Wermus, *Petites blagues juives entre amis* (First éditions, 1997); David Lemberg and Élie Baroukh, *5000 Ans d'humour juif* (First éditions, 1995); Gil Wern and Léon Tzroky, *Le Livre de l'humour goy* (Les Belles Lettres, 1995); Samuel Abraham, *Les Toutes Dernières Histoires juives* (Zélie, 1993); François Lévy, Jean-Jacques Ritz, and Emmanuel Suchet, *Freudlichkeit. Recueil d'histoires judéo-psychanalytiques* (Comp'Act, 1991); Guy Konopnicki, Brice Couturier, *Réflexions sur la question goy* (Lieu Commun, 1988); Henry Bulawko, *Anthologie de l'humour juif et israélien* (Bibliophane, 1988); *Popeck raconte les meilleures*

histoires de l'humour juif, ed. Bernard Stéphane, (Le Livre de poche, 1980); *Jüdische Anekdoten und Sprichwörter* (Deutscher Taschenbuch Verlag, 1966).

2 *Comment ça va mal? L'humour juif, un art de l'esprit* (Bréal, 2009).

3 *La Bible de l'humour juif* (Ramsay, 1995).

4 "Aspects psychologiques des 'histoires juives,'" *La Revue de la pensée juive,* 6 (1951).

5 In *Le Rire de Dieu* (Points Seuil, 2010), p. 7.

6 Ibid., p. 17.

7 *L'Humour juif dans la littérature de Job à Woody Allen,* p. 49.

8 *Humour et sagesse judéo-arabes* (Desclée de Brouwer, 1998).

9 *Contes et récits humoristiques du monde juif* (L'Harmattan, 1991).

10 Pierre Birnbaum, *The Jews of the Republic: A Political History of State Jews in France from Gambetta to Vichy,* trans. Jane Marie Todd (Stanford University Press, 1996).

11 *Déportation et génocide. Entre la mémoire et l'oubli* (Hachette, 2003).

12 Jankélévitch, *La Conscience juive* (L'Herne, 2023), p. 7.

13 See Perrine Simon-Nahum, "Penser le judaïsme. Retour sur les Colloques des intellectuels juifs de langue française (1957–2000)," *Archives juives* (2005/1), vol. 38, pp. 79–106.

14 Trans. Stephen Becker (Atheneum, 1960).

15 Gallimard, 1962.

16 https://www.lemonde.fr/archives/article/2004/02/12/rene-gos cinny-asterix-et-le-judaisme_352742_1819218.html.

17 https://www.actuabd.com/Comment-ca-Marcel-vous-etes-juif.

18 *Les Juifs, les musulmans et la République* (Robert Laffont, 2017).

19 See his book *L'Engrenage terroriste* (Fayard, 1981).

20 I analyze the emergence of this in an article in the journal *Esprit* ("Les conditions de formation d'un mouvement juif en France," April 1982).

21 *Contes et récits humoristiques du monde juif,* p. 9.

22 *Une vie de Juif sans importance* (Robert Laffont, 2008).

23 Éditions François Maspero.

24 In the journal *Plurielles,* 10 (2003).

25 *Des Blancs comme les autres ? Les Juifs, angle mort de l'antiracisme* (Stock, 2022), p. 98.

26 Alain Finkielkraut, *The Imaginary Jew,* trans. Kevin O'Neill and David Suchoff (University of Nebraska Press, 1994), p. 6.

VI: The American Decline

1 *The Tears of History: The Rise of Political Antisemitism in the United States,* trans. Karen Santos Da Silva (Columbia University Press, 2023).

VII: In France, a Changed Situation

1 See especially his book *Heureux comme Juifs en France? Étude sociologique* (Elkana, 2007).

2 *Ghetto urbain. Ségrégation, violence, pauvreté en France aujourd'hui* (Robert Laffont, 2008).

3 *L'An prochain à Jérusalem ? Les Juifs de France face à l'antisémitisme* (Éditions de l'Aube, 2016).

4 Mille et une nuits, 2002.

5 *Pieds-noirs de père en fils* (Balland, 2004).

6 The conference led to the book *L'Allemagne nazie et le génocide juif* (Gallimard/Le Seuil, 1985).

7 Michel Wieviorka, *The Lure of Anti-Semitism: Hatred of Jews in Present-Day France,* trans. Kristina Couper Lobel and Anna Declerck (Brill, 2007).

8 For more on the history of the CRIF, I refer the reader to the book by Samuel Ghiles-Meilhac, based on his dissertation (for which I served as director), *Le CRIF. De la Résistance juive à la tentation du lobby. De 1943 à nos jours* (Robert Laffont, 2011).

9 Max Milo, 2018.

10 Don Quichotte, 2010.

11 Don Quichotte/Le Seuil, 2021.
12 In *Understanding Terror Networks* (University of Pennsylvania Press, 2004).
13 Rue de Seine, 2022.
14 "On ne combat pas des dérives en faisant la guerre à l'intelligence," *Le Monde*, January 19, 2022. ["One can't fight abuse by waging war on intelligence."]
15 Verso, 2000.
16 See the Wikipedia article on this at: https://en.wikipedia.org /wiki/Amendment_to_the_Act_on_the_Institute_of_National _Remembrance – Trans.

VIII: What About Israel?

1 December 17, 2022.
2 "La démocratie est en danger en Israël en raison de l'avènement sournois d'un régime autocratique illiberal," *Le Monde*, March 9, 2023. ["Democracy in Israel is in danger due to the insidious rise of an illiberal autocratic regime."]
3 "Plus qu'Itamar Ben-Gvir, c'est la dérive droitière de l'opinion publique en Israël qui est inquiétante," *Le Monde*, January 7, 2023. ["More than Itamar Ben-Gvir, it is the right-wing drift of public opinion in Israel that is worrying."]
4 In his *La Fin du peuple juif?*, which appeared in English as *The End of the Jewish People?*, trans. Eric Mosbacher (Doubleday, 1967).
5 Ibid., p. 273.
6 "Le judaïsme, problème intérieur," in Jankélévitch, *La Conscience juive* (L'Herne, 2023), pp. 12–13.
7 Harvard University Press, 1970.
8 "Le judaïsme, problème intérieur," p. 13.

Conclusion: The Last Jewish Joke

1 Fayard, 2022.
2 Freud, *Jokes and Their Relation to the Unconscious*, p. 107.
3 *Rire pour réparer le monde* (La Nuée bleue, 2021), p. 12.

4 See Eliezer Ben-Rafaël, *Qu'est-ce qu'être juif?*, followed by *50 Sages répondent à Ben Gourion (1958): document inédit* (Balland, 2001).

5 Trans. George J. Becker (Schocken, 1995).

6 *Dictionnaire amoureux de l'humour juif,* p. 463.

AMY EDMONDSON

Bestselling Author of *The Fearless Organization*

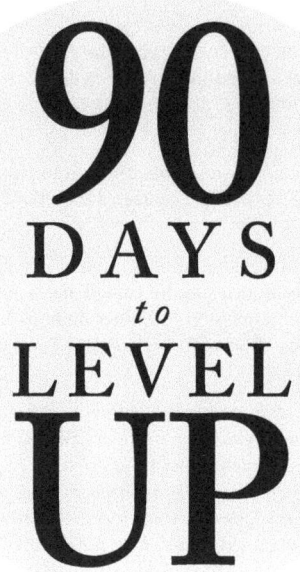

90
DAYS
to
LEVEL
UP

YOUR
TEAMWORK

WILEY

Published by John Wiley & Sons, Inc., Hoboken, New Jersey.
Published simultaneously in Canada.

The manufacturer's authorized representative according to the EU General Product Safety Regulation is Wiley-VCH GmbH, Boschstr. 12, 69469 Weinheim, Germany, e-mail: Product_Safety@wiley.com.

For general information on our other products and services or for technical support, please contact our Customer Care Department within the United States at (800) 762-2974, outside the United States at (317) 572-3993 or fax (317) 572-4002.

Wiley also publishes its books in a variety of electronic formats. Some content that appears in print may not be available in electronic formats. For more information about Wiley products, visit our web site at www.wiley.com.

Library of Congress Cataloging-in-Publication Data is Available:

ISBN 9781394257959 (Cloth)
ISBN 9781394335527 (ePub)
ISBN 9781394372317 (ePDF)

Cover design: Paul McCarthy

Contents

90-Day Plan

Each week, you'll focus on one element of teamwork that will help you achieve your performance goals. This 90-Day Plan outlines these skills and topics so you can pace yourself, track your progress, and identify the areas that will have the most impact for you. Add your personal goals and vision for success at the bottom of this plan.

Your 90-Day Plan to Level Up Your Teamwork Skills
Performance Goals
• Get ready to learn, innovate, and compete.   • Team fearlessly with psychological safety.   • Innovate with teaming.
Benchmark Goals
Days 1–30   Get ready to learn, innovate, and compete.   Week 1: Understand how teaming is different than teamwork.   Week 2: Learn the four pillars of teaming and why they work.   Week 3: Lead through teaming.   Week 4: Discover how to team across boundaries.

Days 31–60

Team fearlessly with psychological safety.

Week 5: Grasp the power of psychological safety.

Week 6: Make it safe to team.

Week 7: Frame your team for success.

Week 8: Create a fearless organization.

Days 61–90

Innovate with teaming.

Week 9: Aim high.

Week 10: Team up.

Week 11: Fail well.

Week 12: Learn fast.

Personal Goals and Vision for Success

What do you hope to achieve by leveling up?

_____

_____

_____

How could your life change by reaching these goals?

_____

_____

_____

Are you ready to level up? Let's get started!

Introduction

Welcome to *90 Days to Level Up Teamwork*, your guide to taking your leadership skills to the next level in only 90 days. In this guide, I challenge you with actionable, practical goals to build your teamwork skills week by week. You don't have to wait to see results: you'll be learning and growing every week of this 90-Day Plan.

In this guide, I challenge you to do the following:

- Get ready to learn, innovate, and compete.
- Team fearlessly with psychological safety.
- Innovate with teaming.

These overarching performance goals are broken down into benchmark goals for each week: rigorous but achievable targets to let you see immediate progress on your journey.

Each weekly goal comes with insightful readings, engaging activities, and opportunities for self-reflection.

Part I describes the basic activities and conditions that help organizations succeed through teaming, a dynamic kind of teamwork designed to fit the needs of the fast-paced modern workplace. I cover how work gets done, how leaders help make it happen, and how a safe interpersonal environment frees up people to focus on innovation. The model and guidelines presented throughout this part provide

readers with a supportive framework for understanding and responding to the dynamics of collective learning. I examine and describe the mindset required to successfully incorporate teaming within an organizational setting and provide a set of leadership practices that can help develop a team-based learning infrastructure.

In Part II, I look at what psychological safety is and why it matters, as well as why it's not the norm in many organizations. I discuss how crucial it is to create an environment where everyone feels free to speak up honestly and mistakes can be admitted without fear. I also talk about what psychological safety *isn't* and why it doesn't mean immunity from consequences. Leaders have a special responsibility to create the conditions of psychological safety, and I discuss what those are. Last, I cover the importance of framing work well and how to actually go about creating a psychologically safe environment.

In Part III, I discuss the four requirements to build a team for innovation: aim high, team up, fail well, and learn fast. Aiming high involves choosing a worthy goal for your team, and I cover what that means and how it spurs innovation. Successful teaming often requires diverse (in many ways) team members, and that diversity brings risks as well as benefits. You will learn how to maximize the benefits and minimize risks. I also explain why "fail well" isn't an oxymoron and the many learning benefits that you can derive from an *intelligent* failure.

In Part I, you will get ready to learn, innovate, and compete with teaming.

In week 1, I define teaming and explain how teaming is different than teamwork. How does it work? What does it take for people to learn how to team? What do people do when teaming? How does teaming produce organizational learning? This week describes the challenges to teaming and shows what it looks like when it's done well. I define teaming and examine why it's so crucial in today's complex organizations.

In week 2, you learn the four pillars of teaming and why they are a must: speaking up, collaboration, experimentation, and reflection. I also look at why those four pillars aren't as easy to achieve as you might think. I review the benefits of teaming and talk about some of the barriers you must overcome to team effectively.

In week 3, I show you how to lead with teaming. My years of research have established four key responsibilities that leaders have to set the stage for successful teaming:

- Frame the situation for learning.
- Make it psychologically safe to team.
- Learn to learn from failure.
- Span occupational and cultural boundaries.

I cover all of these in more depth throughout this 90-Day Plan. In week 3, I also offer strategies for learning from failure.

In week 4, you discover how to team across boundaries. There are many barriers or boundaries to successful teaming. In the modern workplaces, workers are often widely dispersed geographically, have different cultural backgrounds, have varying educational backgrounds, and have widely differing status. But in order to get the results you want, you'll need to overcome these stumbling blocks to successful teaming. In this week, you look at the common types of boundaries, how they interfere with successful teaming, and, most important, how to overcome them.

In Part II, you will discover teaming fearlessly with psychological safety.

In week 5, we begin a deep dive into psychological safety—what it is and why it's important. You will also learn the dangers of an environment where people don't feel psychologically safe. Finally, I

explain why psychologically safe high-performing teams only *seem* to make more errors than other teams.

In week 6, you will learn the many benefits of psychological safety. In addition, you will see why it can be so difficult for workers to feel comfortable in speaking up and how interpersonal risk plays into that. I also explain how everyone, but especially leaders, can help encourage psychological safety throughout the organization.

In week 7, you look at the subject of framing and the important responsibilities that leaders have to frame work and the team effectively. Considerable research has shown that when a project is framed well by leadership, successful outcomes are more likely. In this week, you learn what successful framing looks like and strategies for achieving it. I also explain why the "ideal employees" might not be who you think they are.

In week 8, I dive into the hows of psychological safety. How does a leader create a fertile environment for it? One key factor is encouraging employees to use their voice. I examine how to do that and why it matters. You will also read about an interesting case where an employee was fired from Google for expressing an (unpopular) opinion. I examine how it could have been handled differently and how Google could learn from this situation in the future.

In Part III, you will learn how to innovate with teaming by discovering four key concepts to innovation: aim well, team up, fail well, and learn fast.

In week 9, you begin to learn about the first of the key concepts that set the stage for innovation: aiming well. When you are looking to do something that has never been done before, it helps to have a worthy goal. A leader is responsible for not only pointing the team in the direction of an inspiring or meaningful goal but also helping to frame it that way for everyone on the team.

In week 10, I discuss the second key to innovation: teaming up. Contrary to popular belief, some of the most successful teams are composed of strange bedfellows. You will learn about one fascinating real-life example that formed the basis of the movie *Argo*. Diverse skills and backgrounds are often necessary for a successful team, but those differences can create challenges, too. I also cover how to address those boundaries to successful teaming.

In week 11, I cover the third key to innovation: failing well. Despite what you might think, not all failure is created equal. Sometimes, failures can be an essential and productive learning opportunity, but not all failures fall into this category. In this week, I explain the different types of failures and how to make sure that your failures are the right kind. I also cover the responsibilities of a leader in managing failures.

In week 12, I look at the fourth key to innovation: learning fast. When you have those productive failures that you learned about in week 11, it's vital that you learn from them and learn fast. In this week, you discover how to learn fast and how to overcome barriers to it. You will also discover your responsibilities as a leader to prepare your team for learning from its mistakes and setbacks.

If you are ready to level up your teamwork, turn the page and get started!

Performance goal: Get ready to learn, innovate, and compete.

Teaming, coined deliberately to capture the *activity* of working together, presents a new, more flexible way for organizations to carry out interdependent tasks. Unlike the traditional concept of a team, *teaming* is an active process, not a static entity. Imagine a fluid network of interconnected individuals working in temporary teams on improvement, problem-solving, and innovation. Teaming blends relating to people, listening to other points of view, coordinating actions, and making shared decisions.

The following table summarizes the skills you will sharpen over the next 30 days. To keep yourself motivated, consider your personal goals and vision for success. What does teamwork mean to you?

Days 1–30
Performance Goal: Get ready to learn, innovate, and compete.

Week 1	**Benchmark Goal: Understand how teaming is different than teamwork.** • What was psychologist Richard Hackman's perspective on teams? • How is teaming different than that traditional understanding? • Do you agree that fear is no longer an effective management strategy in the workplace? • What is the difference between organizing to execute and organizing to learn?
Week 2	**Benchmark Goal: Learn the four pillars of teaming and why they work.** • What are the four pillars of teaming? • What are the benefits of teaming compared to a traditional structured team? • Which of the social and cognitive barriers of teaming have you struggled with in the workplace? • Were you able to handle the barrier effectively? If not, can you think of a better way to handle such a barrier in the future?
Week 3	**Benchmark Goal: Lead through teaming.** • How can leaders promote teaming? • Can you think of a time when you learned a valuable lesson from failure? • Can you recall a failure you should have learned from but didn't?

90 Days to Level Up Your Teamwork

Days 1–30	
Performance Goal: Get ready to learn, innovate, and compete.	
Week 4	**Benchmark Goal: Discover how to team across boundaries.** • What are some of the biggest boundaries or barriers to teaming? • What are some of the challenges of teaming across boundaries of physical distance? • Have you found status a serious boundary in your experience of teamwork?
Personal Goals and Vision for Success	
What do you hope to achieve by leveling up?	
How could your life change by reaching these goals?	

Teaming Is a Verb

Benchmark goal: Understanding how teaming is different than teamwork.

Say the word *team* and the first image that comes to mind is probably a sports team: football players huddled in the mud, basketball players swarming in a full-court press, or baseball players turning a game-saving double play. In sports, great teams consist of individuals who have learned to trust one another. Over time, they have discovered each other's strengths and weaknesses, enabling them to play as a coordinated whole. Similarly, musicians form bands, chamber groups, and orchestras that rely on interdependent talents. A symphony falls apart unless the string section coordinates with the woodwinds, brass, and percussionists. Even when a soloist is featured on stage, the orchestral score has a part for every musician. A successful performance is one in which the musicians complement one another and play in harmony. Like all good teams, they display synergy. The whole is greater than the sum of its parts. The players understand that they succeed or fail together—they win or lose as a team.

In today's complex and volatile business environment, corporations and organizations also win or lose by creating wholes that are

greater than the sum of their parts. Intense competition, rampant unpredictability, and a constant need for innovation are giving rise to even greater interdependence and thus demand even greater levels of collaboration and communication than ever before. Teaming is essential to an organization's ability to respond to opportunities and to improve internal processes. Week 1 aims to deepen your understanding of why teaming and the behaviors it requires are so crucial for organizational success in today's environment.

Delving into Teaming

Sports teams and musical groups are both bounded, static collections of individuals. Like most work teams in the past, they are physically located in the same place while practicing or performing together. Members of these teams learn how to interact. They've developed trust and know each other's roles. Advocating stable boundaries, well-designed tasks, and thoughtfully composed membership, many seminal theories of organizational effectiveness explained how to design and manage just these types of static performance teams.

Harvard psychologist Richard Hackman, a preeminent scholar of team effectiveness, established the power of team structures in enabling team performance. According to this influential perspective, well-designed teams are those with clear goals, well-thought-out tasks that are conducive to teamwork, team members with the right skills and experiences for the task, adequate resources, and access to coaching and support. Get the design right, the theory says, and the performance will take care of itself. This model focused on the team as an entity, looking largely within the well-defined bounds of a team to explain its performance. Other research, notably conducted by MIT professor Deborah Ancona, showed that how much a team's members interact with people outside the team boundaries was also an

important factor in team performance. Both perspectives worked well in guiding the design and management of effective teams, at least in contexts where managers had the lead time and the run time to invest in composing stable, well-designed teams.

In these prior treatments, *team* is a noun. A team is an established, fixed group of people cooperating in pursuit of a common goal. But what if a team disbands almost as quickly as it was assembled? For example, what if you work in an emergency services facility where the staffing changes every shift, and the team changes completely for every case or client? What if you're a member of a temporary project team formed to solve a unique production problem? Or you're part of a group of managers with a mix of individual and shared responsibilities? How do you create synergy when you lack the advantages offered by the frequent drilling and practice sessions of static performance teams like those in sports and music?

The answer lies in *teaming*.

Teaming is a verb. It is a dynamic activity, not a bounded, static entity. It is largely determined by the mindset and practices of teamwork, not by the design and structures of effective teams. Teaming is teamwork on the fly. It involves coordinating and collaborating without the benefit of stable team structures, because many operations, such as hospitals, power plants, and military installations, require a level of staffing flexibility that makes stable team composition rare. In a growing number of organizations, the constantly shifting nature of work means that many teams disband almost as soon as they've formed. You could be working on one team right now, but in a few days, or even a few minutes, you may be on another team.

Fast-moving work environments need people who know how to team, people who have the skills and the flexibility to act in moments of potential collaboration when and where they appear. They must

have the ability to move on, ready for the next such moments. Teaming still relies on old-fashioned teamwork skills such as recognizing and clarifying interdependence, establishing trust, and figuring out how to coordinate. But there usually isn't time to build a foundation of familiarity through the careful sharing of personal history and prior experience, nor is there time for developing shared experiences through practice working together. Instead, people need to develop and use new capabilities for sharing crucial knowledge quickly. They must learn to ask questions clearly and frequently. They must make the small adjustments through which different skills and knowledge are woven together into timely products and services.

Why should managers care about teaming? The answer is simple. Teaming is the engine of organizational learning. By now, everyone knows that organizations need to learn—to thrive in a world of continuous change. But how organizations learn is not as well understood. Organizations are complex entities; many are globally distributed, most encompass multiple areas of expertise, and nearly all engage in a variety of activities. What does it mean for such a complex entity to "learn"? An organization cannot engage in a learning process in any meaningful sense—not in the way an individual can. Yet, when individuals learn, this does not always create change in the ways the organization delivers products and services to customers.

In spite of the obvious need for change, most large enterprises are still managed according to a powerful mindset I call *organizing to execute*.

Organizing to Execute

If you stood on a main street in Detroit around 1900, you would have seen electric trolleys sharing the streets with horse-drawn carriages.

A mere decade later, cars had arrived in force. Though inefficient and unreliable, these increasingly popular cars brought with them the promise of a new, exciting world. For a short time, however, both horse and mechanical horsepower tried to share the streets, sometimes with devastating consequences. Many people found the collision of old and new worlds difficult, especially when those streets became even more crowded with young men from the countryside drawn to the city by the promise of manufacturing jobs.

In this transitional period, it was not obvious to the average worker how much the new industrial era would disrupt the social order by calling for new forms of obedience, unprecedented conformity to routine, and a new mindset that revered systems of control. Self-sufficient farmers and shopkeepers, who had for generations confronted vicissitudes of weather and illness and found ways to survive, would subtly but inexorably be transformed into order followers collecting paychecks from impersonal enterprises.

Organizing to execute found its seminal momentum in Henry Ford's invention of the assembly line: workers focused on fitting cog to component and component to cog. Emphasizing routine procedures, Ford's approach made the working life of employees menial and tedious. Reliable and predictable, Ford's assembly line process was as much a novelty as its product. With the new century, age-old structures for self-reliance were being replaced with the small, repetitive steps that made mass production possible and brought about the modern world of products and services we know today. Ford's success was contingent on a high level of managerial control over employee practices known today as command-and-control management, or top-down management. The practice of top-down management is one component of a broader organizational methodology known as scientific management.

Scientific Management

Ford's intellectual partner as a pioneer in mass production was management expert Frederick Winslow Taylor, who complemented Ford's assembly line with his efficiency methods and scientific measurement. Taylor and his followers devised ways to transform unpredictable and expensive customized work into efficient, economical systems of mass production. Long product life cycles enabled ample payback for the time invested in designing near-foolproof execution systems like the machine-paced assembly line. Periods of stability could be counted on. Products, processes, and even customers were mercifully uniform, minimizing the need for real-time improvisation to respond to unexpected problems, technological changes, or customer needs. Promoting the use of empirical methods, Taylor advocated his model of management and production in two influential monographs, *Shop Management* and *The Principles of Scientific Management*.

As managers today well know, an advantage of these new small, repetitive tasks was their transparency. Small, repetitive tasks are easy to monitor. They make the performance of the individual worker easy to measure. The assumption that firm performance was the cumulative result of thousands and thousands of well-designed and well-executed individual tasks dominated managerial theory and matched the economic reality. Even today, when it comes to issues like efficiency and productivity, most managers and corporate leaders are driven by taken-for-granted beliefs that were first promulgated by Ford and Taylor. For example, many consider the ability to measure and reward the specific, differentiated performance of individuals crucial to good management—a belief that is inaccurate and unhelpful in certain settings.

Ford and Taylor's Legacy

Devotion to efficiency and productivity resulted in two major workplace changes. First, it spurred a demand for professional managers who could oversee a vast complex of work activity. Second, it instilled a basic distrust of the worker. To ensure that workers did their jobs according to specified procedures, objective measurements of individual performance were relatively easy for managers to develop and implement. And, for the most part, workers who tried harder performed better. In mass production settings like the one designed by Ford, opportunities for worker decision-making or creativity were nonexistent. With this transparency, fear worked reasonably well to motivate employees. Whether through a fear of supervisor sanction or loss of material rewards, managers were able to coerce and intimidate workers to ensure high productivity. If there were costs to this approach for the enterprise or corporation, they were not in plain view.

The primary problem this legacy creates for managers today is that these systems produced an overreliance on fear in management practice. As Taylorism gained a foothold in factories across the country, the corporate mood became dour. Taylorism was ruthless. The individual's worth was measured by their contribution to enterprise gains. A history of the United Auto Workers union described factory life in these early days as follows: "Every Ford worker is perfectly aware that he is under constant observation—that he will be admonished if he falls below the fast pace of the department." Even in 1940, decades after the early days of the Ford miracle, a worker could be fired for smiling.

Fear in the Modern Workplace

Unfortunately, draconian management practice is not relegated to the distant past. Consider the rash of employee suicides that brought Foxconn's factory conditions to the public eye in May 2010.

(continued)

Fear and routine have never been limited to blue-collar work. Ford's factory worker can be seen as the precursor to the 1950s' *organization man*, a term coined by sociologist William Whyte. Deindividuating labor was not all that different from deindividuating white-collar work. Much like the assembly line worker, the office-bound organization man was bound by rules, processes, hierarchical structures, and fear. Moreover, the image of the organization man wasn't just promulgated by sociologists. Novelists and writers have portrayed work in large organizations as replete with both monotony and anxiety. American literature has long presented bankers and other managers as organization men, experiencing the same cog-in-the-machine dehumanization as their blue-collar counterparts.

As a society, we are still largely inured to a fear-based work environment. We believe (most of the time, erroneously) that fear increases control. Control reinforces certainty and predictability. We don't immediately see the costs of fear. In fact, many managers believe that without fear people will not work hard enough.

Thriving in the Face of Uncertainty

As customer expectations continue to shift and competition becomes increasingly global, many companies struggle to succeed in a drastically

changing landscape. Rapid developments in technology and changes in the legal environment greatly reduce the barriers to entry in a variety of industries, thus introducing new, nimble competitors. Now you see supermarkets, department stores, and funeral homes offering financial services that were formerly the exclusive purview of banks and banking institutions. Likewise, telephone companies offer television service, while television companies offer phone service. Heightened competitive pressure means that even in previously stable industries unexpected changes are occurring in a compressed period of time and creating new, unprecedented challenges.

Consequently, as management and system dynamics expert Peter Senge put it, "The organizations that will truly excel in the future will be the organizations that discover how to tap people's commitment and capacity to learn at all levels in an organization."[1] Learning new skills in an uncertain environment where knowledge is a moving target is now a competitive imperative in most industries. Consider the astonishing expansion of medical knowledge. If you were practicing medicine in 1960, you could subscribe to a few leading professional journals and most likely keep up with the literature in your field. In 1960, there were just 100 articles published on randomized control trials, the gold standard for best practices in medicine. Today more than 10,000 articles reporting on randomized control trials are published annually. An average engineer today sports a wristwatch with more computing power and memory than was available to the team of engineers working in the Apollo program at NASA in the 1960s.

Good-Bye Taylor and Ford . . . Hello Complex Adaptive Systems

The point is that knowledge in fields related to health care, technology, science, and engineering, as well as a host of others, is growing at such

a pace that today's workplace is significantly different from that of the industrialized manufacturing era of Ford and Taylor. By now, most leaders and managers recognize that organizations that don't learn are left behind their more innovate and adaptive competitors. In this dynamic environment, successful organizations need to be managed as complex adaptive systems rather than as intricate controlled machines.

The term *complex adaptive system* describes systems that are dynamic and adaptable, much like those found in nature. A system is complex when it has many interacting parts. Feedback loops are a hallmark of complex systems. Feedback loops mean that part A has an impact on part B, which may then affect part C, which feeds back in turn to have an impact on part A. Taken together, these interactions create unpredictable dynamics. Trying to understand, much less predict, what happens in such systems when one is expecting linear, unidirectional relationships—where A influences B, which may influence C, and that is the end of the chain—will produce flawed results.

Complex adaptive systems self-regulate. Not always in preferred ways, mind you, but they change in response to both external and internal triggers. Examples of such systems range from an embryo to an ant colony to a hospital. What these systems have in common is that they encompass a number of similar elements (cells, ants, people) and they self-organize in reaction to external and internal disruptions (often called *perturbations*).

The learning imperative requires relinquishing control as the ultimate goal. It requires embracing the creation of adaptive capabilities as a fundamental organizational competence. It requires flexibility and judgment. It requires a managerial approach that works when organizations face uncertainty created by new technologies, shifting customer preferences, or complex systems. Success requires a shift from organizing to execute to a new way of working that supports collaboration, innovation, and organizational learning.

Learning to Team, Teaming to Learn

Simply put, *teaming* is a way of working that brings people together to generate new ideas, find answers, and solve problems. But people have to learn to team; it doesn't come naturally in most organizations. Teaming is worth learning, because it is essential for improvement, problem-solving, and innovation in a functioning enterprise. The complex interdependencies involved in learning and innovating require the interpersonal skills necessary to negotiate disagreements, overcome technical jargon, and revisit ideas or problems until solutions emerge—all activities supported by teaming. Learning in today's organizations involves what's called *reciprocal interdependence*, where back-and-forth communication and coordination are essential to getting the work done.

Although teaming can help any enterprise improve, it is absolutely critical to success when any of the following conditions are present:

- The work requires people to juggle multiple objectives with minimal oversight.

- People must be able to shift from one situation to another while maintaining high levels of communication and tight coordination. This situation literally defines the practice of teaming.

- It is helpful to integrate perspectives from different disciplines.

- Collaborating takes place across dispersed locations.

- Preplanned coordination is impossible or unrealistic due to the changing nature of the work.

- Complex information must be processed, synthesized, and put to good use quickly.

Though teaming refers to a dynamic activity rather than to a traditional, bounded group structure, many of its purposes and benefits are grounded in basic principles of teams and teamwork. Among the benefits of teams is their ability to integrate diverse expertise as needed to accomplish many important tasks. Historically, the focus of team research and project implementation was on reorganizing production processes. Increasingly, however, teamwork extends beyond the factory floor.

Using teams to solve problems or shape new strategic directions has been popular in organizations since the early 2000s. In 2003, the Census of Manufacturers from the Manufacturing Performance Institute (MPI) reported that 70 percent of respondents used teams to accomplish their business goals.

Yet all is not perfect with teams and teaming. Despite the fact that team use is steadily increasing, team effectiveness is not keeping up at the same pace. In the previously cited MPI report, only about 14 percent of organizations surveyed rated their teaming efforts as "highly effective," while just over half (50.4 percent) rated their teams as "somewhat effective." Thus, over a third of teams were rated as ineffective. This, in addition to scores of other reports and studies, indicates that although using teams to get interdependent work done can be valuable, achieving the tremendous potential of teams is far more challenging than many expect—and successful teamwork is thus still elusive in many organizations.

Organizing to Learn

Staying competitive, as we have seen, requires learning. Organizing to learn is a way of leading that encourages critical teaming behaviors to promote collective learning. It supports the collaboration needed to solicit employees' knowledge, apply it to new situations or challenges,

and to analyze outcomes. Organizing to learn is a way of moving forward in spite of uncertainty. Taking action without certainty can be a daunting prospect in organizations where stability and success are valued over variance and experimentation. Collective learning includes such activities as collecting, sharing, or analyzing information; obtaining and reflecting on feedback from customers or others; and active experimentation. Individual learning behaviors within a collective learning experience include the following:

- Asking questions
- Sharing information
- Seeking help
- Experimenting with unproven actions
- Talking about mistakes
- Seeking feedback

These learning behaviors enable groups to obtain and process the data needed to adapt and improve. Through collective learning, organizations can detect changes in the environment, learn about customers' requirements, improve members' collective understanding of a situation, or discover the consequences of their previous actions. They require a willingness to take interpersonal risks such as discussing mistakes. This requires leaders who work to create environments that support and encourage sharing, experimenting, and learning.

The old mindset, organizing to execute, has been a century in the making, so it's no wonder that many leaders adopt it by force of habit and training. Organizing to execute has many strengths, especially in its emphasis on discipline and efficiency. However, it also has many risks, particularly when used in highly uncertain or complex contexts.

In these settings, organizing to learn is critical to success. Table 1.1 highlights key differences between the approaches and identifies two distinct mindsets, and the corresponding management practices that leaders can adopt when they are responsible for guiding people and organizations.

Table 1.1   Organizing to Execute Versus Organizing to Learn

Management Approach	Organizing to Execute	Organizing to Learn
Hiring	Conformers, rule followers	Problem-solvers, experimenters
Training	Learn before doing.	Learn from doing.
Measuring performance	Did YOU do it right?	Did WE learn?
Structuring work	Separate expertise	Integrated expertise
Employee discretion allowed	Choose among options.	Experiment through trial and error.
Empowerment means	Employees can deviate from the script if special circumstances make it necessary.	There is no script. Improvise!
Process goal	Drive out variance.	Use variance to analyze and improve.
Watercooler conversation	About the weather	About the work
Business goal	Make money now.	Make money later.
Works when	Path forward is clear.	Path forward is not clear.

Teaming to Learn

The ability to learn is critical for organizations operating in today's fast-paced business environment. Relying on existing knowledge and skills succeeds only if you know exactly what should be done in a job and you expect the process to remain relatively fixed for a significant amount of time. In today's environment, that's the exception, not the rule. In this activity, you delve into teaming and how it works with today's business climate.

Activity

Reflect on the following questions:

How do you define the difference between teaming and teamwork?

_____

_____

_____

What conditions make it necessary to team (as opposed to simply working as a team)?

_____

_____

_____

Do you think teaming is necessary for your organization? If not, do you still think it will be beneficial?

_____

_____

_____

Do you feel fear is a good motivator in the workplace?

_____

_____

_____

Identifying the Fundamentals of Teaming

Benchmark goal: Learn the four pillars of teaming and why they work.

Teaming occurs when people apply and combine their expertise to perform complex tasks or develop solutions to novel problems. Often a fluid process, teaming may involve performing with others, disbanding, and joining another group right away. An episode of teaming ends once some or all of the work is complete, but teaming as a mindset—and approach to work—can continue indefinitely. Teaming is normal in the temporary organizations that characterize creative endeavors, such as making a film, or in the coordination of complex events, such as producing a professional conference. In such efforts, a mix of planned and spontaneous coordination often brings multiple players together to team.

Proficient teaming often requires integrating perspectives from a range of disciplines, communicating despite the different mental models that accompany different areas of expertise, and being able to manage the inevitable conflicts that arise when people work together. Fundamentally, this is a matter of developing interpersonal skills related to learning (inquiry, curiosity, listening) and teaching (communicating,

connecting, clarifying). Teaming is thus both a mindset that accepts working together actively and a set of behaviors tailored to sharing and synthesizing knowledge. Sometimes teaming requires coordinating across distant locations, which both increases the potential for miscommunication and gives rise to new opportunities for innovation.

Driving Teaming Success

Whether face-to-face or mediated by communication technologies, successful teaming involves these four pillars:

- **Speaking up:** Teaming depends on honest, direct conversation between individuals, including asking questions, seeking feedback, and discussing errors.

- **Collaboration:** Teaming requires a collaborative mindset and behaviors—both within and outside a given unit of teaming—to drive the process.

- **Experimentation:** Teaming involves a tentative, iterative approach to action that recognizes the novelty and uncertainty inherent in every interaction between individuals.

- **Reflection:** Teaming relies on the use of explicit observations, questions, and discussions of processes and outcomes. This must happen on a consistent basis that reflects the rhythm of the work, whether that calls for daily, weekly, or other project-specific timing.

Speaking Up

Candid communication enables teams to incorporate multiple perspectives and tap into individual knowledge. This includes asking

questions, seeking feedback, talking about errors, asking for help, offering suggestions, and discussing problems, mistakes, and concerns. Speaking up is particularly crucial when confronting problems or failures of any kind. When people are willing to engage with each other directly and openly, they are better able to make sense of the larger shared work and more likely to generate ideas for improving work processes. Speaking up in this context refers to an interpersonal behavior that enables the development of shared insights from open conversation. It is essential for determining appropriate courses of action in any teaming encounter. Speaking up is also essential for helping people grasp new concepts and methods. Conversing about experiences, insights, and questions builds understanding of new practices and how to perform them. Although many people think of themselves as direct and straightforward, speaking up in the workplace is less common than you might think.

Speaking Up Is Less Common Than You Think

My research with Professor Jim Detert at Cornell University on voice and silence in the workplace shows that speaking up at work is less common than most people think. Through interviews with hundreds of executives, managers, and supervisors in a global high-tech company, we discovered that almost everyone could think of specific instances of not speaking up about a potentially important work-related issue. Most were well-educated, thoughtful people who spanned corporate departments, areas of expertise, and even countries of origin. To explain why people frequently don't speak up, we analyzed hundreds of specific episodes and identified taken-for-granted beliefs about appropriate behavior in hierarchies that are far-reaching in their implications.

(continued)

(continued)

Although most people we studied thought of themselves as pretty straightforward, rather than hesitant or fearful, they still held back potentially important ideas at work. In this study, and several that followed, we showed that there is a remarkable paucity of directness in the workplace. It appears that reluctance to speak up is overdetermined by human nature and by specific realities of the modern economy. From an evolutionary point of view, we're hardwired to overestimate rather than underestimate certain types of risk: it was better for survival to "flee" from threats that weren't really there than to not flee when there was a real risk. And we appear to have inherited emotional and cognitive mechanisms that lead us to avoid perceived risks to our psychological and material well-being. In the workplace, fear of offending people above us in the hierarchy is both natural and widespread, and it means the speaking-up behavior on which teaming depends must be cultivated rather than assumed to be present.

Collaboration

Collaboration is a way of working with colleagues that is characterized by cooperation, mutual respect, and shared goals. It involves sharing information, coordinating actions, discussing what's working and what's not, and perpetually seeking input and feedback. Teaming depends on collaborative behaviors within and between departments or organizations. Clearly, without collaboration, teaming easily breaks down. Plans are less well informed, and the execution of plans suffers from poor coordination. A collaborative attitude is also essential to shared reflection that may occur following coordinated action, because it enables full and thoughtful sharing of expertise and promotes the

development of broader and deeper lessons from any experience. Imagine a product development team that doesn't collaborate with the marketing group and thereby fails to incorporate vital customer preferences or feedback!

Experimentation

Experimentation means expecting not to be right the first time. Borrowed from the experiments of scientists, experimentation behavior is a way of acting that centrally involves learning from the results of action. In teaming, experimentation behavior involves reaching out to others to assess the impact of one's actions on them, and also testing the implications of one's ideas with respect to what others are thinking. Experimentation is a vital aspect of teaming because of the uncertainty inherent in interdependent action. It's also a crucial part of learning.

Reflection

Reflection is the habit of critically examining the results of actions to assess results and uncover new ideas. Some teams engage in reflection on a daily basis. Others reflect at a natural break in the project, such as at halftime for sports teams, or when documenting aspects of a patient's care in a chart after a medical visit. Project teams may explicitly engage in a reflection exercise only when a project is completed. The after-action reviews conducted by the US Army following military exercises are explicit reflection sessions that use a rigorous structured approach to assess what occurred against what was planned or expected. Reflection does not necessarily mean extensive sessions to thoroughly analyze team process or performance, but rather is often quick and pragmatic. Reflection in action, for example,

is the critical, real-time examination of a process so it can be adjusted based on new knowledge or, more often, in response to subtle feedback received from the work itself. Reflection as a basis for effective teaming is more a behavioral tendency than a formal process. In one study of surgical teams, for example, I found no differences in outcomes for teams with formal reflection sessions compared to those without such sessions; the teams that succeeded were those that were constantly reflecting aloud on what they were observing and thinking, as a way of figuring out how to work together more effectively. For some types of teams, however, it may be more appropriate to wait for outcomes to be available before stopping to reflect on team process, in which case a more structured approach, such as a formal project review, is extremely valuable.

These four behaviors are the pillars of effective teaming. The challenges encountered on the factory floor, in the operating room, and around the glass-topped tables in corporate conference rooms differ significantly in look and feel, as well as in the nature of the work. Yet speaking up, collaboration, experimentation, and reflection are crucial behaviors across these disparate settings. In all of them, leaders who themselves embrace these behaviors make it easier for others to act in ways that support teaming. In addition to these behavioral tendencies, however, leaders must also understand the cyclical, recursive nature of the actual teaming process.

The Benefits of Teaming

One of the most successful product launches in history, Motorola's 2004 RAZR mobile phone, was the result of successful teaming. Battling fierce global competition in the mobile phone market in 2003, Motorola set out to create the thinnest phone ever released. Electrical engineer Roger Jellicoe was chosen to lead the team. In addition to

designing the thinnest phone ever, Jellicoe's instructions were to create a thing of beauty, a device more like jewelry than a mere utilitarian object. To partner in leading the project, he chose mechanical engineer Gary Weiss, with whom he knew he could work well. Twenty Motorola engineers were invited to join the teaming effort with its ambitious deadline. They came from different groups and locations to collaborate in an otherwise unremarkable facility an hour from Chicago.

Speaking up and experimentation were critical to their success. Neither ideas nor criticisms were held back, as perpetual experimentation and debate led to possibilities and prototypes that were attempted, rejected, altered, tweaked, and refined. A core challenge was the integration of style and technology. Numerous trade-offs, mostly between appearance and functionality, were considered, and the team resisted easy compromises, pushing instead for elegant solutions to the tough problems they confronted. By experimenting with different configurations, the team hit on the idea of putting the battery next to the circuit board (prior phones had them stacked) to reduce thickness. It worked, allowing the ultra-thin design that gave the phone its appeal and its name.

The team's innovative solution ignored existing human factors experts who had strong views about how wide a cell phone could be to feel right in a person's hand. Experimenting with a wider mock-up of the phone, the team decided the experts were wrong. Reflection was built into the teaming process from the beginning. Meeting every afternoon at 4:00 p.m., the group discussed the day's progress, and reported on the status of such components as the antenna, speaker, keypad, or light source. Scheduled for an hour, the meetings frequently ran past 7:00 p.m. These meetings were a primary mechanism for the team's focused conversation and debate. Reporting on failures as easily as successes and breakthroughs, everyone was engaged in the process of offering ideas and criticisms.

The project's biggest setback occurred when it missed its ambitious initial deadline, but the result, only a few months later and still within a fast time line, was worth waiting for: Motorola unveiled the RAZR, the thinnest phone ever produced, before the end of 2004, and went on to sell 50 million RAZR mobile phones within the next two years and 110 million over four years.

Performance

Whether a new product development team made up of designers, marketers, and engineers, or a cardiac surgery team made up of surgeons, nurses, perfusionists, and anesthesiologists, the benefits of teaming for organizational learning and performance are significant. In particular, teaming helps organizations develop new routines and implement new technologies to meet the demands of a changing context. These kinds of organizational changes call for teaming because they require understanding and coordination across departments and disciplines. Teams are an organization's best change agents. Most models of change management call for a change leadership team or a change implementation team to promote better ideas and greater buy-in. But it shouldn't stop there. What really matters is not just the creation of a team, but how those selected work with each other and with other members of the organization to help create change in a dynamic, learning-oriented way. These change agents must listen, coordinate, and continually make adjustments in plans to accommodate each other's input. This naturally gives rise to uncertainty and requires attention and sensitivity to feedback. The core behaviors of teaming thus drive organizational performance by facilitating the creation of new knowledge, new processes, and new products. Performance improves when new knowledge is put to good use, also enabled by teaming.

Engaged Employees

Teaming has a positive effect on people's experience at work. Interacting directly with people who have different knowledge and skills makes work more interesting, enriching, and meaningful. In organizations where teaming is common, employees learn from each other, enjoy a broader understanding of the work and how it gets done from start to finish, and can better see and act on opportunities for improvement. For example, Simmons Mattress Company introduced team training to raise employee technical and interpersonal skills, which in turn led to greatly increased awareness of the contributions of other employees working in different parts of the manufacturing process. Once everyone began to understand what unseen colleagues did all day, why it was difficult, and how the combined tasks came together to make an entire mattress, not to mention an entire sales and distribution operation, they enjoyed the work more, and were also more productive.

Social and Cognitive Barriers to Teaming

I've spent an inordinate amount of time studying people in hospitals. People working in hospitals face some particularly challenging work environments. Demands for coordination are great, time is tight, and the stakes are high. As a result, the rest of us can learn a lot from understanding how the best hospitals manage these inherent challenges effectively. Medical knowledge and best care practices, which are vast and constantly updated, must be consulted to inform high-stakes, cross-disciplinary communication and action, often under immense time pressure. And, unfortunately, even in a hospital—a setting that calls for nearly constant teaming—cooperation and trust face many challenges.

Serious Work Means Serious Tension

As Wynton Marsalis, artistic director for Jazz at Lincoln Center, says of his work with other jazz musicians, "There are always tensions that come up. Part of working is dealing with tensions. If there's no tension, then you're not serious about what you're doing."

Certainly, teaming sometimes goes well in today's organizations. People recognize their interdependence and work effectively together. They offer their ideas freely, carrying out their part of the collective work and responding thoughtfully to others' ideas and actions. At other times, however, teaming breaks down and coordination fails. Signals get crossed or conflicting opinions derail the conversation. Many teaming efforts—whether in routine, complex, or innovation operations—start with high hopes, only to falter. What are some of the obstacles to effective teaming?

People Don't Always Get Along

Teaming requires participants to productively manage the inevitable conflicts that arise when people work together in serious endeavors. Well-functioning teams are powerful, but rarely static. They are as hard to create as to sustain. Many tasks are technically complex to begin with and present interdependencies that make them even more so. Personality, leadership, resource allocation, differences in knowledge and background—any problems encountered in these areas can give rise to misunderstanding or dysfunction. Fear is a major barrier to teaming. Similarly, lacking a clear, shared objective also inhibits the effortful behaviors that comprise teaming. Organizational factors, such as bureaucracy, layers of management, or contradictory incentive systems, also get in the way. Teaming is as difficult as it is necessary.

It's far easier for an individual to have a clear and well-bounded task to do over and over again than to figure out how to carry out more complex and interdependent work with others. Interdependent work requires coordination through back-and-forth communication to do it well. When we are interdependent, it necessarily means we cannot do everything that must be done alone. This is a rather humbling realization, and many shy away from embracing it. It can be hard for people to muster both the humility and the genuine curiosity that is needed to really learn from others. It turns out that cognitive, interpersonal, and organizational factors all get in the way of effective learning in teams. It's a cruel irony—our success depends on effective collaboration and learning, the essence of teaming, but these don't come naturally either for individuals or the social systems we create. The following sections examine the cognitive and structural factors that inhibit teaming.

Silence Is Easier Than Speaking Up

When leaders fall into a default "do-it-my-way" management style, it silences nearly everyone except the person with the loudest voice or the largest office. But silence in today's economic environment is deadly. Silence means good ideas and possibilities don't bubble up, and problems don't get addressed. Silence stymies teaming. Most people feel a need to manage what I call interpersonal risk—a risk that others will think less of them—so as to minimize harm to their image, especially in the workplace, and especially in the presence of bosses and others who hold formal power. One way to minimize risk to one's image is simply to avoid speaking up unless you're sure you're right, avoid admitting mistakes, and, of course, never ask questions or raise tentative ideas that you're not sure have merit. Although this approach may work for individuals—protecting them from being seen by others in an unfavorable light—it is clearly problematic for organizations and their customers.

Shhhh, Here Comes the Boss

Research shows that hierarchy, by its very nature, dramatically reduces speaking up by those lower in the pecking order. We are hardwired, and then socialized, to be acutely sensitive to power, and to work to avoid being seen as deficient in any way by those in power. Most of this behavior is unconscious. As a result, in most organizations, even if leaders at the top of the hierarchy say they welcome employee feedback, and even if people have the knowledge and training to say something of importance, they still may remain silent out of fear of negative consequences.

Research does show, however, that leaders can promote speaking up through particular behaviors and actions. Most important, when leaders explicitly communicate that they respect employees, it makes it easier for employees to volunteer their knowledge. More specifically, by acknowledging the need for the knowledge and skills that others bring, leaders issue a credible invitation for people to speak up. Mistakes, in particular, require active encouragement if they are to be reported or discussed. In sum, speaking up is not natural in organizations, but it can and does happen, particularly when leaders actively model, invite, and reward candor and openness. By contrast, inaccessibility or a failure to acknowledge vulnerability can contribute to a reluctance to incur the interpersonal risks of teaming behavior.

Disagreement

Speaking up brings challenges, too. As soon as people speak up and communicate freely with one another, there is bound to be disagreement and sometimes seemingly irresolvable conflict. The problem with disagreement is not that it occurs; the problem is the sensemaking in which people spontaneously engage when disagreement occurs. All of us have at one point or another spontaneously attributed

unflattering motives, traits, or abilities to those who disagree with our strongly held view. In such cases, we might say something like "She doesn't get it" or "He's just out for himself."

Naïve Realism

We are all prone to *naïve realism*, a term coined by psychologist Lee Ross (1977), which is a person's "unshakable conviction that he or she is somehow privy to an invariant, knowable, objective reality—a reality that others will also perceive faithfully, provided that they are reasonable and rational."[1] So, when others misperceive our "reality," we conclude that it must be because they are unreasonable or irrational and "view the world through a prism of self-interest, ideological bias, or personal perversity." And therein lies the trouble.

One outcome of naïve realism is that people tend to see their own views as more common than they really are, leading them to falsely assume that others share their views. For example, someone might say, "We need to dramatically curb carbon emissions to prevent further global warming." Or, "Everyone knows we have the best medical system in the world." Social psychologists call this the *false consensus effect*. And such assumptions usually go unnoticed—until unexpectedly refuted when someone disagrees. This means, if someone replies, "I don't think human activity is contributing to climate change. Temperature fluctuations have gone on for millennia," the original speaker may spontaneously conclude that the responder is closed-minded, wrong-headed, or worse. Similarly, someone might respond to the second statement, "If we have the best medical care, why do we rank 36th in the world for life expectancy?" while privately viewing the original speaker as ignorant or misguided. For most people, finding out that a friend or colleague disagrees with us on something we care about is usually an unpleasant surprise.

The Fundamental Attribution Error

The second cognitive error that makes it hard to cope with conflict productively was dubbed the *fundamental attribution error* by Lee Ross. The term describes our failure to recognize situational causes of events and our tendency instead to overattribute individuals' personality or ability as likely causes. An outgrowth of this cognitive error is that we tend to explain others' shortcomings as related to their ability or attitude, rather than to the circumstances they face. That is, we blame the people for things that go wrong—not the situation. Every parent of more than one child has heard, "Don't blame me, it's his fault." In the workplace, the same thing happens, even if the words are less direct and unambiguous.

It's almost amusing to realize that we do exactly the opposite in explaining our own failures. That is, we spontaneously attribute them to external factors. For example, if we show up late for a meeting, we may blame circumstances outside our control, like rush-hour traffic. If a subordinate is late for a meeting, however, we think he is not committed to the project, or that he's disorganized. On both sides of the attribution coin, we make judgments effortlessly—remaining largely unaware that there was an alternative cause to consider. As natural and sometimes humorous as this asymmetry is, it creates a couple of problems for teaming. First, when we blame others for things that go wrong, productive discussion of the issues is less likely to occur. Worse, we tend to believe we have sized up the situation and its causes accurately. Second, we begin to think less of others, and then may be less motivated to engage wholeheartedly in teaming with them.

Tension and Conflict

The fundamental problem with disagreements, and the cognitive structures that exacerbate them, is that they create tensions in a group. Tensions are to be expected when teaming. Although rarely fun, tensions

are not always bad. They can evoke creativity, sharpen ideas, and refine analyses. But there's a catch: patience, wisdom, and skill are needed to transform tensions into positive results. This is because most of us naturally resist tensions and the conflict they invariably bring.

Teaming to Learn

Teaming in organization can often be successful, but it can often be stymied by various barriers. In this activity, spend some time thinking about your own career and the barriers to teaming that you've encountered.

Activity
Reflect on the following questions:

Can you think of a time when you were guilty of naïve realism? How do you think you can safeguard against this in the future?

_____

_____

_____

Of the major barriers to teaming, which seems most insurmountable to you?

_____

_____

_____

Can you think of a time when interpersonal conflict got in the way of a team working effectively? Did the team handle it well? If not, what could they have done differently?

_____

_____

_____

Supporting Teaming as a Leader

Benchmark goal: Lead through teaming.

Teaming and learning do not happen automatically. Instead, they require coordination and some structure to ensure that insights are gained from members' collective experience and used to guide subsequent action. As research demonstrates across varied cases and settings, teaming and learning both depend on the deliberate exercise of leadership. It takes leadership to understand and resolve conflict and to instigate thoughtful conversations about errors. It takes leadership to adhere to process discipline and to help people remember to explore and experiment. In short, leadership is needed to help groups build shared understanding and coordinate action.

In nearly two decades of research, I've discovered that leaders have four main responsibilities to set the stage for successful teaming:

- Frame the situation for learning.

- Make it psychologically safe to team.

- Learn to learn from failure.

- Span occupational and cultural boundaries.

These four actions are not solely practices intended for teaming and learning. In fact, these individual practices translate directly to improved leadership and performance under nearly any circumstance. Taken together, however, they form the foundation for leading a successful teaming effort and provide a path forward for integrating learning into everyday execution.

In addition, leaders play a key role in making sure that the team learns from those (inevitable) failures. This week, you focus on the special responsibility that a leader has to support successful teaming.

Frame the Situation for Learning

Framing is crucial for leading the kind of change necessary to engage people as active learners. Leaders seeking to facilitate teaming and produce organizational learning must frame their project in a way that motivates others to collaborate. Researchers agree, however, that many of our spontaneous frames at work are inherently about self-protection. These self-protective frames dramatically inhibit opportunities to collaborate, learn, and improve. However, people can learn to reframe and shift from spontaneous, self-protective frames to reflective, learning-oriented frames. Doing so involves interdependent team leaders, empowered teams, and an aspirational purpose.

Make It Psychologically Safe to Team

An environment of psychological safety is an essential element of organizations that succeed in today's complex and uncertain world. The term *psychological safety* describes a climate in which people feel free to express relevant thoughts and feelings without fear of being penalized. Although it sounds simple, the ability to ask questions, seek help, and tolerate mistakes while colleagues watch can be

unexpectedly difficult. Because coordinating and integrating complex tasks requires people to ask questions, share thoughts openly, and act without excessive concern about what others think of them, teaming flourishes with psychological safety and diminishes without it.

Learn to Learn from Failure

An essential, if difficult, teaming activity is learning from failure. Failure, broadly defined, encompasses both the small and large events in organizations that don't go as planned. Examples include a defect occurring in an assembly process, a new drug failing in clinical trials, or a strategy meeting breaking down. Learning from failures of all kinds is as vital as it is difficult. No one wants to look bad in front of their peers, and few of us want to admit failure. Yet failure is a necessary aspect of both teaming and organizational learning. Failures of many kinds offer the chance to gain new insights into how to improve a process or product. The secret for organizations is to figure out how to gather and act on, rather than ignore or suppress, this potentially valuable information.

Span Occupational and Cultural Boundaries

Teams that succeed today don't merely work well around a shared conference table; they also have the ability to collaborate across boundaries and reach people who have the knowledge and information to help them apply resources effectively. Rapid developments in technology and the greater emphasis on globalization have dramatically increased the significance of boundary spanning in today's work environment. The information technology that has enabled us to communicate instantaneously across continents, however, sometimes

leaves us with a false sense of confidence that productive teamwork is merely a click away. Education and other socializing processes lead people to favor their own group, discipline, location, or department. Ignoring such boundaries can easily blindside even the most well-intentioned teaming efforts.

Leading Through Failure

Teaming rarely unfolds perfectly, without any bumps, glitches, or failures. This means that the ability to learn from failure is an essential teaming skill. And although most leaders say they understand the importance of failure to the learning process, not many truly embrace it. In my research, I've found that even companies that have invested significant money and effort into becoming learning organizations struggle when it comes to the day-to-day mindset and activities of learning from failure. Managers in these companies were highly motivated to help their organizations learn in order to avoid recurring failures and mistakes. In some cases, they and their teams had devoted many hours to after-action reviews and post-mortems. Even these types of painstaking efforts fall short, however, if managers or leaders think about failure the wrong way.

Most leaders I've talked to believe that failure is bad. They also believe that if failure does occur, learning from it is pretty straightforward: simply ask people to reflect on what they did wrong and instruct them to avoid similar actions in the future. Or, better yet, assign a team to review what happened and develop a report to distribute. Unfortunately, these widely held beliefs are misguided. Here's the simple truth about failure: it is sometimes bad, sometimes good, and often inevitable. Good, bad, inevitable—learning from organizational failures is anything but straightforward.

To learn from mistakes and missteps, organizations must employ new and better ways to go beyond lessons that are superficial (procedures weren't followed) or self-serving (the market just wasn't ready for our great new product). This requires jettisoning old cultural beliefs and stereotypical notions of success and replacing them with a new paradigm that recognizes that some failures are inevitable in today's complex work organizations and that successful organizations will be those that catch, correct, and learn from failures quickly.

Developing a Learning Approach to Failure

Because psychological and organizational factors inhibit both failure identification and analysis, a fundamental reorientation is needed to successfully learn from failure. Individuals and groups must be motivated to embrace the difficult and often emotionally challenging lessons that failures reveal. Doing so requires a spirit of curiosity and openness, as well as exceptional patience and a tolerance for ambiguity. These traits and behaviors are best characterized by what, in the management literature, has been termed an *inquiry orientation*. This type of orientation is presented as a contrast to an *advocacy orientation*. Both terms describe contrasting communication behaviors and distinct approaches to group decision-making.

Advocacy and Inquiry Orientations

Organizational structures and processes can hinder the ability of a group to learn from failure. In groups characterized by an advocacy orientation, these structures and processes support a top-down management approach and the organizational status quo. Therefore, when

trying to incorporate the unique knowledge of different members, the unintentional results often include antagonism, a lack of listening and learning, and limited psychological safety for challenging authority.

An inquiry orientation is characterized by the perception among group members that multiple alternatives exist and that frequent dissent is necessary. These perceptions result in a deeper understanding of issues, the development of new possibilities, and an awareness of others' reasoning. This orientation can counteract common group tensions and process failures. Learning about the perspectives, ideas, and experiences of others when facing uncertainty and high-stakes decisions is critical to making appropriate choices and finding solutions to novel problems. But how can leaders promote an inquiry orientation to facilitate learning? The terms *exploratory response* and *confirmatory response* have recently been used to describe distinct ways that leaders can orient individuals and groups to respond to potential failures.

Confirmatory and Exploratory Responses

Leaders play an important role in determining a group's orientation to a perceived failure. Facing small or ambiguous problems, leaders can respond in one of two basic ways: confirmatory or exploratory responses. A confirmatory response by leaders reinforces accepted assumptions, naturally triggering an advocacy orientation. When individuals seek information in this mode, they look for data that confirms existing beliefs, which is a natural human response. Leaders encourage or reinforce a confirmatory response, when they act in ways consistent with established frames and beliefs. This often means they're passive or reactionary rather than active and forward-looking.

In uncertain, risky, or novel situations, an exploratory response is more appropriate. Rather than supporting existing assumptions,

an exploratory response requires a deliberate shift in the mindset of a leader. This alters the way a leader interprets and diagnoses the situation at hand. This shift involves challenging and testing existing assumptions and experimenting with new behaviors and possibilities. When leaders adopt an exploratory approach, they embrace ambiguity and openly acknowledge gaps in knowledge. They recognize that their current understanding may require revision, and so they actively search for evidence in support of alternative hypotheses. Rather than seeking to prove what they already believe, exploratory leadership encourages inquiry and experimentation. This deliberate response helps to accelerate learning through proactive information gathering and simple, rapid experimentation.

It would be nice if transforming an organization into a learning enterprise was just a matter of altering the orientation and perspective of a single leader. But of course it's not that simple. A productive approach to failure requires leadership, exercised by many individuals, to cultivate diagnostic acumen. In this way, an organizational culture of curiosity and analysis can be developed and nurtured. This helps people to develop a clearheaded understanding of what happened, rather than just identifying "who did it" when something goes wrong. Doing this well means insisting on consistent reporting of failures, encouraging deep and systematic analysis, and promoting the proactive search for opportunities to experiment.

Strategies for Learning from Failures

Failure tolerance is a smart strategy for any organization wishing to gain new knowledge. Because organizations are more and more likely to encompass complex work and face unpredictable environments, a growing number of failures are of the complex type, and it's crucial to anticipate and respond to them quickly. Moreover, great strategic

advantage can be gained from intelligent failures. But neither type of failure can be put to good use without a rational approach to diagnosis and discussion. Given that failure is inherently emotionally charged, responding to it requires specific, purposeful strategies. Three activities—detection, analysis, and experimentation—are critical to learning from failures. As Table 3.1 shows, these three activities apply to all types of failures, although how they're carried out varies in important ways.

Table 3.1 Strategies for Learning from Failure

	Detect Failure	Analyze Failure	Promote Failure
Strategies for learning from preventable failures	Make it safe for employees to check with managers and peers when unsure what to do. Reward problem detection. Reward false alarms (potential failures that turn out fine) for their value in learning and practicing.	Develop and employ classic techniques for process improvement.	Encourage small tests to ensure process viability, especially in the face of gradual changes in technology or customer preferences.

90 Days to Level Up Your Teamwork

Table 3.1 *(continued)*

	Detect Failure	Analyze Failure	Promote Failure
Strategies for learning from complex failures	Make it safe to report errors and problems. Reward finding system vulnerabilities. Reward rapid reporting of small and large failures.	Convene cross-functional groups to identify what happened from multiple perspectives.	Encourage offline tests to identify new failure modes so as to add new fail-safe mechanisms into processes.
Strategies for learning from intelligent failures	Make it safe to experiment. Reward early detection of failed experiments. Reward early declaration of failed projects.	Employ scientific method to analyze data systematically. Avoid superficial insights from quick assessment of trends or patterns. Include multiple perspectives.	Experiment more often, with more variety. Conduct pilots as experiments to identify failure modes rather than as demonstrations of success.

Failure Detection: Support Systems for Identifying Failure

The first crucial strategy to master is the proactive and timely identification of failure. This is especially true of the type of small and seemingly inconsequential failures that lead to large, often catastrophic, failures. Any organization can detect big, expensive failures. It's the little ones that often go unnoticed. In many organizations, any failure that can be hidden is hidden, so long as it's unlikely to cause immediate or obvious harm. Even more common is the tendency to withhold bad news related to pending failures as long as humanly possible.

Recognizing this, Allan Mulally, soon after being hired as CEO of Ford Motors, created a new system for identifying failures. Understanding how difficult it is for early-stage failures to make it up the corporate hierarchy, he asked his managers to color code their reports: green for good, yellow for caution, red for problems. Mulally was frustrated when, during the first couple of meetings, managers coded most of their operations green. He reminded managers how much money the company had recently lost and asked pointedly whether everything was indeed going along well. It took this prodding for someone to speak up, tentatively offering a first yellow report. After a moment of shocked silence in the group Mulally clapped, and the tension was broken. After that, yellow and red reports came in regularly.

Ford's is not an isolated story. In companies around the world, even the most senior executives can be reluctant to convey bad news to bosses and colleagues. Shooting the messenger remains an enduring and problematic phenomenon, so it's essential for leaders to proactively create conditions in which messages of failure travel up and across an organizational hierarchy. To do this, leaders need to engage in three essential activities: embrace the messenger, gather data and solicit feedback, and reward failure detection.

Embrace the Messenger

Savvy managers understand the risks of unbridled toughness. An overly punitive response to an employee mistake may be more effective in stifling information about problems than in making your organization better. This is obviously not a good result. Managers' ability to quickly diagnose and resolve problems depends on their ability to learn about them. Organizations with a habit of punishing mistakes or errors will discourage this process. This means that psychological safety (Part II of this 90-Day Plan) is the bedrock of any genuine failure identification and analysis effort.

Gather Data and Solicit Feedback

My research has found that a lack of access to data on failures is the most important barrier to managers learning from them. This is especially true for preventable and complex failures. In these circumstances, people often believe that no failures are acceptable, so hiding them can seem the only feasible approach. That inaccessibility can be due as much to human resistance to identifying failure as to technical difficulties in understanding small mistakes. To overcome this barrier, organizational leaders must develop systems, procedures, and cultures that proactively identify failure.

Soliciting feedback is an effective way of gathering data and surfacing many types of failures. Feedback from customers, employees, and other sources can expose failures such as communication breakdowns, the inability to meet goals, or a lack of customer satisfaction. Proactively seeking feedback from customers often helps manufacturers and service providers identify and address failures in a timely manner. If you believe identifying customer dissatisfaction is a luxury, bear in mind that only 5–10 percent of dissatisfied customers choose to complain following a service failure. Instead, most simply switch

providers. This means that if service companies fail to learn from their failures, they're guaranteed to lose customers.

Reward Failure Detection

Failures must be exposed as early as possible to enable learning in an efficient and cost-effective way. This requires a proactive effort on the part of managers to surface available data on failures and use it in a way that promotes learning. The detection challenge for intelligent failures lies in knowing when to declare defeat in an experimental course of action. The human tendency to hope for the best impedes early failure identification and is often exacerbated by strict organizational hierarchies. As a result, fruitless research projects are frequently kept going much longer than is scientifically rational or economically prudent. We throw good money after bad, hoping to pull a rabbit out of a hat. In innovation operations, this happens more often than most managers realize. Engineers' or scientists' intuition can be telling them for weeks that a project has fatal flaws, but making the formal decision to call it a failure may be delayed for months. Considerable resources are saved when such projects are stopped in a timely way and people are freed up to explore the next potential innovation.

Teaming as a Leader

Leaders have a special responsibility to encourage teaming. In this activity, you will examine the leader's role in encouraging teaming.

Activity

Reflect on the following questions:

Of a leader's four main responsibilities to promote teaming, which do you think is most important?

_____

_____

_____

Do you agree that many of our spontaneous frames are self-protective? Why or why not?

_____

_____

_____

Can you think of a failure you learned from? Describe the failure and what you learned from it. Do you think that failure was inevitable?

_____

_____

_____

Breaking Through Barriers

Benchmark goal: Discover how to team across boundaries.

When teaming across boundaries works, the results can be awe-inspiring. Managing a complex rescue operation, launching a space shuttle, producing a big-budget movie, or delivering a large engineering and construction project are all examples of complex uncertain work that requires multiple areas of expertise, and even multiple organizations, for its completion. The problem is that all too often teaming is thwarted by communication failures that take place at the boundaries between professions, organizations, and other groups. People think they're communicating, they participate in endless meetings, and they work hard, only to have their projects fail. Why? As individuals bring diverse expertise, skills, perspectives, and goals together in unique team configurations to accomplish challenging goals, they must overcome the hidden challenge of communicating across multiple types of boundaries. Some boundaries are obvious—like 2,000 feet of rock, or being in different countries with different time zones. Others are subtle, such as when two engineers working for the same company in different facilities unknowingly bring different taken-for-granted assumptions about how to carry out a particular technical procedure to a collaboration.

This week, I describe the boundaries that team members frequently must cross while working together on complex problems. After examining why boundaries matter, I describe three types of boundaries that confront teaming in today's global organizations. I then provide guidelines for successfully teaming across boundaries to create possibilities for organizational learning.

Visible and Invisible Boundaries

Boundaries refer to the divisions between identity groups. An identity group exists for any meaningful category in which a person belongs, such as gender, occupation, or nationality. Some identity groups, and their corresponding boundaries, are more visible than others. Gender, for example, is visible. Occupation is less visible—except when clothing gives it away. What is invisible, however, are the taken-for-granted assumptions and mindsets that people hold in different groups. For teaming to be successful, managers and team members must be aware that they come together with different perspectives, often taking for granted the "rightness" of their own beliefs and values. This means it's not enough to simply say, let's band together and it will all work out. No matter how much goodwill may be involved, boundaries limit collaboration in ways that are often invisible but nonetheless powerful.

Taken-for-Granted Assumptions

Processes of education, licensing, hiring, and socializing contribute to beliefs that lead people to favor their own group or location, and to unconsciously view the knowledge of their own group as especially important. It's as if there's a wall that separates engineers from marketers, nurses from doctors, and designers in Beijing from designers

in Boston. Most people take knowledge that lies on their side of a boundary for granted, making it hard to communicate with those on the other side. Paraphrasing an observation once made by communications theorist Marshall McLuhan, we don't know who discovered water, but it wasn't the fish. In other words, the context in which we work, day in and day out, is often invisible to us. Presumably, fish don't think much about water; they take it for granted.

Communication with anyone from a different group, whether the difference is demographic or organizational, is fraught with small hurdles. Teams within organizations often must coordinate objectives, schedules, or resources with other teams, departments, or locations. This requires discovering and revealing taken-for-granted assumptions to avoid misunderstanding and error. But by their very nature, taken-for-granted assumptions are notoriously hard to recognize, so it helps to be aware that they exist and to be on the lookout for them.

Specialization and Globalization

Two related trends have increased the need for teaming across boundaries. First, knowledge and expertise evolve ever more rapidly. In most fields, the rate of new knowledge development requires people to invest considerable time just to stay current in their own area of expertise. Especially in technical fields, the explosion of new knowledge leads inexorably to greater specialization. Fields spawn new subfields, and new subfields spawn even more specialized subfields. For example, electrical engineering, once a subfield of physics, became its own discipline by 1900, and today splits into the several distinct subfields of power systems, signal processing, and computer architecture. More generally, technical knowledge and specialized jargon proliferate, making it difficult to keep up with other, even closely related, fields of inquiry. Highly specialized professionals thus find

themselves needing to collaborate to carry out the important work of the organization, whether developing a new cell phone or caring for a cancer patient.

Second, global competition has led to ever more compressed time frames: product life cycles are shrinking, lead times for getting new products to market are shorter, and scientific researchers face more threats of being scooped in their work by a lab halfway around the world. Time pressures mean that a structured approach, in which managers plan each aspect of a large development project with specialized tasks to be accomplished separately in carefully structured phases, are unrealistic. This planning becomes even less realistic when completed tasks are "thrown over the wall" to other functions or disciplines. Instead, the walls between disciplines have come down, and simultaneous work on related tasks must be coordinated and negotiated in a dynamic teaming journey.

Individuals or departments cannot accomplish meaningful results in isolation. The chances of individual components, developed separately, coming together into meaningful, functional wholes—new product, feature film, or rescue operation—without intense communication across the boundaries are exceedingly low. Considering these two factors—increasing specialization and global competition—there are numerous benefits to learning how to transcend boundaries that exist between people, departments, or specialties. Understanding how to break down these walls includes developing a deeper understanding of the varieties of diversity and how they relate to the boundaries that exist both within and between work groups.

Three Types of Boundaries

Diversity is an important topic in research on teams and teaming, yet researchers lack consensus on a single clear definition of diversity.

Katherine Klein and Dave Harrison, professors at Wharton and Penn State, respectively, defined diversity as "the distribution of differences among the members of a unit with respect to a common attribute X."[1] Common attributes include gender, ethnicity, professional status, and educational degree. A team is considered diverse if its members differ in respect to at least one attribute. Conceptually, Klein and Harrison grouped diversity into three basic groups—separation, disparity, and variety—which provides a helpful starting point. Here are three common boundaries that often confront teaming in complex organizations:

- **Physical distance:** *Separation diversity* includes differences in location—different time zones or the building down the street.

- **Status:** *Disparity diversity* ranks people according to the social value of a particular attribute. Teaming often confronts differences in status between people who need to work together to get a job done.

- **Knowledge:** *Variety diversity* describes differences in experience, knowledge, expertise, or education. When teaming, the major boundaries confronted in this category are differences in knowledge based on organizational membership or expertise.

The following sections look at examples of each of these types of boundaries and consider their impact on collaboration. Of course, sometimes people must cross multiple boundaries at once, such as when two team members have differences in terms of nationality, profession, gender, and time zone. Fortunately, leadership that helps establish process discipline and good communication can help overcome the challenges.

Physical Distance

An increasingly common teaming challenge is created by the need to span geographic distance. In many global companies, work teams in geographically dispersed locations all over the world, so-called virtual teams, are relied on to integrate expertise. A virtual team is a group of individuals who work across physical and organizational boundaries through the use of technology. Geographic regions in some organizations present nearly impermeable boundaries, even within the same country. At the Internal Revenue Service (IRS), for example, before Commissioner Charles Rossotti led the agency in an ambitious organizational transformation during his five-year tenure under President Bill Clinton, regional centers had acted like fiefdoms for decades, sharing neither information nor resources, despite the need to do both. Service representatives were unable to respond to the volume and variety of complex tax questions that would come into the regional center. The result was poor service and frustrated customers. Rossotti took down the regional barriers by combining all service representatives into one centralized national call center. Employees did not physically move. They still lived and worked in the old geographic locations, but they became part of one large virtual service team that was able to spread the workload in sensible and equitable ways. This organizational change enabled taxpayers' technical queries to be routed to those individuals with expertise in a particular aspect of the tax code—no matter where they were located.

Status

Disparity diversity may be the most challenging boundary to cross in teaming. When those at the top have the most power and those at the bottom have the least, lower-power individuals usually find it hard to

speak up. Perhaps the most common power differences within work teams are professional status and ethnicity. Professional status can significantly affect beliefs about taking interpersonal risks and speaking up. In health care, for example, physicians have more status and power than nurses, who in turn have more status than technicians. Yet members of these professions often must team to take care of patients. Even people from the same profession can have status differences. Consider resident-level and senior ("attending") physicians working together to care for patients. Fears about taking interpersonal risk can prohibit candid discussion and hinder collaboration.

Note that demographic differences (differences based on gender, race, religion, and other social categories), which may readily be seen as variety diversity, sometimes also enforce a power hierarchy due to the nature of social power in various cultures and countries. For example, power and status differences in organizations have been documented for both gender and race. In addition, individuals aware of negative stereotypes associated with cultural identity may become hindered by self-fulfilling prophecies or a perceived need to overcome negative stereotypes. Similarly, unconscious negative stereotypes significantly hinder group performance because individuals tend to skirt or avoid the issue, allowing negative stereotypes to arise in other, more subtle ways.

Knowledge

Work teams often confront differences in expertise. In product and process development teams, for example, it is increasingly common to bring together people from different organizational functions for a limited period of intense teaming. The value of teaming is that different experts bring different knowledge and skills to the

collaborative task. In product development, engineering offers insight into design and technology; manufacturing into feasible production processes, accurate cost estimates, pilot and full-scale production; and marketing into customer receptivity, customer segments, product positioning, and product plans. Teaming is the process of integrating these diverse skill sets and perspectives, as well as coordinating timelines and transferring resources across groups, when appropriate. However, diverse groups often have difficulty accessing and managing disparate knowledge, for two reasons. Misunderstandings arise due to different meanings embedded in different disciplines, and mistrust arises between groups.

Teaming Across Common Boundaries

Sharing knowledge across boundaries may not be natural in large organizations, but it's certainly worth the effort. Successfully overcoming the obstacles of teaming across boundaries offers valuable learning for individuals and provides a vital competitive advantage for organizations. Working across the three types of boundaries described in the previous section requires attention to their unique challenges and to techniques for overcoming them. For reference, Table 4.1 summarizes these common boundaries and their accompanying tactics.

As shown in Table 4.1, physical and status differences arise from distance and hierarchy, respectively, whereas knowledge boundaries arise from two distinct origins: membership in different organizations and membership in different occupations. The following sections explore the implications of teaming across each boundary and present strategies for successful teaming and learning within diverse groups.

Table 4.1 Common Boundaries That Impede Teaming and Organizational Learning

Boundary Type	Physical Distance	Status	Knowledge-Based	
Arises due to . . .	Dispersed geographic locations	Hierarchy	Different organizations collaborating	Different experts collaborating
Composition of team:	Geographically dispersed team members	Different levels of power or status	From different companies or different sites within a company	Diverse skills and expertise from education or function
Team challenges:	Misunderstandings, miscommunication, and coordination difficulty	Social norms of deference to authority	Competing taken-for-granted assumptions derived from organizational goals or values Competing incentives	Team member allegiance to expertise-based subgroups
Collaboration enabled by . . .	Periodic visits to other sites Focus on shared goal Knowledge repositories and exchanges	Leadership inclusiveness to minimize experienced status gaps	Explicitly sharing individual perspectives Emphasizing value brought by each organization Focus on shared goal	Proactive sharing of expertise-based knowledge Use of boundary objects like drawings, models, and prototypes

Teaming Across Distance Boundaries

"Sharing is not a natural thing," said Benedikt Benenati, the organizational development director at the multinational food company Groupe Danone. With subsidiaries in 120 countries, Groupe Danone is a multinational corporation that sought to promote teaming across the geographical boundaries of its many divisions. In addition to sharing common problems, such as getting retailers to stock the right amounts of Danone products at the right time, managers in different countries were focused on their own regions, and they rarely considered the opportunity to seek ideas from their counterparts in other regions. As Benenati pointed out, the company's senior managers may be part of the problem: "Managers may be reluctant to let their teams discuss among themselves. If members of their team find solutions, then perhaps managers are of no further use." Such reactions and fears are very human, of course, but they also leave opportunities for small process improvements around the globe to go untapped.

The information technology that enables us to shrink global distances by sending emails hurtling through cyberspace and to fax documents to machines across continents gives us a false sense of security, lulling us into believing that teamwork among geographically dispersed employees requires nothing more than a fast internet connection or new videoconferencing equipment. In fact, there are substantial barriers to sharing and integrating knowledge that virtual teams must overcome. In some organizations, however, it's the different mindsets across geographic regions, rather than the actual physical distance between them, that present nearly impermeable boundaries. In addition to the obvious challenges brought on by language and time zone differences, some types of knowledge just do not travel well. This is because certain, often very valuable, information is taken for granted by those who are closest to it. This tacit knowledge can be situated in ways that make it invisible to distant team members.

Teaming Across Status Boundaries

Most organizations contain vestiges of hierarchical boundaries. Although a command-and-control model of authority may have been productive in the past, the knowledge economy increasingly requires interactive communication and collaboration. The principal strategy for developing the necessary level of collaboration is leadership inclusiveness, in which higher-status individuals in a group actively invite and express appreciation for the views of others.

Consider the case of Patti Bondurant, senior clinical director at the Regional Center for Newborn Intensive Care at Cincinnati Children's Hospital. Bondurant felt that having the respiratory therapists, rather than the physician-director of the unit, lead an improvement project was a key driver to their improvement. She described this new relationship as follows:

> The turning point for us was when our respiratory therapy clinical managers in all three of the units said, "With all due respect, doctor, this is our expertise and you need to let us do our job." It was a really defining moment for this group. The doctor sat back and said, "I believe you're right. I don't need to hang onto control when there are people willing to do the work." . . . Those doctors were open to say, "Yes, you're the experts and we're going to let you do your job." The dynamic shifted from doctor sitting at the head of the table, to all of us becoming common denominators at the table.[2]

This is a textbook moment of teaming across hierarchical boundaries. The respiratory therapy clinical managers, lowest on the ladder, felt valued enough to speak clearly and directly to their institutional superiors with both expertise and a point of view. The doctors, at the

top of the ladder, were able to sit back, listen, agree, and learn, thereby relinquishing control over every aspect of the project. Most important, spanning this boundary enabled a renegotiation of responsibilities, which in turn enabled improved care for the newborn patients.

Teaming Across Knowledge Boundaries

Organization and occupation are two important sources of knowledge boundaries. The former exists anytime people from different companies—or even sites within companies as we saw at the IRS—have to work together. The latter is driven by differences in areas of expertise, within and between organizations.

Organization-Based

Organizational membership brings with it taken-for-granted, or tacit, knowledge shared by other members of the same organization. People working together acquire shared experiences and practices that begin to seem (to them) like the obvious right way to do things. This tacit knowledge might consist of expectations about a particular supplier's reliability, the performance of a particular piece of equipment, or even awareness of who knows what in a given facility. Some things you just have to be on site to know. And because this kind of knowledge is taken for granted, people often don't realize that what they know is important to share. It is also the case that these kinds of knowledge boundaries often coexist with distance boundaries, which further raises the communication hurdle.

Consider the example of a new product development team in a large highly technical business charged with carrying out a project to develop a polymer for a new customer in a strategic market sector. With seven people dispersed across five sites on three continents, teleconferencing

enabled the team to share extensive brainstorming and discussion, yet one ingredient for the new polymer proved unexpectedly difficult to source. One member of the team, an engineer in the United Kingdom whom I'll call David Thompson, turned to his local, on-site colleagues for help. As Thompson tells it, he was "just talking" when a colleague at his site happened to mention that he was making the difficult-to-source ingredient and could reserve a barrel for Thompson's team. It's the "just talking" around the proverbial watercooler that is situational, often crucial, and easily misunderstood by distant colleagues.

Occupation-Based

Training for any one profession is often a long process of mastering a specialized body of knowledge, terminology, and, above all, a mindset or way of knowing. Business students learn about marketing, management, and how to interpret company problems. Medical students learn about ligaments, blood vessels, and how to recognize disease. Writers learn about how to use language. Each profession is trained to make particular assumptions and epistemological assertions, which often become taken for granted. Jargon, acquired in specialized education and practice, often means that occupations speak different languages. This makes sharing across the "thought worlds" of occupational communities highly vulnerable to misunderstanding. In many cases, meaning is lost, errors are made, and synergy fails to materialize.

Expertise diversity is a key source of innovation. Individuals from different groups weave their ideas and knowledge into new, integrated forms. This type of synthesis is tricky even in mature industries, but particularly when confronting new or novel problems. Colocation, along with a lot of communication, and excitement about the innovative building they were trying to build, were essential to the team's ability to build trust across occupational boundaries that had long been

antagonistic in the industry. Working across occupational boundaries is replete with technical and interpersonal challenges. It also comes with the territory of cross-functional teams.

Teams with occupational and expertise differences aligned with organizational departments or functions are called *cross-functional teams*. Such teams are on the rise in organizations, especially for innovation projects. The goal of cross-functional teaming is to bring together experts of various kinds who can combine knowledge gleaned from their distinct training to produce results that can't be achieved by any single discipline. Cross-functional teams are useful in organizations because they serve as a mechanism for combining different sets of highly specialized skills into one cohesive group. The obvious benefit of this form of collaboration is the qualified, high-level information that can be provided by each team member.

Research has shown that the challenge of occupational boundary spanning can be mitigated through the use of what are called *boundary objects* around which diverse groups can coalesce. Boundary objects like drawings, prototypes, and components are tangible representations of knowledge. Professor Paul Carlile of Boston University studied knowledge barriers in new product development teams in the automotive industry. He found that boundary objects facilitated spanning occupation and expertise boundaries. By pointing to and discussing elements in a model or schematic, the obfuscating qualities of jargon can be overcome. Similarly, University of California, Davis, professor Beth Bechky has found that while working face-to-face in a production, facility engineers, technicians, and assemblers can cocreate meaning, reaching across the boundaries between practices to do so. This process, which generates fuller understanding of the products and problems they face, involves more than just discussion but also shared action, for example, convening around a common machine or drawing

to articulate different perspectives and develop a shared understanding. It also facilitates sharing expertise-based knowledge.

Occupation and Organization Combined

When knowledge boundaries based on expertise or profession are confounded with knowledge boundaries that exist between companies, the challenge intensifies. A complex building project, for example, brings together multiple areas of expertise as well as multiple companies to produce a customized product with unique constraints and goals. Participants in this process—owners, architects, engineers, and builders—have traditionally managed the manifold risks they face through legal contracts rather than through teaming, leaving the industry with a history of deep mistrust between professions.

Some recent innovative building projects have attempted to change the counterproductive dynamics in the construction industry by teaming across boundaries from the beginning of a project until the very end. The goal is to avoid the small failures that are nearly inevitable in complex, unique projects, and, of course, to avoid large failures, too. My colleague Faaiza Rashid and I studied a project that employed such an approach, called Integrated Project Delivery. Individuals from the multiple companies and professions in a large building project agreed to work together closely from project start to completion. Locating together in one workplace near the building site, everyone signed a single legal contract. Despite aggressive targets in budget, deadline, aesthetics, and environmental sustainability that made the project especially challenging, the teaming worked, trust grew, and the result was an award-winning building for the Boston area headquarters of software company Autodesk.

Teaming across boundaries of all kinds has the potential to help participants increase their knowledge of other fields. Working in

diverse teams can expand participants' networks of colleagues from other areas of the organization and improve their boundary-spanning skills. This last point is particularly important because most teams must work across more than one diversity type or organizational boundary to solve today's most complex problems.

Team Across Boundaries

Every team must cross many kinds of boundaries to work effectively. Use this activity to think about the boundaries you have faced or are likely to face in your work.

Activity

Reflect on the following questions:

What are the three types of boundaries? Which have you had experience working across?

_____

_____

_____

How has specialization increased the need for teaming across boundaries?

_____

_____

_____

What type of boundary do you find most challenging to work across? Why?

_____

_____

_____

Performance goal: Get ready to learn, innovate, and compete.

Teaming and its associated interpersonal behaviors support organizational learning and require the right leadership mindset to optimize outcomes. This way of working allows employees to grow personally and professionally, whereas traditional top-down and assembly line models treated workers like children who must be told what to do.

Questions

1. Although teaming is imperative in today's organizations, neither teams nor organizations naturally do it well. Have you had an experience with unsuccessful teaming in your career?

2. There are several benefits to teaming. These benefits fall into two categories: better organizational performance and more engaging and satisfying work environments. Which category do you think is more important?

Activity

For this activity, get a paper and pen to write answers to these prompts.

Teaming is a dynamic way of working that provides the necessary coordination and collaboration without the luxury (or rigidity) of stable team structures. Do you see benefits to this approach? What about drawbacks? Do the benefits outweigh the drawbacks in your opinion? Why or why not?

Boundary spanning involves deliberate attempts to reach across the barriers that exist within and between groups of all kinds. Rapid developments in technology and the greater emphasis on globalization have greatly increased the significance of boundary spanning in today's work environment. What actions would you take to help span boundaries, such as workers located in different areas around the country or world?

Days 31–60

Performance goal: Team fearlessly with psychological safety.

Teaming is the art of communicating and coordinating with people across boundaries of all kinds: expertise, status, and distance, to name the most important. But whether you're teaming with new colleagues all the time or working in a stable team, effective teamwork happens best in a psychologically safe workplace.

The following table summarizes the goals you will pursue over the next 30 days. To keep yourself motivated, consider your personal goals and vision for success. What does psychological safety mean to you?

Days 31–60	
Performance Goal: Team fearlessly with psychological safety.	
Week 5	**Benchmark Goal: Grasp the power of psychological safety.** • Can you think of the last time you made an "unconscious calculation" to stay silent because of a lack of psychological safety? • What would have been different if you'd felt psychologically safe? • What does a psychologically safe workplace look like to you? • How does psychological safety boost performance?

Days 31–60
Performance Goal: Team fearlessly with psychological safety.

Week 6	**Benchmark Goal: Make it safe to team.** • What risks do you face at work? • What are some of the benefits of psychological safety? • Can you think of a time when hierarchy affected psychological safety for the worse? • Of the tools for cultivating psychological safety, which do you think you need to improve on the most?
Week 7	**Benchmark Goal: Frame your team for success.** • What is framing versus reframing? • What's a leader's role in framing? • How does framing play a role in teaming?
Week 8	**Benchmark Goal: Create a fearless organization.** • What's the leader's toolkit for creating a fearless organization? • How do you set the stage for psychological safety? • How do you get your organization excited about establishing psychological safety?
Personal Goals and Vision for Success
What do you hope to achieve by leveling up?
How could your life change by reaching these goals?

Teaming Without Fear

Benchmark goal: Grasp the power of psychological safety.

The tiny newborn twins seemed healthy enough, but their early arrival at only 27 weeks' gestation meant they were considered high-risk. Fortunately, the medical team at the busy urban hospital where the babies were delivered included staff from the neonatal intensive care unit (NICU): a young neonatal nurse practitioner named Christina Price (all names in this story are pseudonyms) and a silver-haired neonatologist named Dr. Drake. As Christina looked at the babies, she was concerned. Her recent training had included, as newly established best practice, administering a medicine (a prophylactic surfactant) that promoted lung development as soon as possible for a high-risk baby. Babies born very prematurely often arrive with lungs not quite ready for fully independent breathing outside the womb. But the neonatologist had not issued an order for the medicine. Christina stepped forward to remind Dr. Drake about the surfactant and then caught herself. Last week she'd overheard him publicly berate another nurse for questioning one of his orders. She told herself that the twins would probably be fine—after all, the doctor probably had a reason for avoiding the surfactant, still considered a judgment call—and she dismissed the idea of bringing it up. Besides, he'd already turned on his heel, off for his morning rounds, white coat billowing.

Unconscious Calculations

In hesitating and then choosing not to speak up, Christina was making a quick, not entirely conscious, risk calculation—the kind of micro-assessment most of us make numerous times a day. Most likely she was not even aware that she had weighed the risk of being belittled or berated against the risk that the babies might in fact need the medication to thrive. She told herself the doctor knew better than she did, and she was not confident he would welcome her input. Inadvertently, she had done something psychologists call *discounting the future*—underweighting the more important issue of the patients' health, which would take some time to play out, and overweighting the importance of the doctor's possible response, which would happen immediately. Our spontaneous tendency to discount the future explains the prevalence of many unhelpful or unhealthy behaviors—whether eating that extra piece of chocolate cake or procrastinating on a challenging assignment—and the failure to speak up at work is an important and often overlooked example of this problematic tendency.

Like most people, Christina was spontaneously managing her image at work. As noted sociologist Erving Goffman argued in his seminal 1957 book, *The Presentation of the Self in Everyday Life*, as humans, we are constantly attempting to influence others' perceptions of us by regulating and controlling information in social interactions. We do this both consciously and subconsciously.

Put another way, no one wakes up in the morning excited to go to work and look ignorant, incompetent, or disruptive. These are called *interpersonal risks*, and they are what nearly everyone seeks to avoid, not always consciously. In fact, most of us want to look smart, capable, or helpful in the eyes of others. No matter what our line of work, status, or gender, all of us learn how to manage interpersonal risk relatively early in life. At some point during elementary school,

children start to recognize that what others think of them matters, and they learn how to lower the risk of rejection or scorn. By the time we're adults, we're usually really good at it! So good, we do it without conscious thought. Don't want to look ignorant? Don't ask questions. Don't want to look incompetent? Don't admit to mistakes or weaknesses. Don't want to be called "disruptive"? Don't make suggestions. While it might be acceptable at a social event to privilege looking good over making a difference, at work this tendency can lead to significant problems—ranging from thwarted innovation to poor service to, at the extreme, loss of human life. Yet avoiding behaviors that might lead others to think less of us is pretty much second nature in most workplaces.

As influential management thinker Nilofer Merchant said about her early days as an administrator at Apple, "I used to go to meetings and see the problem so clearly, when others could not." But worrying about being "wrong," she "kept quiet and learned to sit on my hands lest they rise up and betray me. I would rather keep my job by staying within the lines than say something and risk looking stupid." In one study investigating employee experiences with speaking up, 85 percent of respondents reported at least one occasion when they felt unable to raise a concern with their bosses, even though they believed the issue was important.

If you think this behavior is limited to those lower in the organization, consider the chief financial officer recruited to join the senior team of a large electronics company. Despite grave reservations about a planned acquisition of another company, the new executive said nothing. His colleagues seemed uniformly enthusiastic, and he went along with the decision. Later, when the takeover had clearly failed, the executives gathered with a consultant for a post-mortem. Each was asked to reflect on what they might have done to contribute to or avert the failure. The CFO, now less of an outsider, shared his earlier

concerns, acknowledging that he had let the team down by not speaking up. Openly apologetic and emotional, he lamented that the others' enthusiasm had left him afraid to be "the skunk at the picnic."

The problem with sitting on our hands and staying within the lines rather than speaking up is that although these behaviors keep us personally safe, they can make us underperform and become dissatisfied. They can also put the organization at risk. In the case of Christina and the newborns, fortunately, no immediate damage was done, but the fear of speaking up can lead to accidents that were in fact avoidable. Remaining silent due to fear of interpersonal risk can make the difference between life and death. Airplanes have crashed, financial institutions have fallen, and hospital patients have died unnecessarily because individuals were, for reasons having to do with the climate in which they worked, afraid to speak up. Fortunately, it doesn't have to happen.

Envisioning the Psychologically Safe Workplace

Had Christina worked in a hospital unit where she felt psychologically safe, she would not have hesitated to ask the neonatologist whether or not he thought treating the newborns with prophylactic lung medicine was warranted. Here, too, she might not even be aware of making a conscious decision to speak up; it would simply seem natural to check. She would take for granted that her voice was appreciated, even if what she said didn't lead to a change in the patient's care. In a climate characterized by psychological safety—which blends trust and respect—the neonatologist might quickly agree with Christina and call the pharmacy to put in a request, or he might have explained why he thought it wasn't warranted in this case. Either way, the unit would be better off as a result. The patients would have received

life-saving medication, or the team would have learned more about the subtleties of neonatal medicine. Before leaving the room, the doctor might thank Christina for her intervention. He'd be glad he could rely on her to speak up in case he slipped up, missed a detail, or was simply distracted.

Finally, as she gave the medicine to the babies, Christina might come up with the idea that the NICU could institute a protocol to make sure that that all babies who need a surfactant would get it. She might seek out her manager to make this suggestion during a break in the action. And because psychological safety exists in work groups, rather than between specific individuals (such as Christina and Dr. Drake), it's likely her nurse manager would be receptive to her suggestion.

Speaking up describes back-and-forth exchanges people have at work—from volunteering a concern in a meeting to giving feedback to a colleague. It also includes electronic communication (for example, sending an extra email to ask a coworker to clarify a particular point or seek help with a project). Valuable forms of speaking up include raising a different point of view in a conference call, asking a colleague for feedback on a report, admitting that a project is over budget or behind schedule, and so on—the myriad verbal interactions that make up the world of twenty-first century work.

There is, of course, a range of interpersonal riskiness involved in speaking up. Some cases of speaking up occur after significant trepidation; others feel reasonably straightforward and feasible. Still others simply don't occur—as in the case of Christina in the NICU—because one has weighed the risk (consciously or not) and come out on the side of silence. The free exchange of ideas, concerns, or questions is routinely hindered by interpersonal fear far more often than most managers realize. This kind of fear cannot be directly seen. Silence— when voice was possible—rarely announces itself! The moment passes, and no one is the wiser except the person who held back.

I have defined psychological safety as the belief that the work environment is safe for interpersonal risk-taking. The concept refers to the experience of feeling able to speak up with relevant ideas, questions, or concerns. Psychological safety is present when colleagues trust and respect each other and feel able—even obligated— to be candid.

In workplaces with psychological safety, the kinds of small and potentially consequential moments of silence experienced by Christina are far less likely. Speaking up occurs instead, facilitating the open and authentic communication that shines the light on problems, mistakes, and opportunities for improvement and increases the sharing of knowledge and ideas.

As you will see, our understanding of interpersonal risk management at work has advanced since Goffman studied the fascinating micro-dynamics of face saving. We now know that psychological safety emerges as a property of a group, and that groups in organizations tend to have very interpersonal climates. Even in a company with a strong corporate culture, you will find pockets of both high and low psychological safety. Take, for instance, the hospital where Christina works. One patient care unit might be a place where nurses readily speak up to challenge or inquire about care decisions, while in another it feels downright impossible. These differences in workplace climate shape behavior in subtle but powerful ways.

An Accidental Discovery

As much as I'm passionate about these ideas, I didn't set out to study psychological safety on purpose. As a first-year doctoral student in the process of clarifying my research interests for my eventual dissertation, I had been fortunate to join a large team studying medical error in several hospitals. This was a great way to gain research experience

82

90 Days to Level Up Your Teamwork

and to sharpen my general interest in how organizations can learn and succeed in an increasingly challenging, fast-paced world. I had long been interested in the idea of learning from mistakes for achieving excellence.

My role in the research team was to examine the effects of teamwork on medical error rates. The team had numerous experts, including physicians who could judge whether human error had occurred and trained nurse investigators who would review medical charts and interview frontline caregivers in patient care units in two hospitals to obtain error rates for each of these teams. These experts were, in effect, getting the data for what would be the dependent variable in my study—the team-level error rates. This was a great arrangement for me, for at least two reasons. First, I lacked the medical expertise to identify medical errors on my own. Second, from a research methods perspective, it meant that my survey measures of team effectiveness would not be subject to experimenter bias—the cognitive tendency for a researcher to see what they want to see rather than what is actually there. So the independence of our data collection activities was an important strength of the study.

The nurse investigators collected error data over a six-month period. During the first month, I distributed a validated instrument called the *team diagnostic survey* to everyone working in the study units—doctors, nurses, and clerks—slightly altering the language of the survey items to make sure they would make sense to people working in a hospital, and adding a few new items to assess people's views about making mistakes. I also spent time on the floor (in the patient care units) observing how each of the teams worked.

Going into the study, I hypothesized, not surprisingly, that the most effective teams would make the fewest errors. Of course, I had to wait six months for the data on the dependent variable (the error rates) to be fully collected. And here is where the story took an unexpected turn.

First, the good news (from a research perspective anyway). There was variance! Error rates across teams were strikingly different; indeed, there was a 10-fold difference in the number of human errors per 1,000 patient days (a standard measure) from the best to the worst unit on what I sincerely believed was an important performance measure. A wrong medicine dose, for example, might be reported every three weeks on one ward but every other day on another. Likewise, the team survey data also showed significant variance. Some teams were much stronger—their members reported more mutual respect, more collaboration, more confidence in their ability to deliver great results, more satisfaction, and so on—than others.

When all of the error and survey data were compiled, I was at first thrilled. Running the statistical analysis, I immediately saw that there was a significant correlation between the independently collected error rates and the measures of team effectiveness from my survey. But then I looked closely and noticed something wrong. The direction of the correlation was exactly the opposite of what I had predicted. Better teams were apparently making more—not fewer—mistakes than less strong teams. Worse, the correlation was statistically significant. I briefly wondered how I could tell my dissertation chair the bad news. This was a problem.

No, it was a puzzle.

Did better teams really make more mistakes? I thought about the need for communication between doctors and nurses to produce safe, error-free care. The need to ask for help, to double-check each other's work to make sure, in this complex and customized work environment, that patients received the best care. I knew that great care meant that clinicians had to team up effectively. It just didn't make sense that good teamwork would lead to more errors. I wondered for a moment whether better teams got overconfident over time and then became sloppy. That might explain my perplexing result. But why else might better teams have higher error rates?

And then came the eureka moment. What if the better teams had a climate of openness that made it easier to report and discuss error? The good teams, I suddenly thought, don't *make* more mistakes; they *report* more. But having this insight was a far cry from proving it.

I decided to hire a research assistant to go out and study these patient care teams carefully, with no preconceptions. He didn't know which units had made more mistakes, or which ones scored better on the team survey. He didn't even know my new hypothesis. In research terms, he was "blind" to both the hypothesis and the previously collected data.

Here is what he found. Through quiet observation and open-ended interviews about all aspects of the work environment, he discovered that the teams varied wildly in whether people felt able to talk about mistakes. And these differences were almost perfectly correlated with the detected error rates. In short, people in the better teams (as measured by my survey, but unbeknownst to the research assistant) talked openly about the risks of errors, often trying to find new ways to catch and prevent them. It would take another couple of years before I labeled this climate difference *psychological safety*. But the accidental finding set me off on a new and fruitful research direction: to find out how interpersonal climate might vary across groups in other workplaces, and whether it might matter for learning and speaking up in other industries—not just in health care.

Over the years, in studies in companies, hospitals, and even government agencies, my doctoral students and I have found that psychological safety does indeed vary, and that it matters very much for predicting both learning behavior and objective measures of performance. Today, researchers like me have conducted dozens of studies showing greater learning, performance, and even lower mortality as a result of psychological safety.

In that initial study over two decades ago, I learned that psychological safety varies across groups within hospitals. Since that time, I

have replicated this finding in many industry settings. The data are consistent in this simple but interesting finding: psychological safety seems to live at the level of the group. In other words, in the organization where you work, it's likely that different groups have different interpersonal experiences; in some, it may be easy to speak up and bring your full self to work. In others, speaking up might be experienced as a last resort—as it did in some of the patient care teams I studied. That's because psychological safety is very much shaped by local leaders.

Understanding Psychological Safety

Psychological safety makes it possible to give tough feedback and have difficult conversations without the need to tiptoe around the truth. In psychologically safe environments, people believe that if they make a mistake, others will not penalize or think less of them for it. This activity explores your own experience with psychological safety in the workplace.

Activity

Reflect on the following questions:

Can you think of a time at work when you made a conscious or unconscious calculation to stay silent rather than speaking up? What held you back from speaking up?

_____

_____

_____

How do you spontaneously manage your image at work? What kind of image do you try to project? How does that lead to actions (or nonactions) that may negatively affect the quality of the work in your team or organization?

_____

_____

_____

Have you worked on a psychologically safe team? Do you agree that such an environment makes it easier to report errors?

_____

_____

_____

Creating Psychological Safety

Benchmark goal: Make it safe to team.

On January 16, 2003, the space shuttle *Columbia* was successfully launched from the Kennedy Space Center on a 16-day research mission. The next day, shuttle engineer Rodney Rocha reviewed a video of the launch and became deeply concerned about the size and position of a chunk of insulating foam that appeared to have fallen off the shuttle's external tank and struck its left wing. The video images were grainy, and it was impossible to be sure what had happened. To determine whether damage had occurred, Rocha hoped to obtain photographic images of the shuttle's wing from spy satellites. Although the photos would have to be authorized by the Air Force, the request would require neither a technical nor financial miracle. It did mean that NASA would have to ask for help from the Department of Defense.

Rocha initially expressed the need for the satellite images in an email to his immediate superior, emphasizing the urgency by using boldfaced type. When he learned that his request was unlikely to be honored, Rocha wrote a scathing email: "Remember the NASA safety poster everywhere around, stating, 'If it's not safe, say so?' Yes, it's that serious." He didn't send the email to the mission manager, however;

he only shared it with fellow engineers. Later, he explained that "engineers were often told not to send messages much higher than their own rung in the ladder."

Discouraged by his early efforts to call attention to the foam-strike issue and convinced that voicing concerns was career limiting at NASA, Rocha refrained from sharing his anxiety in a critical mission management team meeting, eight days into the flight. He fervently hoped others with more clout might offer their concerns. The opportunity passed, however, and the issue was never formally revisited in a mission management team meeting.

Just eight days after this lost opportunity to speak up, the shuttle burned up on reentry into the Earth's atmosphere, resulting in the death of all seven astronauts. Much later, asked in a television interview with ABC News anchor Charlie Gibson why he didn't voice his doubts about the safety of the shuttle in that mission management team meeting, Rocha replied, "I just couldn't do it. I'm too low down . . . and she [mission management team leader Linda Ham] is way up here," gesturing with his hand held above his head.

The 2003 *Columbia* space shuttle tragedy reflects an unusually dramatic consequence of not speaking up in the workplace—especially with tentative concerns or unproven ideas—an all-too-common organizational dynamic. Instances where people are reluctant to voice concerns or engage in behaviors that could threaten their image occur within a wide spectrum of industries and organizations. Although it's understandable to keep silent about mistakes when not much is at stake, in many situations errors can be deadly.

The term *psychological safety* describes a climate in which people feel free to express relevant thoughts and feelings. Although it sounds simple, the ability to seek help and tolerate mistakes while colleagues watch can be unexpectedly difficult. Yet, frank conversations and public missteps must occur if teaming is to realize the promise of collaboration across differences.

Promoting Trust and Respect

Simply put, psychological safety makes it possible to give tough feedback and have difficult conversations without the need to tiptoe around the truth. In psychologically safe environments, people believe that if they make a mistake others will not penalize or think less of them for it. They also believe that others will not resent or humiliate them when they ask for help or information. This belief comes about when people both trust and respect each other, and it produces a sense of confidence that the group won't embarrass, reject, or punish someone for speaking up. Thus psychological safety is a taken-for-granted belief about how others will respond when you ask a question, seek feedback, admit a mistake, or propose a possibly wacky idea. Most people feel a need to manage interpersonal risk to retain a good image, especially at work, and especially in the presence of those who formally evaluate them. This need is both instrumental (promotions and rewards may depend on impressions held by bosses and others) and socio-emotional (we simply prefer approval over disapproval).

Psychological safety does not imply a cozy situation in which people are necessarily close friends. Nor does it suggest an absence of pressure or problems. Psychological safety does not mean a group has to be cohesive or in agreement about things. As research has shown, group cohesiveness can reduce people's willingness to disagree with or challenge each other. The term *groupthink* refers to this problem. Specifically, in many cohesive groups, people are reluctant to disturb the feeling of harmony created by the group's apparent agreement about an important issue. This leads them to hold back or fail to admit to holding a different view, and thus contributes to poor decision-making. Yale professor Irving Janis attributed President Kennedy's ill-fated plan to send Cuban exiles to invade the Bay of Pigs in 1961 to groupthink. By contrast, psychological safety describes a

climate in which raising a dissenting view is expected and welcomed. A tolerance of dissent enables productive discussion and early detection of problems.

I have found that many people are genuinely pained and frustrated by keeping silent at work. For the most part, the people I've studied aren't failing to provide ideas or input because they've "checked out" or don't care, but because of a subtle but pervasive fear of what others, particularly those in power, might think of them. As most people intuitively recognize, each of us engages in a tacit calculus in which we assess the risk associated with a given interpersonal behavior, quickly and effortlessly, as we face a micro-behavior decision point. To illustrate what I mean by a micro-behavior decision point, imagine that while you are in a conversation with your boss, you consider fleetingly, "Should I say something about this?" In this almost imperceptible thinking process, you weigh the potential gain against the potential loss. You wonder, "If I do this, will I be hurt, embarrassed, or criticized?" If you quickly conclude that the answer is no, then you have a sense of psychological safety, and you proceed to voice your thoughts. (If you believe that the answer might be that you could be hurt but you speak anyway, then you are demonstrating courage.) Typically, proceeding means being authentic. It means expressing the work-relevant thoughts and feelings on your mind without excessive self-censorship.

Consider the fact that admitting a mistake or asking for help may be unthinkable in one work setting and yet readily accepted, even valued, in another setting. The difference between the two situations is what psychological safety is all about.

The easy solution to minimizing image risk at work is to avoid doing or saying anything unless you're absolutely sure you're right. This is obviously a facetious solution. Not only does it limit creativity, stifle innovation, and preclude authentic relationships but it also

creates important risks of another kind: risks to performance and safety. This is especially true in dangerous industries such as nuclear power, where admitting errors and asking for help may be critical for avoiding catastrophe. The human tendency to favor silence over voicing concerns is also particularly troubling in organizations where lives are at stake, such as in hospitals. Extensive research on hospitals and other high-risk organizations has shown that rules and required procedures are not enough to eradicate errors that were not caught or corrected due to a lack of psychological safety. This isn't because people deliberately break rules, but rather because of the subtle ways in which we make sense of uncertainty and view each other at work.

Weighing Interpersonal Risks in the Work Environment

Whether frequently or infrequently, overtly or implicitly, most people in organizations are being evaluated in an ongoing way. The presence of others with more power or status makes the threat associated with being evaluated especially powerful, but it by no means disappears in the presence of peers and subordinates.

The four following concerns powerfully shape our willingness to speak up:

- **Being seen as ignorant:** When individuals ask questions or seek information, they run the risk of being seen as ignorant. Most of us can think of a time when we hesitated to ask a question because it seemed that no one else was asking, or perhaps we believed the information was something we were already expected to know.

Creating Psychological Safety

- **Being seen as incompetent:** When admitting mistakes, asking for help, or accepting the high probability of failure that comes with experimenting, people risk being seen as incompetent. For example, if you admit that something you tried didn't work as expected, it could possibly signal to others that you're not skilled or smart enough to reliably perform your job.

- **Being seen as negative:** To learn and improve, it's essential to critically evaluate current and past activities and performance. The risk of being seen as negative, however, often stops people from providing critical assessments. People often believe that critiquing others' performance will make them appear overly critical or hard to work with. In addition, it is well known that bad news rarely travels well up the hierarchy.

- **Being seen as disruptive:** Fearful of disrupting or imposing on others' time, people avoid seeking feedback, information, or help. In particular, individuals are often reluctant to seek feedback about their performance, despite the personal gains that can be obtained from feedback. Although this reluctance can be attributed to the possibility of hearing something negative, it also stems from a wish not to be seen as intrusive or lacking in self-sufficiency.

The Benefits of Psychological Safety

The benefits of psychological safety include the following:

- **Encourages speaking up:** Psychological safety alleviates concern about others' reaction to behaviors or actions that have the potential for embarrassment.

- **Enables clarity of thought:** When the brain is activated by fear, it has less neural processing power for exploration, design, or analysis.

- **Supports productive conflict:** Psychological safety enables self-expression, productive discussion, and the thoughtful handling of conflict.

- **Mitigates failure:** A climate of psychological safety makes it easier, and therefore more common, to report and discuss errors.

- **Promotes innovation:** Removing the fear of speaking up enables people to suggest the novel ideas and possibilities that are integral to developing innovative products and services.

- **Removes obstacles to pursuing goals for achieving performance:** With psychological safety, individuals can focus on achieving motivating goals rather than on self-protection.

- **Increases accountability:** Rather than supporting a permissive atmosphere, psychological safety creates a climate that supports people in taking the interpersonal risks necessary to pursue high standards and achieve challenging goals.

Those are clearly some powerful benefits. But how do you establish an environment of psychological safety?

Cultivating Psychological Safety

How do leaders raise the level of psychological safety in an organization? This is the question that Arthur Ryan, CEO of Prudential, asked himself after taking the 100-year-old insurance and investment company public. Ryan looked around at the increasingly complex

and competitive financial services industry and concluded that the Prudential culture—dubbed *Pru-polite* by employees for its cautious feel—would have to change to succeed. In particular, Ryan believed that operating successfully as a public company would require direct, honest communication among employees. This meant creating a psychologically safe environment that enabled them to openly debate issues and analyze customer needs.

In an effort to increase levels of psychological safety, Ryan asked a team from the human resources department to create a program focused on encouraging employees to speak up and share their thoughts. Calling the program the *Safe-to-Say* initiative, the team worked energetically to design and implement a series of integrated training programs and recurring staff meetings that would make the work climate more psychologically safe. Many at Prudential, including senior managers and frontline representatives, spoke positively of the efforts, but substantial change in the culture was slow. An internal survey revealed remarkably stable scores on items relevant to the ability to speak up. The primary lesson here: you cannot metaphorically snap your fingers with short-term initiatives, no matter how well intentioned, and expect psychologically safety to suddenly exist.

Leadership Cultivating Psychological Safety

Leaders—at all levels, but particularly those in the middle of an organization—play crucial roles in creating a psychologically safe organization. The impact of leaders on organizational culture is well established by research. Studies have shown that leaders' responses to events influence other members' perceptions of appropriate and safe behavior. It's clear that signals sent by people in power are critical to shaping others' ability and willingness to offer their ideas

and observations. When a leader of a team is supportive, coaching oriented, and nondefensive in response to questions and challenges, team members are likely to feel that the team constitutes a safe environment. By contrast, team leaders who act authoritarian or punitive reduce others' psychological safety and, as a consequence, hinder their ability to contribute everything they can to the collective effort.

The most important influence on psychological safety is the nearest manager, supervisor, or boss. These authority figures, in subtle and not so subtle ways, shape the tone of interactions in a team or group. Therefore, they also must be engaged as the primary drivers in establishing a more open work environment. They must take practical steps to make the workplace psychologically safe. That is the key phrase: take practical steps.

Be Accessible and Approachable

Leaders encourage team members to learn together by being accessible and personally involved. In one of the cardiac surgery teams I studied, an operating room nurse made this association by describing the surgeon leading her team as "very accessible. He's in his office, always just two seconds away. He can always take five minutes to explain something, and he never makes you feel stupid." In striking contrast, the surgeon in one of the less successful teams requested that nonphysician team members go through his residents (junior physicians who are still in training) if they had something to say, rather than speak to him directly. Through their behaviors, these two surgeons conveyed very different messages to their teams: the first surgeon increased the likelihood that people would speak up openly both in and outside of the operating room when they had concerns and questions, whereas the second surgeon obviously made the process of communication more difficult.

Acknowledge the Limits of Current Knowledge

Explicitly acknowledge the lack of answers to the tough problems your group or team faces. Strange as it may seem, many leaders are unwilling to publicly express the fact that they don't have the answers to every issue or challenge. It's not that they don't recognize the imperfect state of knowledge; they just fail to mention it. Acknowledging uncertainty may seem like a weakness, but in fact it's usually an intelligent and accurate diagnosis of a murky situation. Moreover, it creates an implied invitation to offer information or expertise.

Display Fallibility

To create psychological safety, team leaders must demonstrate a tolerance of failure by acknowledging their own fallibility. Self-disclosure by team leaders is an effective way to reveal one's limitations. For instance, one cardiac surgeon team leader in the previously mentioned study repeatedly told his team, "I need to hear from you because I'm likely to miss things." The repetition of the phrase was as important as its meaning. People tend not to hear or believe a message that contradicts old norms or stances when they hear it only once. Acknowledging one's fallibility and the need for feedback suggests to others that their opinion is respected and contributes to establishing a norm of active participation. Moreover, when managers and supervisors admit that they don't know something or made a mistake, their genuine display of humility encourages others to do the same.

Invite Participation

A logical extension of acknowledging limits and modeling fallibility is inviting others to offer observations and ideas. This means explicitly requesting input from other people on a team or in the organization

more broadly. Team and organizational-level learning both depend on gaining access to a valuable, untapped body of individually held knowledge. Leaders must seek out this individual, internal knowledge, especially from lower-status team members who might otherwise be reluctant to speak. Team leaders can play a role in drawing out members' thoughts by setting up reflective sessions where job and time pressures are temporarily removed. In these types of sessions, ask questions. But be sure to ask real questions, not leading or rhetorical ones. When people believe leaders and managers want to hear from them and value their input, they're more responsive.

Highlight Failures as Learning Opportunities

By avoiding punishing others for having taken well-intentioned risks that backfired, leaders inspire people to embrace error and failure and deal with them in a productive manner. Vivid examples of purposefully refraining from penalizing failure exist throughout management literature. Apocryphal stories prevalent in many organizations capture the ways in which senior management can powerfully influence views of psychological safety in the organization as a whole. One such story involves Tom Watson Jr. at IBM and a field executive responsible for a $10 million mistake. Called into the chairman's office, the executive was understandably anxious. As retold by Paul Carroll, "Watson asked, 'Do you know why I've asked you here?' The man replied, 'I assume I'm here so you can fire me.' Watson looked surprised. 'Fire you?' he asked. 'Of course not. I just spent $10 million educating you.' He then reassured the executive and suggested he keep taking chances."

Truth or myth, such stories have lasting effects in an organization. The sent message is that failure is inevitable and the point is to learn, to share the learning, and to try again. As espoused by Watson, "You really aren't committed to innovation unless you're willing to

fail. . . . The fastest way to succeed is to double your failure rate." One of the best-known examples is the story of 3M's wildly successful Post-it product. As nearly everyone has heard by now, the adhesive used in Post-it notes came from a botched attempt to create a super-strong adhesive. Similarly, a well-known public relations firm has a ritual of opening monthly meetings by recognizing the "Mistake of the Month." This is a lighthearted way to both build a sense of community and acknowledge the value of learning from mistakes.

Use Direct Language

In knowledge work, people can't afford to avoid critiques due to a fear of sounding negative, criticizing the boss, or making the company appear fallible. Strategy teams, new product development, and other project teams often face crucial decisions that require evaluating the current situation and suggesting difficult changes. A major challenge in these discussions is to be objective and blunt. Often, however, the language is anything but direct. For example, the top management team of a manufacturing company that I studied engaged in a series of meetings to develop a new strategy. In these conversations, I observed a persistent pattern of using metaphors, rather than direct language, to describe the company's strategic options. As one executive commented during one meeting:

> Listening to Bob talk about the ship, I'd like to explore the difference between the metaphor of the ship and how the rudder gets turned and when, in contrast to a flotilla, where there's lots of little rudders and we're trying to orchestrate the flotilla. I think this contrast is important. At one level, we talk about this ship and all the complexities of trying to determine not only its direction but also how

to operationalize the ship in total to get to a certain place, versus allowing a certain degree of freedom that the flotilla analogy evokes.

Although metaphors can provoke new ideas and elicit creativity, they can sometimes obscure the real issues and preclude direct or contentious discussion. In this team, members rarely asked for clarification of each other's words or tried to identify areas of disagreement. Instead, the team continued to discuss the company and its situation abstractly, avoiding disagreement and postponing resolution. By the end of six months of regular meetings, little progress had been made; the team's abstract ruminations had failed to translate into any sort of action.

Set Boundaries

Paradoxically, when leaders are as clear as possible about what constitutes blameworthy acts, people feel more psychologically safe than when boundaries of acceptable action are subject to guesswork. This means leaders must establish and clarify boundaries at the outset of a teaming or learning effort. In a financial institution, this may mean never exceeding a particular investment limit without approval. In a hospital setting, it may mean never failing to ask for help when there is any doubt about a patient's condition or medication. For the team at Motorola, it meant never violating the code of secrecy about the project, until the product was publicly unveiled. Establishing this clear restriction helped promote a sense of freedom and expression within the delineated boundaries, including the willingness to ignore the recommendations of human factors experts about the phone's width. Regardless of the situation, by setting clear boundaries for action and behavior within the team, leaders contribute to building an environment of psychological safety.

Hold People Accountable

It's the job of leaders to help people understand that unacceptable behaviors do occur and must be equitably addressed. When leaders take the difficult step of punishing or even firing someone, they must clearly explain what happened and why, while observing rules for confidentiality as appropriate. Providing the justification behind such difficult actions helps protect other people against fear that the actions were arbitrary and could happen to them, without warning. In most cases, people understand both the rationale and the need for sanctions to preserve the team or organization's integrity so that it can effectively fulfill its purpose. Although it is more about avoiding the destruction of psychological safety than about creating it in the first place, holding people accountable builds fairness and responsibility, which removes the fear of leader arbitrariness. This is why psychological safety and accountability are both essential to a "just culture," an increasingly central concept in health care and other high-risk operations. The idea of a just culture was developed to acknowledge that "competent professionals make mistakes and . . . even develop unhealthy norms (shortcuts, 'routine rule violations')" while maintaining "zero tolerance for reckless behavior." In short, psychological safety is not created through lax standards or permissiveness, but rather through sober recognition that any workplace presents both challenges and constraints that must be discussed openly if progress is to be made.

Setting boundaries and holding people accountable are critical for a leader hoping to cultivate an environment of psychological safety. It may seem counterintuitive, but think of these two actions as being like guardrails on a bridge. If the guardrails are missing, you're likely to drive as close to the center line as possible. It's obviously frightening to drive near the bridge's edge without rails in place. When teaming and learning, the equivalent is sticking to safe, tractable behaviors that

shield you from possible punishment, while avoiding behaviors with interpersonal risk, like admitting mistakes, that may be interpreted as "outside the lines." But when the guardrails are in place, there's less risk in venturing to the outside lanes and gaining a broader, more informed perspective. With clear boundaries and the structures that enforce them, you're more likely to test the limits of current processes and knowledge. In doing so, team members and teams greatly increase their ability to collaborate, learn, and innovate.

Setting the Stage for Psychological Safety

Psychological safety means no one will be punished or humiliated for errors or questions in the service of reaching ambitious performance goals. The following activity helps you probe your experiences and thoughts of psychological safety.

Activity

Reflect on the following questions:

Of the seven benefits of psychological safety, which do you think is most valuable in your current work?

_____

_____

_____

Has your organization or a past organization you worked for promoted psychological safety? Did the effort succeed or fail? Why?

_____

_____

_____

(continued)

Creating Psychological Safety

(continued)

If you are not in a leadership position, what can you do to promote psychological safety on your team? How might these actions matter? Why?

_____

_____

_____

Framing for Learning

Benchmark goal: Frame your team for success.

Teaming behavior is often at odds with the demands of formal organizational structures, which divide people by specialty and focus more of their attention on bosses than on peers. Natural cognitive biases can get in the way, too; for many kinds of knowledge work, effective teaming requires suspension of the spontaneous assumption that one's own perspective is more accurate than those of others. In many workplaces, therefore, engaging in teaming may feel like an unnatural act; thus, leadership is needed to create an environment conducive to teaming.

Framing is a crucial leadership action for enrolling people in any substantial behavior change. It is especially important for promoting teaming and learning. Framing helps people interpret the ambiguous signals that accompany change in a positive and productive light, and facilitates understanding of new performance expectations. This week, I explore what leaders can do to frame a new initiative or project in a way that supports successful teaming and engages people in the learning and problem-solving challenges that lie ahead.

Cognitive Frames

A *frame* is a set of assumptions or beliefs about a situation. Most of the time, framing occurs automatically. We rarely recognize the power of the automatic frames we've superimposed on situations, because we take them for granted. Frames nearly always exist, shaped by past experiences. Without our realizing it, these prior experiences affect how we think and feel about the current situation. Framing is neither bad nor good; it is simply inevitable. We interpret what is going on around us through an invisible lens shaped by our personal history and social context. The problem is that we tend to assume that our framing represents the truth, rather than merely presenting a subjective map. In truth, however, each frame offers its own image of reality.

Tacit Interpretations

In complex situations, such as a busy hospital ward, an improvement project, or a strategy session, people interpret ambiguous cues and draw conclusions about what is happening. Cognitive research shows that many of these effortlessly drawn interpretations are tacit (taken for granted, not explicitly recognized), yet extremely powerful. Once we interpret a situation, we think we know its true meaning. In addition, when we work closely with others, we develop shared interpretations, and these are also taken for granted. As a result, people in a particular workplace often look at what's going on through tacit, shared frames. In studies of workplace conversation, in particular, researchers have identified frames that shape how we talk to each other. These frames feel natural, but make it difficult for people to learn much from each other, especially when they have conflicting points of view. In a conflict, most people have a tacit goal of winning (few of us enter a

conflict with a goal of learning as much as we can about the merits of the other person's point of view). Within this frame, conflict is viewed as a competition to be won rather than a problem to be understood and solved.

Others have used the term *mental model* or *taken-for-granted assumption* to convey a similar idea, but the terminology of framing applies particularly well to understanding teaming behavior. The terms *frame* and *framing* suggest the idea of looking through something at something else. A frame directs attention to features of the object of interest in a subtle way. Although our focus is on the painting, its frame can enhance or diminish our appreciation of the painting's colors and shapes without our conscious attention. Similarly, leaders and managers can use cognitive frames to highlight or encourage specific traits that help promote behaviors necessary for teaming and learning.

In a well-known example of the power of framing, Viktor Frankl, a Nazi concentration camp survivor, endured Auschwitz by imagining himself sharing the stories of courage he saw around him to friends and family on the outside. Frankl, a psychiatrist, later described the moment of transformation that enabled him to persevere in these worst of conditions: it was when he recognized the opportunity to reframe his experience from one of minute-to-minute suffering and fear to one of future-oriented visioning and hope. It's an extreme example, but Frankl's remarkable story of courage and resilience illustrates the potential consequences of reframing—seeing the same situation one way rather than another, very different way.

Reframing for Learning

Psychologists and behavioral scientists have established the power of a variety of alternative cognitive frames. For instance, when people frame a task as a "performance situation" they are more risk averse

and less willing to persist through obstacles than when the same task is framed as a "learning situation." Not only do people adopting a learning frame persist longer in unfamiliar, challenging tasks but also they ultimately learn more as a result. In addition, people with a performance frame engage in less experimentation and innovation and are less likely to formulate new strategies in difficult situations. Instead, they're more likely to fall back on ineffective strategies they have used previously. Similarly, other research distinguishes between a "promotion" and a "prevention" orientation in approaching a task or challenge. A promotion orientation is characterized by ideals, goals, and eagerness to attain them. It reflects a tendency to frame new situations in terms of what can be gained. Conversely, a prevention orientation is characterized by a sense of obligation and by vigilance against loss. It indicates an inclination for framing new situations as opportunities to lose ground.

Fortunately, frames can be changed. Behavioral scientists and therapists have studied the process of reframing to help people change their tacit frames and obtain better results in their lives. One approach—rational behavioral therapy—teaches people to try out more productive, learning-oriented ways of framing themselves. Managerial research has also explored the process of framing, how it works, and how powerful it can be for improving results. Notably, Chris Argyris, one of the seminal scholars of organizational learning, conducted research over many years with managers to identify and challenge the tacit frames that shaped how they interacted with each other in difficult, confrontational conversations. Similarly, Donald Schön, another pioneering researcher and a longtime colleague of Argyris, showed that how people framed their roles shaped their behavior and, correspondingly, helped determine the results they achieved.

Team Members' Roles

When temporary teams form, it's natural for people to assume roles according to position, expertise, or personality. Due to this inevitability, thoughtfully framing the roles that different people should play in a joint effort is important to building a cohesive team and an effective process. In particular, in a setting where jobs have traditionally been highly segmented—such that task interdependence is managed in advance by clear role boundaries—making a shift to a way of working characterized by back-and-forth communication can be extremely challenging. Getting people to start teaming requires a new frame.

Intellectual and Emotional Commitment

A critical part of framing people's roles in a temporary team project is to communicate that they are being selected for the project for a reason. This builds intellectual and emotional commitment to the implementation process and acts as an invitation to others to participate in shaping the specifics of the effort, in addition to helping execute it. It also represents an implicit awareness that new technology imposes a need for change, that change is hard, and that everyone affects whether or not the change succeeds. When leaders emphasize that they have handpicked great people for a project, it builds intellectual and emotional commitment.

By contrast, when leaders fail to convey that others play vital roles in the project, team members may not believe they can or will make genuine contributions to its success. This compromises their ability to envision and help shape how a new technology or process can transform the work to help the organization or its customers. Framing powerfully influences commitment and motivates people to exert the effort and take the risks that change requires. These observations

point to a simple but incontrovertible fact: teaming works when everyone makes it work. Learning happens when individuals commit to cooperating in a unified effort to overcome the inevitable setbacks that accompany innovation and implementation. Deliberate, positive reframing motivates team members to communicate more intensively, thus lessening the confines of hierarchy. Individual motives become more closely aligned with the purpose of the project.

The Project Purpose

Even when individual employees are aware of problems, a collective effort focused on solving them is unlikely to occur when people do not understand and care about a common purpose. Therefore, effectively framing a task involves providing a compelling answer to the question of why a particular project exists. What purpose does it serve? What value does the project offer to employees, customers, or society? The leader's job is to articulate and help people cohere around this shared purpose. Whether or not the effort to create a sense of purpose is effective hinges on the leader's ability to connect the teaming effort to goals and objectives that motivate people to persist during a novel, uncertain endeavor. Just as individuals have a promotion or prevention orientation, projects are often framed in either an aspirational or a defensive way.

Aspirational or Defensive Purpose

Many teams I've studied fell into one of two groups in terms of team beliefs—explicit or inferred—about the reason for implementing the new technology. Members of successful teams shared a sense of purpose that can be described as aspirational—driven by a desire to accomplish compelling goals. By contrast, unsuccessful teams' goals

were fundamentally preventative and reactive. These teams were driven by concerns about competition and encumbered by the anxiety of coping with technological change. This latter belief seemed to be the default state in the absence of leadership effort to impose a new, inspiring belief.

Communicating a Clear and Compelling Purpose

Engaging others' willing contribution is a core leadership task. This means that leaders in uncertain, dynamic contexts have to stimulate and guide a collective learning process. To do so, leaders must communicate a clear and compelling purpose that resonates with all members of the team. The type of purpose that motivates teaming generally has meaning beyond making money or self-preservation, providing a clear, aspirational goal that energizes others and encourages a focus on collective responsibility for teaming and learning. An aspirational purpose encapsulates the excitement of doing something that aids others and helps team members endure the hardships of learning. By explicitly communicating growing confidence in a new process or technology, leaders ensure that team members recognize that they are making progress toward achieving the purpose.

Together, these three dimensions of framing—establishing the leader's role, others' roles, and a shared purpose—play a crucial part in determining success or failure in a substantial change effort. By helping shape others' perceptions of roles and objectives, deliberate framing can make the difference between the creation of an environment that supports collaboration and encourages persistence or a defensive environment that implicitly presents change as a burden to be endured. The framing makes all the difference between individuals who see themselves as embarking on a valued learning journey and those who are merely trying to get the work done.

A Learning Frame Versus an Execution Frame

Leaders who frame themselves as interdependent with others in accomplishing important changes, view others as crucial partners, and put forward an aspirational purpose are employing a learning frame. By contrast, leaders who present themselves as experts who are more important than others in completing the journey ahead, and see others as supporting actors, can be characterized as having an execution frame. Table 7.1 directly contrasts the three dimensions of a learning frame with those of an execution frame.

Table 7.1 Learning Frame Versus Execution Frame

Project Dimension	Learning Frame	Execution Frame
Leader's view of self in carrying out the project	Important and interdependent in overcoming the challenges ahead	Knows what to do and in a position to tell others what to do
Leader's view of others in carrying out the project	Valued partners with essential input for overcoming the challenges ahead	Coactors or subordinates
Overall view of the situation created by the project and corresponding tacit goal for the project	Challenging, full of unknowns, and an opportunity to try out new concepts and techniques; the tacit goal is to learn as much as possible so as to figure out what to do next	Same as, or "not that different from," normal situation; the tacit goal is to get the job done

90 Days to Level Up Your Teamwork

When managing a project in which risk and uncertainty are high, leaders who employ and communicate a learning frame help launch a rewarding collaborative effort that promotes learning and innovation. By contrast, when, by design or by default, work is framed as an opportunity to "get it right" on the first try, people are less able to learn during the process and ultimately get it right. Any implementation process that involves uncertainty is most successful when participants are open to change, eager to find the best fit, and recognize that other people may have different perspectives. When people are very aware that others may have observed or interpreted something in a different way, they are more likely to be curious and to engage each other in relevant discussions about what to try. This is the very essence of a learning frame. To even consider this possibility, however, requires either an innate or trained habit of being self-aware, collaborative, and curious. Unfortunately, these traits and their corresponding cognitive frame rarely appear spontaneously in corporate and other organizational settings.

Changing Frames

In general, researchers agree that many of the spontaneous frames we bring to work are inherently about self-protection. Unfortunately, protection comes at a cost. Self-protective frames dramatically inhibit the opportunity to learn and improve. Research shows that people can learn to reframe and shift from spontaneous self-protective frames to reflective or learning-oriented frames. When this happens, the new frames are no longer tacit—at least not at first—but rather explicitly imposed on a situation or project in an effort to be effective. Following are steps for developing and reinforcing a learning frame,

along with specific tactics to help individuals embrace a new way of interpreting their roles.

Establishing a Learning Frame

In successful organizations that adopted learning frames, the collective learning process consisted of four tightly coupled, recurring steps. The first step was enrollment of carefully selected team members by the leader, followed by team preparation, and then by multiple cycles of trial and reflection. Table 7.2 summarizes these steps and shows specific activities that successful implementers of the new technology had in common. It also suggests underlying cognitions supportive of these activities.

Table 7.2   Activities and Cognitive Frames for Successful Implementation

Step	Activities	Frames (Implicit Cognitions)	Effects
Enrollment	Communicate deliberateness in project team selection. Communicate purpose of project.	The project will create significant change in this organization or in people's jobs. Others play an important role in whether or not it succeeds.	Participants feel part of a team, have a shared sense of purpose, and feel committed to the project.

Table 7.2 *(continued)*

Step	Activities	Frames (Implicit Cognitions)	Effects
Preparation	Offline sessions to safely explore implications of the new technology or other change. Practice with new behaviors.	We need to learn how to work together and to anticipate problems if the project is going to succeed.	Participants develop an increasing willingness to take interpersonal risks in the project team and are motivated to expend effort on novel and uncertain actions.
Trial	Try out new concepts, processes, and tools. Pay close attention to what happens.	Actions at this stage of implementation are experiments. It's not about getting it right the first time. I feel a sense of curiosity about what will happen.	Every event, every action is seen as an opportunity to learn; people pay attention and are alert for possible changes that could be made.

(continued)

Table 7.2 (*continued*)

Step	Activities	Frames (Implicit Cognitions)	Effects
Reflection	Discuss trial results.	It will help me/us to learn from the past trials. I wonder what others may have seen that I missed.	Participants discuss what they did and what happened. Then they analyze what it means and brainstorm alternatives if needed.

Enrollment

A critical feature of enrollment is communicating to others that they are being specifically selected for a project or role. This builds intellectual and emotional commitment to the work. Enrollment is also about building awareness that a new technology imposes change, that change is challenging, and that everyone involved will affect whether or not the change succeeds. Enrollment, which is a fundamental leadership action, sets the tone of the journey that follows. It may be the first communication about a proposed change, enabling team members to form first impressions about what lies ahead for them and for the organization. When first impressions contain excitement or confidence that one's participation matters to outcomes, it can have a lasting effect.

Preparation

Preparation may involve attendance at an off-site training, or in-house team practice sessions, or it may be a quick team-building meeting to get to know others' strengths, weaknesses, hopes, and fears. Depending on the nature of the project, preparation sessions should include discussion of how existing routines may need to be altered in order to collect ideas for getting this to happen. More important, having an explicit practice session reduces the real and perceived risks of trying new things in "real" situations where customers or other outsiders could be harmed or receive a negative impression. Practice also enables team members to refine their own skills and integrate their actions with those of other participants. Other activities that should take place during the preparation phase include the establishment of team norms, a thorough discussion of how the team should work together, how to encourage speaking up with concerns and observations, and how power relations might affect the group.

Trial

The next step in the team learning process is a first, real trial of the new technology or other change. This means doing actual work while actively framing that work as an experiment from which much may be learned. In the trial step, people will begin to envision and enact how the new process or technology transforms the way work is done in the organization. The goal here is not to execute perfectly on the first try, but rather to quickly identify what adjustments or changes may be necessary for future success. Trials work well when those involved are curious and inquisitive.

Reflection

Paired with the previous step, reflection constitutes an opportunity to learn from what worked and what failed. Salient observations should then be used to make potential improvements after each round of trials. Together, these last two steps, trial and reflection, are the basis of a learning cycle that fuels successful implementation or innovation. Until such time as a new process or technology is completely routine, each use of it is an experiment, and each may be subtly different from prior use. Such differences are only useful if they are noticed, analyzed for their impact, and considered in the design of the next trial. In this way, the design of subsequent action continuously benefits from the knowledge gained in the prior cycle. Change happens through iteration.

Reinforcing a Learning Frame

One factor that facilitates deeper acceptance of a learning frame is making its use public rather than practicing it privately. Whether leading or participating in implementation projects, individuals seeking to follow the tactics for reframing can be open with others about what they are trying to do—enabling others to understand, provide feedback about, and even experiment with the learning frame themselves. Note that this is not the typical way leaders act; more often, they keep their strategy for engaging others (even when noble) to themselves. Here are five leadership tactics for reinforcing a learning frame:

- Use verbal and visual discourse to promote the learning frame.
- Reinforce this framing by explaining and modeling the desired interpersonal and collaborative behaviors.
- Explain these desired behaviors in practical terms, such as "Speak up if you see something wrong" or "Just pick up the phone and ask if you have a question."

- Initiate activities, for example, a kick-off meeting, a meeting to identify personal goals within the teaming or learning effort, and training on how to efficiently deal with interpersonal conflict. These can facilitate new processes or routines and help team members build confidence.

- Use artifacts such as a prominent sign in the project work area to visually reinforce the learning frame.

The Ideal Employee?

This week has emphasized the use of deliberate framing. But it's the unconscious frames that may exert the strongest influence on learning in an organization. Many managers have a taken-for-granted concept of an ideal employee. Consider the following: an ideal employee can handle with ease any problem that comes along (without bothering managers, of course), quietly corrects errors (their own and others') without making a fuss, performs flawlessly, and is deeply committed to the organization and its processes. I often pose this hypothetical person to managers, and I ask, "What's wrong with this employee?" They nearly always respond, "They don't exist!" My response is, no, that's not the problem. They exist. Every large organization has a few of these tireless and unassuming souls. But that's not the real problem. What's wrong with this so-called ideal employee is that they are making it more difficult for the organization to learn.

In the learning organization, problems and errors must be reported so everyone can learn. Flawless performance means not stretching enough. And the organization's processes need to be challenged, not blindly followed and enforced. In reflecting on our study explaining why hospitals don't learn from failures, Anita Tucker and I suggested, provocatively, that managers who want to build a learning organization must reframe the ideal employee in their own minds—and get ready to celebrate the disruptive questioner who simply won't leave

well enough alone. This organizational-learning enabler is constantly questioning and improving, not accepting and using, current practices.

Tactics for Individual Reframing

Until this point, framing has been discussed as a leaders' job. Indeed, framing is one of the most important ways leaders can positively influence others and shape outcomes. However, anyone involved in a change initiative, in any role, can exert leadership in the form of helping to establish or reinforce a learning frame. Facing significant change, formal leaders should not be the only ones to actively frame the work ahead as a collaborative learning journey. General participation in cocreating a learning mindset not only ensures that it is widely shared but also helps others build their own leadership skills.

Here are four tactics that anyone confronted with the challenge of teaming, learning, implementing new technology, or driving organizational change can use to help adjust an existing cognitive frame:

- Tell yourself that the project is different from anything you've done before and presents an exciting opportunity to try out new approaches and learn from them.

- See yourself as critical to a successful outcome and yet as unable to achieve success without the willing participation of others.

- Tell yourself that others are vitally important to a successful outcome and may provide key knowledge or suggestions that you can't anticipate in advance.

- Communicate with others exactly as you would if the preceding three statements were true.

Framing the Picture of Success

Framing helps people interpret change in a positive and productive light and facilitates understanding of new performance expectations. In this activity, we examine the power of framing to improve results.

Activity

Reflect on the following questions:

Can you think of a time that you've worked on a task with as aspirational purpose? How about one with a defensive purpose? Which one felt better and why?

_____

_____

_____

What does a leader see as their role in a learning frame? How does this differ from the leader's role in an execution frame?

_____

_____

_____

What makes for the "ideal employee" in most managers' minds? What explains this tacit belief? Do you agree that this type of employee is truly ideal? Why or why not?

_____

_____

_____

Working Without Fear

Benchmark goal: Create a fearless organization.

Whenever you are trying to get people on the same page, with common goals and a shared appreciation for what they're up against, you're setting the stage for psychological safety. The most important skill to master is that of framing the work. If near perfection is what is needed to satisfy demanding car customers, leaders must know to frame the work by alerting workers to catch and correct tiny deviations before the car proceeds down the assembly line. If zero worker fatalities in a dangerous platinum mine is the goal, leaders must frame physical safety as a worthy and challenging but attainable goal. If discovering new cures is the goal, leaders know to motivate researchers to generate smart hypotheses for experiments and to feel okay about being wrong far more often than right.

Setting the Stage for Psychological Safety

Leaders have a special responsibility for creating psychological safety for their teams, but they also have special tools for doing so. In this week, we look at the tools leaders have for creating an environment where team members feel psychologically safe, productive mistakes

are allowed, people can speak their minds, and every employee understands they make a contribution. Table 8.1 is a summary of the leader's tool kit.

Table 8.1 The Leader's Tool Kit for Building Psychological Safety

Category	Setting the Stage	Inviting Participation	Responding Productively
Leadership tasks	**Frame the Work** • Set expectations about failure, uncertainty, and interdependence to clarify the need for voice. **Emphasize Purpose** • Identify what's at stake, why it matters, and for whom.	**Demonstrate Situational Humility** • Acknowledge gaps. **Practice Inquiry** • Ask good questions. • Model intense listening. **Set Up Structures and Processes** • Create forums for input. • Provide guidelines for discussion	**Express Appreciation** • Listen. • Acknowledge and thank. **Destigmatize Failure** • Look forward. • Offer help. • Discuss, consider, and brainstorm next steps. **Sanction Clear Violations**
Accomplishes	Shared expectations and meaning	Confidence that voice is welcome	Orientation toward continuous learning

Framing the Work

Because fear of (reporting) failure is such a key indicator of an environment with low levels of psychological safety, how leaders present the role of failure is essential. Astro Teller at Google X observed that "the only way to get people to work on big, risky things . . . is if you make that the path of least resistance for them [and] make it safe to fail." In other words, unless a leader expressly and actively makes it psychologically safe to do so, people will automatically seek to avoid failure. So how did Teller reframe failure to make it okay? By saying, believing, and convincing others that "I'm not pro failure, I'm pro learning."

Note that failure plays a different role in different kinds of work. In high-volume repetitive work, such as in an assembly plant, a fastfood restaurant, or even a kidney dialysis center, many failures are avoidable. Failing to correctly plug a patient into a dialysis machine or install an automobile airbag in precisely the right manner can have disastrous consequences. So in this kind of work it's vital that people eagerly catch and correct deviations from best practice. Here, celebrating failure is a matter of viewing such deviations as "good-catch" events and appreciating those who noticed tiny mistakes as observant contributors to the mission.

In innovation and research, however, little is known about how to obtain a desired result. Creating a movie, a line of original clothing, or a technology that can convert seawater to fuel are all examples. In this context, dramatic failures must be courted and celebrated because they are an integral part of the journey to success. Between these two extremes, where much of the work done today falls, are complex operations, such as hospitals or financial institutions. Here, vigilance and teamwork are both vital to preventing avoidable failures and celebrating intelligent ones.

Reframing failure starts with understanding types of failures:

- Basic failures (never good news)
- Complex failures (still not good news)
- Intelligent failures (not fun, but must be considered good news because of the value they bring)

Basic failures are deviations from recommended procedures that produce bad outcomes. If someone fails to don safety glasses in a factory and suffers an eye injury, this is a basic failure. Complex failures occur in familiar contexts when a confluence of factors come together in a way that may never have occurred before; consider the severe flooding of the Wall Street subway station in New York City during Superstorm Sandy in 2012. With vigilance, complex failures can sometimes, but not always, be avoided. Neither basic nor complex failures are worthy of celebration.

By contrast, intelligent failures, as the term implies, must be celebrated so as to encourage more of them. Intelligent failures, like the basic and complex, are still results no one wanted. But, unlike the other two categories, they are the result of a thoughtful foray into new territory. An important part of framing is making sure people understand that failures will happen. Some failures are genuinely good news; some are not, but no matter what type they are, our primary goal is to learn from them.

Clarifying the Need for Voice

Framing the work also involves calling attention to other ways, beyond failure's prevalence, in which tasks and environments differ. Three especially important dimensions are uncertainty, interdependence, and what's at stake—all of which also have implications for

failure (e.g. expectations about its frequency, its value, and its consequences). Emphasizing uncertainty reminds people that they need to be curious and alert to pick up early indicators of change in, say, customer preferences in a new market, a patient's reaction to a drug, or new technologies on the horizon.

Emphasizing interdependence lets people know that they're responsible for understanding how their tasks interact with other people's tasks. Interdependence encourages frequent conversations to figure out the impact their work is having on others and to convey in turn the impact others' work has on them. Interdependent work requires communication. In other words, when leaders frame the work, they are emphasizing the need for taking interpersonal risks like sharing ideas and concerns.

Finally, clarifying the stakes is important whether the stakes are high or low. Reminding people that human life is on the line—say, in a hospital, a mine, or at NASA—helps put interpersonal risk in perspective. People are more likely to speak up—thereby overcoming the inherent asymmetry of voice and silence—if leaders frame its importance. Similarly, reminding people that the only thing that is at stake is a bruised ego when a lab experiment doesn't go as hoped is a good way to get them to be willing to go for it—offer possibly crazy ideas and figure out which ones to test first!

Finally, how most people see bosses presents a crucial area for reframing. As a default, bosses are viewed as having answers, being able to give orders, and being positioned to assess whether the orders are well executed. With this frame, others are merely subordinates expected to do as they are told. The default set of frames makes interpersonal fear sensible.

In a world in which bosses have the answers and absolute authority over how your work is judged, it makes sense to fear the boss and to think very carefully about what you reveal. The reframe, by

contrast, spells out logic that clarifies the necessity for a psychologically safe environment. This logic applies to the successful execution of work in most organizations today.

The reframe shows that leaders must establish and cultivate psychological safety to succeed in most work environments today. The leader is obliged to set direction for the work, to invite relevant input to clarify and improve on the general direction that has been set, and to create conditions for continued learning to achieve excellence.

In the reframe, those who are not the boss are seen as valued contributors—that is, as people with crucial knowledge and insight. When a leader asks people to speak up about patient error or orchestrates staff meetings to give everyone a chance to speak, they do so because it will improve decision-making and execution—not because they want to be nice. Leaders in a volatile, uncertain, complex, and ambiguous (VUCA) world, who understand that today's work requires continuous learning to figure out when and how to change course, must consciously reframe how they think, from the default frames that we all bring to work unconsciously to a more productive reframe.

Framing the work is not something that leaders do once, and then it's done. Framing is ongoing. Frequently calling attention to levels of uncertainty or interdependence helps people remember that they must be alert and candid to perform well.

Emphasizing Purpose

Emphasizing a sense of purpose is another key element of setting the stage for psychological safety. Motivating people by articulating a compelling purpose is a well-established leadership task. Leaders who remind people of why what they do matters—for customers, for the world—help create the energy that carries them through challenging moments. Note that even when it seems obvious (for instance, taking care of vulnerable patients) that the work is meaningful, leaders still

must take the time to emphasize the purpose the organization serves. This is because anyone can get tired, distracted, and frustrated and lose sight of the larger picture of what's at stake.

Meaning can be defined and framed in other ways, too. Most leaders would be well served by stopping to reflect on the purpose that motivates them and makes the organization's work meaningful to the broader community. Having done so, they should ask themselves how often and how vigorously they are conveying this compelling rationale for the work to others. Our primal need to feel purpose and meaning in our lives, including at work, has been demonstrated by numerous studies in psychology.

Inviting Participation So People Respond

The second essential activity in the leaders' tool kit is inviting participation in a way that people find compelling and genuine. The goal is to lower what is usually a too-high bar for what's considered appropriate participation. Realizing that self-protection is natural, the invitation to participate must be crystal clear if people are going to choose to engage rather than to play it safe. Two essential behaviors that signal an invitation is genuine are adopting a mindset of situational humility and engaging in proactive inquiry. Designing structures for input, another powerful tool I discuss in this section, also serves as an invitation for voice.

Situational Humility

The bottom line is that no one wants to take the interpersonal risk of imposing ideas when the boss appears to think they know everything. A learning mindset, which blends humility and curiosity, mitigates this risk. A learning mindset recognizes that there is always more to learn.

Frankly, adopting a humble mindset when faced with the complex, dynamic, uncertain world in which we all work today is simply realism. The term *situational humility* captures this concept well (the need for humility lies in the situation) and may make it easier for leaders, especially those with abundant self-confidence, to recognize the validity, and the power, of a humble mindset. MIT Professor Ed Schein calls this *here-and-now humility.* Keep in mind that confidence and humility are not opposites. Confidence in one's abilities and knowledge, when warranted, is far preferable to false modesty. But humility is not modesty, false or otherwise. Humility is the simple recognition that you don't have all the answers, and you certainly don't have a crystal ball. Research shows that when leaders express humility, teams engage in more learning behavior.

In our study of neonatal intensive care units, Ingrid Nembhard, Anita Tucker, and I found that neonatal intensive care units with high psychological safety had substantially better results from their quality improvement work than those with low psychological safety. A factor we called *leadership inclusiveness* made the difference.

Building on this work, Israeli researchers Reuven Hirak and Abraham Carmeli and two of their colleagues surveyed employees from clinical units in a large hospital in Israel on leader inclusiveness, psychological safety, units' ability to learn from failures, and unit performance. They found that units in which leaders were perceived as more inclusive had higher psychological safety, which led to increased learning from failure and better unit performance. In sum, leaders who are approachable and accessible, acknowledge their fallibility, and proactively invite input from others can do much to establish and enhance psychological safety in their organizations. Powerful tools, indeed.

Practice Proactive Inquiry

The second tool for inviting participation is inquiry. Inquiry is purposeful probing to learn more about an issue, situation, or person. The foundational skill lies in cultivating genuine interest in others' responses. Why is this hard? Because all adults, especially high-achieving ones, are subject to a cognitive bias called *naïve realism*, which gives us the experience of "knowing" what's going on. We believe we are seeing "reality," rather than a subjective view of reality. As a result, we often fail to wonder what others are seeing. We fail to be curious.

Worse, many leaders, even when they are motivated to ask a question, worry that it will make them look uninformed or weak. Further exacerbating the challenge, some companies sport "a culture of telling," as a senior executive in a global pharmaceutical company put it in a recent conversation we had about his company. In a culture of telling, asking gets short shrift. Yet when leaders overcome these biases to ask genuine questions, it fosters psychological safety. Contrary to what many may believe, asking questions tends to make the leader seem not weak but thoughtful and wise.

All of us can benefit from introducing more inquiry into our work. The essential skill of inquiry involves picking the right type of question for a situation. For instance, questions can go broad or deep. To broaden understanding of a situation or expand an option set, ask, "what might we be missing?", "what other ideas could we generate?", or "who has a different perspective?" Such questions ensure that more comprehensive information is considered and that a larger set of options is generated related to a problem or decision. Other questions are designed to deepen understanding. Ask, "what leads you to think so?" or "can you give me an example?" Such questions are crucial to

helping people learn about each other's expertise and goals. Moreover, when asked thoughtfully, a good question indicates to others that their voices are desired—instantly making that moment psychologically safe for offering a response.

Designing Structures for Input

A third way to invite participation and reinforce psychological safety is to implement structures designed to elicit employee input. One way to chip away at interpersonal fear is through employee-to-employee learning structures, as Google has done with its creation of the "g2g" (Googler-to-Googler) network, consisting of more than 6,000 Google employees who volunteer time to helping their peers learn. Participants in g2g do one-on-one mentoring, coach teams on psychological safety, and teach courses in professional skills ranging from leadership to Python coding. Google claims that g2g has helped develop the skills of countless employees. It is also helping to build a psychologically safe culture where everyone is both a learner and a teacher.

The global food company Groupe Danone created structured conference events called *knowledge marketplaces* to foster inquiry and knowledge sharing across country business units. Although many good ideas and practices that improved operational performance came out of these workshops, the executives who sponsored them saw the most important outcome as a shift in the organizational culture toward speaking up, asking for help, and sharing good ideas.

Responding Productively to Voice—No Matter Its Quality

To reinforce a climate of psychological safety, it's imperative that leaders—at all levels—respond productively to the risks people take.

Productive responses are characterized by three elements: expressions of appreciation, destigmatizing failure, and sanctioning clear violations.

Express Appreciation

Stanford Professor Carol Dweck, whose celebrated research on mindset shows the power of a learning orientation for individual achievement and resilience in the face of challenge, notes the importance of praising people for efforts, regardless of the outcome. When people believe their performance is an indication of their ability or intelligence, they are less likely to take risks for fear of a result that would disconfirm their ability. But when people believe that performance reflects effort and good strategy, they are eager to try new things and willing to persevere despite adversity and failure.

Praising effort is especially important in uncertain environments, where good outcomes are not always the result of good process, and vice versa. Although CEOs should take the lead in praising effort, an equally important leadership responsibility for C-suite-level executives is making sure that people throughout the organization respond productively to their colleagues. It helps if everyone understands the logic conveyed in Figure 8.1, which depicts the imperfect relationship between process and outcome.

Clearly, good process can lead to good outcomes, and bad process can lead to bad outcomes. But, good process also can produce bad outcomes (especially facing high uncertainty or complexity, as in VUCA conditions), and bad process can produce a good outcome (when you get lucky) or the illusion of a good outcome. The lack of simple cause-effect relationships in uncertain, ambiguous environments reinforces the importance of productive responses to outcomes of all kinds, but especially to bad news outcomes.

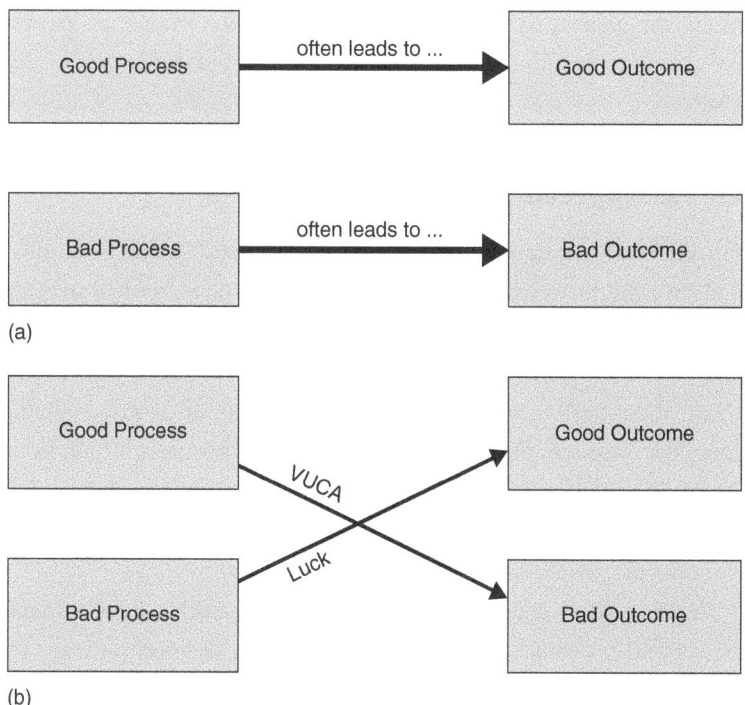

Figure 8.1 The imperfect relationship between process and outcome.

Productive responses often include expressions of appreciation, ranging from the small ("thank you so much for speaking up") to the elaborate—celebrations or bonuses in response to intelligent failure.

Destigmatize Failure

Failure is a necessary part of uncertainty and innovation, but this must be made clear to reinforce the invitation for voice. Leaders

who respond to all failures in the same way will not create a healthy environment for learning. When a failure occurs because someone violated a rule or value that matters in the organization, this is very different than when a thoughtful hypothesis in the lab turns out to be wrong. Although obvious in concept, in practice people routinely get this wrong.

A productive response to *intelligent* failure can mean actually celebrating the news. Some years ago, the chief scientific officer at Eli Lilly introduced "failure parties" to honor intelligent, high-quality scientific experiments that failed to achieve the desired results. Might this be a bridge too far? I don't think so. First, and most obvious, it helps build a psychologically safe climate for thoughtful risks, which is mission critical in science. Second, it helps people acknowledge failures in a timely way, which allows redeployment of valuable resources—scientists and materials—to new projects earlier rather than later, potentially saving thousands of dollars. Third, when you hold a party, people tend to show up—which means they learn about the failure. This in turn lowers the risk that the company will repeat the same failure. An intelligent failure the first time around no longer qualifies as intelligent the second time.

In brief, a productive response to basic failures is to double down on prevention, usually a combination of training and improved system design to make it easier for people to do the right thing. However, there are instances in which a basic failure is the result of a blameworthy action or a repeated instance of deviation from prescribed process, impervious to prior attempts at redirection. In such cases, usually rare, there is an obligation to act in ways that prevent future occurrence. This may mean fines or other sanctions, and in some cases even firing someone.

Sanction Clear Violations

Yes, firing can sometimes be an appropriate and productive response—to a blameworthy act. But won't this kill the psychological safety? No. Most people are thoughtful enough to recognize (and appreciate) that when people violate rules or repeatedly take risky shortcuts, they are putting themselves, their colleagues, and their organization at risk. In short, psychological safety is reinforced rather than harmed by fair, thoughtful responses to potentially dangerous, harmful, or sloppy behavior.

In July 2017, Google engineer James Damore wrote a 10-page memo railing against the company's diversity stance, arguing that biological differences explained why Google had fewer women engineers and paid them less well than men, and circulated it widely within the company. Someone then leaked the memo, creating a public firestorm.

How did Google respond? Damore was promptly and publicly fired a month later, earning the company both praise and criticism. Thoughtful arguments have been made on both sides of the firing debate. Rather than coming out on one side or the other, let's step back to consider when firing constitutes a "productive response," and when it doesn't.

Take this specific case. To begin, it is a shame that Damore chose to share his personal concerns electronically and widely within the company, all but ensuring that someone who disliked the memo would share it publicly. But once the inflammatory memo has been made public, how should a company respond? My intention is not to illuminate the specifics of Damore's memo at Google but rather to suggest a general strategy for productive responses to actions or events in your organization that you wish had not occurred.

If there are clear policies against the use of company email addresses or social media platforms for the expression of personal opinions, an employee who violates these policies commits what we can call a *blameworthy* act. In this case, a productive response indeed involves tough sanctions, which may include terminating the employee. A tough response is productive because it lets people know that the company is serious about its policies and values, which shapes future behavior, and because it constitutes a fair response to a stated violation.

If policies are unclear, however, a productive response is one that turns the unfortunate event into a different kind of learning opportunity—for the company and sometimes for the interested public. In the Damore case, executives might express dismay at the employee's opinion (and perhaps dismay at his ignorance of a larger set of societal forces that have systematically diminished advancement opportunities for certain demographic groups over decades). They might then go on to explain their plans for educating employees on what they believe to be the value of a diverse workforce.

In short, a productive response is concerned with future impact. Punishment sends a powerful message, and an appropriate one if boundaries were clear in advance. Indeed, it is vital to send messages that reinforce values the company holds dear. However, it is equally vital not to inadvertently send a message that says, "diverse opinions simply won't be tolerated here" or "one strike and you're out." Such messages reduce psychological safety and ultimately erode the quality of the work. By contrast, a message that reinforces the values and practices of a learning organization is, "it's okay to make a mistake, and it's okay to hold an opinion that others don't like, so long as

you are willing to learn from the consequences." The most important goal is figuring out a way to help the organization learn from what happened.

Using the Leadership Tool Kit

Leaders have special responsibilities to create psychological safety on their teams, but they also have special tools. In this activity, you will reflect on the leader's tool kit for creating a psychologically safe team.

Activity

Reflect on the following questions:

What are the three types of failure? Do you agree that some types of failure are more productive (and therefore permissible, and even necessary) than others?

_____

_____

_____

Have you ever worked for a manager who avoided the top-down approach? One who actively sought opinions of team members and saw them as valuable contributors? Did it increase your psychological safety? Did it make you more willing to express opinions and admit errors?

_____

_____

_____

Is a firing ever a correct response to an employee expressing an opinion, even one that violates the company's values? Why or why not?

_____

_____

_____

Wrap-Up

Performance goal: Team fearlessly with psychological safety.

Psychological safety is not immunity from consequences, nor is it a state of high self-regard. In psychologically safe workplaces, people know they might fail, they might receive performance feedback that says they're not meeting expectations, and they might lose their jobs due to changes in the industry environment or even to a lack of competence in their role.

But in a psychologically safe workplace, people are not hindered by interpersonal fear. They feel willing and able to take the inherent interpersonal risks of candor.

Questions

1. Twenty-five years of research on psychological safety finds positive benefits for learning, engagement, and performance in a wide range of organizations. Have you worked in an environment where you felt psychologically safe? How did it compare to those where you did not?

2. Creating an environment that values employees yields benefits in engagement, problem-solving, and performance. Why do you think so many organizations create environments where employees don't feel valued?

Activity

For this activity, get a paper and pen to write answers to these prompts.

A lack of psychological safety can create an illusion of success that eventually turns into a serious business failure. Can you think of an example (from your own career or from the news) of a time when an illusion of success was created by fear of speaking out about failure? Do you think things would have been different if employees felt able to speak up?

A culture of silence (where team members are encouraged to keep secrets and cover up problems) is a dangerous culture. It can result in business failures, unnecessary costs, high employee turnover, legal trouble, and even a loss of life in some circumstances. Have you experienced a culture of silence in your career? Did negative consequences come from it?

Days 61–90

Performance goal: Innovate with teaming.

Consider Part III a road map for leaders who wish to inspire or participate in the innovation journey. Each of the following weeks covers one of four overarching recommendations for leaders seeking to enhance innovation in their organization: aim well, team up, fail well, and learn fast.

The following table summarizes the goals you will reflect on over the next 30 days. To keep yourself motivated, consider your personal goals and vision for success. What does innovation mean to you?

Days 61–90 Performance Goal: Innovate with teaming.	
Week 9	**Benchmark Goal: Aim high: Discover how to choose a worthy goal.** • Do you agree that to innovate you need a worthy goal? • How does aiming high help to motivate a team? • Have you ever had a stretch goal that challenged you beyond what seemed feasible? How did you stay motivated?

	Days 61–90 **Performance Goal:** Innovate with teaming.
Week 10	**Benchmark Goal: Team up: Learn the keys to teaming up for innovation.** • Have you ever teamed up with "strange bedfellows" to achieve a challenging goal? How did it work out? • Do you agree that psychological safety is a must for teaming? • How do process guidelines contribute to effective teaming?
Week 11	**Benchmark Goal: Fail well: See how failure sets the stage for success.** • Do you agree that failure is a prerequisite of innovation? • Have you ever experienced a "good failure" in your career? • What did you learn from it? • Why is it important to "fail at the right scale"?
Week 12	**Benchmark Goal: Learn fast: Make the most of your failure.** • What are the four steps to learning fast? Which do you think is more important? • What are some of the barriers to learning? • Can you think of when you've struggled with those barriers?
Personal Goals and Vision for Success	
What do you hope to achieve by leveling up?	
How could your life change by reaching these goals?	

Shooting for the Moon

Benchmark goal: Aim high: Discover how to choose a worthy goal.

Leaders seeking to inspire, enhance, or revive innovation in their organization often wonder what to do. They understand that just asking for innovation will not produce it. They recognize that cross-disciplinary groups do not always come up with terrific new ideas, and synergy is not a necessary outcome of collaboration across boundaries. In fact, without an unusual mix of openness, humility, talent, drive, and creativity, innovation may not occur. It is clear that leadership is needed to nurture these qualities in fluid groupings of people—often both inside and outside the organization—and channel them toward desired ends.

Teaming for innovation is dynamic. It involves identifying (often temporary) collaborators and getting up to speed quickly on what needs to be done and what role each collaborator can play. This kind of flexibility is needed more and more in workplaces across many industries. A growing portion of the work itself—whether product design, patient care, custom software, or strategic decision-making—presents complicated interdependencies that often have to be managed on the fly.

But no matter how flexible and willing one's colleagues may be, effective teaming rarely happens spontaneously. It takes effort. Teaming requires letting down your guard to work interdependently with others. It requires offering your ideas and skills thoughtfully while being equally, if not more, interested in what others have to offer, no matter what their status or position in the hierarchy. It requires accepting that it's simply not possible to look good or be right all the time. Teaming to innovate requires creativity, humility, empathy, and drive. Because these attributes can wax and wane in the real world, especially in the workplace, leaders need to nurture them.

In a nutshell, the leadership task in innovation is to keep people focused on what's at stake—on the purpose the organization seeks to serve and the goals it's striving to achieve—and to be stewards of the contradictory and paradoxical culture of innovation.

Consider this month a road map for leaders who wish to inspire or participate in the innovation journey. Each of the next four weeks look at four overarching recommendations for leaders seeking to enhance innovation in their organization:

- Aim high (this week)
- Team up (week 10)
- Fail well (week 11)
- Learn fast (week 12)

That's basically it. It's simple. (Note that simple doesn't mean easy!) And there is a final recommendation as well: repeat!

Innovation starts with a worthy aspiration. Although invention may occasionally occur as a result of pure brilliance, ingenuity, or the sheer pleasure of discovery, innovation is the result of an effortful and disciplined process. Effort and discipline thrive when people

are motivated to strive for something more. Driven by a desire to do something new and useful, people are able and willing to take the risks that innovation entails. So, to foster innovation in your organization, start with some soul searching to identify a worthy aspiration—one that in some small way relates to creating a better world. Whether to create a brand-new product, service, or solution or merely a substantially better way of doing something we already do, innovation begins as a glimmer. An idea. Aiming high for a worthy goal, no matter how distant, engages and motivates people by involving them in something larger than themselves.

Of course, it's possible to innovate without worthy goals or lofty aims, but if you're interested in engaging smart, motivated people in the uncertain journey of innovation, a worthy aspiration is a valuable source of fuel.

Aiming High for Innovation

On August 5, 2010, more than half a million tons of rock collapsed in the San José copper mine in Northern Chile, completely blocking the entrance. Mining accidents are unfortunately common. But this one was unprecedented for several reasons: the distance of the miners from the surface, the sheer number of miners trapped, and the hardness of the rock, to name just a few. Thirty-three men were buried alive, under 2,000 feet of rock harder than granite. In Chile, initial estimates of the possibility of finding anyone alive were put at 10 percent—odds that diminished sharply two days later when rescue workers narrowly escaped a secondary collapse of the ventilation shaft, which permanently shut down the option of rescuing the miners through that route.

Yet within 70 days all 33 miners would be rescued. This extraordinary result occurred because several leaders committed to the

aspirational goal of a successful rescue, despite the brutal odds against their success. That the rescue required innovation is self-evident— there simply was no existing solution, either inside or outside the mining industry, at the outset. It took the collaborative efforts of over 100 experts in diverse fields innovating to develop and execute a novel solution on the fly.

Innovation occurred in at least two very separate arenas. First, and most painful to consider, were the miners facing the challenge of physical and psychological survival. Innovation here took the form of a new social system—designed to maintain the life and sanity of 33 trapped men in dire circumstances. Second, a network of engineers and geologists came together from multiple organizations and nations to work on the technical problems of locating, reaching, and extracting the trapped miners. Their innovation produced the design and development of a completely novel rescue system. To support the actions of those above and below ground at the San José site, senior leaders in the Chilean government, including the nation's president, made decisions and provided resources and inspiration.

Teaming to Survive

Below ground, amidst shock and fear, leadership and teaming took shape after a tumultuous beginning. Immediately after the collapse, the miners scrambled to safety in the mine's small refuge. Luis Urzúa, who had formal leadership over the group as the shift supervisor, started by checking provisions in the refuge. Calmly and quickly, he focused on crucial survival needs, especially the limited available food (roughly the amount of food two miners would eat over 10 days). However, calm did not prevail. Mario Sepulveda, a charismatic 39-year old, outraged at the state of the mine and the company's long-standing lack of attention to safety, reacted angrily to the collapse. His energy attracted followers; factions and conflict soon emerged. Some wanted

to take action of any kind to reach the outside world rather than sitting helplessly to await rescue. Others wanted to follow Urzúa's guidance. By the end of their first 24 hours, the miners were exhausted by failed attempts to communicate with the outside world and disoriented by the lack of natural light. With scant attention to sanitation or order and subdued by hunger and fatigue, they attempted to sleep.

On the second day, miner José Henríquez stepped in to urge the group to start each day with a collective prayer. Soon this became a sustaining routine and helped unite the group around a shared goal: survival. With no blueprint for how to survive in these conditions, conversation and experimentation were essential to discovering a way forward. In the days that followed, facing darkness, hunger, depression, filth, and illness, the miners cooperated intensely to maintain order, health, sanitation, and sanity.

Teaming to Solve Complex Technical Problems

Above ground, the Chilean Carabineros Special Operations Group—an elite police unit for rescue operations—arrived a few hours after the first collapse. Their initial attempt at rescue led to the ventilation shaft collapse, the rescue effort's dismal first failure. As news of a mine cave-in spread, family members, emergency response teams, rescue workers, and reporters also flooded to the site. Meanwhile, others in the Chilean mining community dispatched experts, drilling machines, and bulldozers. Codelco, the state-owned company overseeing the San José mine, sent Andre Sougarret, an engineer and manager with over 20 years of experience in mining who was known for his composure and ease with people, to lead the operation. Working with numerous other technical experts, Sougarret formed three teams to oversee different aspects of the operation. One team searched for the men, poking drill holes deep into the earth in the hopes of hearing sounds indicating that the men were alive. Another worked on how to

keep them alive if found, and a third worked on how to extract them safely from the refuge. On October 13, miners began to be brought up, one by one, on a 15-minute journey to the surface. Over the next two days, they were hauled up, one after another, in the 28-inchwide escape capsule painted with the red, white, and blue of the Chilean flag. After a few minutes to hug relatives, each miner was taken for medical evaluation.

Neither Top-Down nor Bottom-Up

Reflecting on the Chilean rescue, it is clear that a top-down, command-and-control approach—the kind that can be successfully used in a crisis with a known solution, such as when a large fire breaks out or when an impending hurricane is detected—would have failed utterly. No one person, or even one leadership team, could have figured out how to solve this problem. It's also clear that simply encouraging everyone to try anything they wanted would have produced only chaos and harm. Family members, miners, and others with good intentions had to be held back numerous times from rushing headlong at the rock with pickaxes. Instead, what was required, facing the unprecedented scale of the disaster, was coordinated but flexible teaming—multiple temporary groups of people working separately on different types of problems and coordinating across groups, as needed. Such groups innovate in ways no one can anticipate at the outset. Doing this well involves progressive experimentation, a core discipline of innovation.

Aiming High with Meaning

What drives the hard and interpersonally challenging work of teaming for innovation? Let's face it; it's not easy to get up in the morning and come to work knowing you might fail several times before lunch! The

hard intellectual and emotional work of innovation is fueled by a compelling purpose that addresses questions like, Why care? Why bother? Why should I put aside the momentary comfort of relaxing in order to exert the effort and subject myself to the risks involved in coming up with new solutions to old problems?

Emotions play a role in generating creative ideas. Emotions spark new connections between disparate experiences. Emotions also motivate and provide a foundation to return to when the going gets tough. The most motivating goals are connected to the objectives and frustrations of today's work. This close connection makes tolerable the daily risks and suffering (big and small) in the demanding environment of innovation, where nothing is certain.

Soon after assuming the CEO role at Children's Hospital and Clinics in Minneapolis, Minnesota, Judith Morath assembled a team she called the Patient Safety Steering Committee (PSSC). The PSSC was a select group of key influencers who would help design and launch the "Patient Safety Initiative." To identify those having interest and passion, as well as to communicate with as many people in the hospital as possible, Morath delivered a series of presentations about medical errors, citing the then still unfamiliar fact that as many as 98,000 hospitalized patients in the United States were dying annually from medical errors—more than the number from car accidents, breast cancer, or AIDS. The PSSC was deliberately diverse, comprising doctors and nurses, department heads and frontline staff, union members and executives. It was a group that understood and represented the organization well.

Despite the pedigree of the PSSC and Morath's compelling delivery, many initially pushed back against the idea of a patient safety initiative, reluctant to believe that errors were a problem at Children's. They believed the national statistics but did not believe those numbers applied to Children's. When your work involves taking care of

vulnerable children, it's enormously threatening to be told that you might be doing things that harm them. Quite naturally, they resisted Morath's efforts to promote innovation.

Tempting as it must have been to simply reiterate her message more forcefully (given that she understood that all hospitals, because of their operational complexity, were vulnerable to error), Morath did not try to argue the point. Instead, she thoughtfully responded to the resistance with inquiry. "Okay, this data may not be applicable here," she concurred. Then she probed gently, "Tell me, what was your own experience this week, in the units, with your patients? Was everything as safe as you would like it to have been?"

The Power of Inquiry

This simple inquiry seems to have transformed the dialogue. Note its features. Her question is an invitation, one that is genuine, curious, direct, and concrete. Each caregiver is invited to consider their own patients and experiences, in their own unit, over the prior few days. Moreover, the question is aspirational—not, "Did you see things that were unsafe?" but rather, "Was everything as safe as you would like it to have been?" It respects others' experience while it invites aspiration. Too many would-be leaders forget about the power of inquiry and instead rely on forceful advocacy to bring others along. As Morath showed, inquiry respects and invites. As people began to discuss with her and with others incidents they had thought were unique or idiosyncratic, they realized that most of their colleagues had experienced similar events. As Morath put it, "I found that most people had been at the center of a health care situation where something did not go well. They were quick to recognize that the hospital could be doing better." She led as many as 18 focus groups throughout the organization to enable people to air their concerns and ideas.

Making It Safe to Talk About Problems

To build the psychological safety needed for the inevitably difficult conversations about errors and failures, Morath frequently described her philosophy on patient safety to anyone who would listen. In her words, "Health care is a very complex system, and complex systems are, by their very nature, risk-prone. The culture of health care must be one of everyone working together to understand safety, identify risks, and report them without fear of blame. We must look at ways to change the whole system when we manage to zero defects." By emphasizing the systemic nature of failures, she sought to help people move away from a tendency to find and blame individual culprits.

Morath knew firsthand about the aftershock and emotional pain of medical accidents for health care workers. She never forgot one she'd witnessed 30 years earlier, when she was a young nurse: a four-year-old patient died from an anesthesia error. What Morath remembered, even more than the devastation of the child's death, was that "the nurse who felt responsible 'went home that day and never returned,' giving up the career she loved due to a profound and crushing feeling of guilt. Doctors and other nurses 'just shut down' and never talked to one another about what happened. The hospital's attorneys swooped in to do damage control. 'It just didn't sit right and it plagued me,'" Morath said decades later.

So she introduced a new system for reporting medical incidents called *blameless reporting.* The idea was to allow people to communicate confidentially or anonymously about medical accidents without being punished for doing so, so as to bring as many of these problems as possible to light, to determine their underlying causes, and to keep caring professionals in their positions.

Morath also instituted new words—new ways of talking about safety lapses that would be less emotionally threatening. For example,

she encouraged people to substitute *study* for *investigation*. To Morath, study meant a way of learning how systems work and how the pieces fit together. An investigation, however, was more like a police lineup, assigning blame to someone in a linear search to determine a single cause. By avoiding words that implied blame and encouraging language conducive to learning from failures, Morath was trying to make it psychologically safe to talk about error.

Just as important, she believed that the whole meaning of *error* had to be reframed. She explained to people that in hospitals, *accidents* (a term preferable to *error*) arose from faulty systems rather than faulty persons. Complex systems are failure-prone; individual clinicians involved in a system failure are victims of that complexity, just like their patients.

Last, *blame* was to be replaced by the word *accountable*, defined as being responsible for the duties of a particular job and whatever knowledge it required, as well as for understanding the larger system in which one was a human component. All of these linguistic interventions were designed to make it safe to engage in the interpersonally risky behaviors of innovation.

When leaders successfully engage employees in an innovation process, ideas start to bubble up, experiments start to happen, and activities start to take hold and spread. To a manager seeking to "get the job done," the process might at first seem laborious and slow. But engaging people as active thinkers and learners is the only way to innovate in a complex system like a hospital, where solutions simply don't exist at the outset.

It's a Stretch

On the innovation journey, aiming high means stretching beyond what seems initially feasible. The aspiration must be truly challenging.

At the same time, it's important that it not be completely implausible. The distinction can be a very fine line. The goal should inspire but not turn off or depress those who wish to innovate. Developing systems whereby patients are safe from medical mishap is one such goal. It's enormously challenging, but through innovative ways of changing the culture of reporting and by introducing better mechanisms for catching and correcting small process failures before they reach patients, it is not impossible to dramatically improve patient safety. Morath's innovation journey was both cultural and procedural.

Worthy Aspirations That Motivate Innovation

The opportunity to make a difference turns out to be a key driver of innovation. When people share an ambitious goal—together with a vision of a better future—it gives them a shared identity. It builds camaraderie.

What's so great about camaraderie? First, it makes work more fun. Second, people feel safer, and when people feel safer it's easier to be creative. And third, because innovation is heavy lifting, people must have confidence in each other's abilities. Envisioning a process or a product that has never existed requires conviction. For this reason, the goal, as noted, should be a stretch, but not absurd!

Finally, as any reader who has experienced true teamwork in the pursuit of innovation knows well, there's nothing better. At times, you believe that anything's possible when a group of dedicated people put their minds to doing what was thought to be impossible.

Innovation is a team sport. But teaming to innovate isn't always a smooth ride. Next, I explain why people must span boundaries, build psychological safety, and cool conflict to make teaming work and enable innovation to flourish.

Aiming High and True

If you're interested in engaging smart, motivated people in the uncertain journey of innovation, a worthy aspiration is a valuable source of fuel. In this activity, you examine the role of a laudable goal in spurring innovation.

Activity

Reflect on the following questions:

Have you ever been a part of a team working on a challenge that deeply mattered (to you or someone else)? How did it affect your approach?

_____

_____

_____

Do you agree that emotion plays an important role in innovation? Why or why not?

_____

_____

_____

How important is it to you to feel camaraderie with your team? Do you believe it's possible to be a part of an effective team if there is no camaraderie? Explain your answer.

_____

_____

_____

Coming Together

Benchmark goal: Team up: Learn the keys to teaming up for innovation.

L ike it or not, innovation is a team sport. Few worthy innovations are accomplished alone or even by groups of people who have the same basic knowledge and expertise. This week I look at the second key factor for innovation: teaming up. I look at what it takes to team and explain why teaming is more challenging than it might first appear. I explore the crucial role of psychological safety—along with other enabling factors—in helping people team effectively. And because teaming across disciplinary lines is so vital to innovation, I pay particular attention to the types of boundaries people confront when teaming to innovate and how to bridge them effectively.

Sometimes a Team Calls for Strange Bedfellows

It is hard to imagine two more different thought worlds than Hollywood and the CIA. But what makes the story of the fate of six American hostages in Iran truly gripping is the teaming between these strange bedfellows and how it brought the hostages home. As

you read this story, consider the types of boundaries between these players, the nature of the teaming that occurred, and the innovative solution itself. How did teaming up across boundaries produce innovation?

Early in the morning of November 4, 1979, at the United States Embassy in Tehran, Iran's capital city, a rapidly growing crowd of anti-American student protestors was demanding that ousted monarch (Shah) Mohammad Reza Pahlavi be returned from US exile. They wanted him to be tried by the revolutionary government led by Ayatollah Khomeini. The crowd rushed the embassy gates, chanting, "Allahu Akbar!" (God is great!) and "Marg bar Amrika!" (Death to America!). Soon students were scaling the walls of the embassy. Within minutes, the protestors swarmed the vast compound that contained the ambassador's residence and staff offices.

Consular diplomat Martin Lijek, in Iran on his first consular post, hoped the adjacent visa-processing building where he worked would not be in the protestors' path. He hoped that no one would suspect that a small collection of American embassy staff, Iranian employees, and visa applicants was on the second floor. Martin's group included his wife, Cora (consular assistant), Joseph Stafford (senior foreign service officer), Stafford's wife, Kathleen (consular assistant), and Robert Anders (senior consular officer).

Suddenly, the building went dark as power was cut. Gunshots rang out in the compound. Escaping capture was paramount: Iranian employees had known neighbors who were apprehended and executed by revolutionary guards. As the crowd neared their building, Martin and his peers destroyed the plates used to make visa stamps, improvised an evacuation plan, and ushered both staff and applicants to the back door. This was the sole exit on the embassy compound with direct street access.

The Iranian visa applicants exited first, in small groups, ahead of the American staff. One Iranian group was captured moments later and taken back to the embassy. The Lijeks, Staffords, and Anders headed to the British Embassy, several blocks away. The American escapees had almost reached the embassy when they encountered another demonstration.

Eventually, the group found refuge in the residence of Ken Taylor, the Canadian ambassador. The six became known at the State Department and CIA as the "houseguests." Aware that the lives of the Canadian ambassador and his so-called houseguests were at risk if the presence of the Americans became known, experts in Washington, DC, were considering a number of rescue plans, mostly involving overland routes bypassing roads and checkpoints.

Tony Mendez, Graphics Authentication Division head at the CIA, was called in to come up with a plan for bringing the hostages home. False identities were Mendez's specialty. He had spent 14 years in the CIA's Office of Technical Service—a real-world version of James Bond's "Q" branch—and had helped more than 100 agents and others escape life-threatening situations abroad.

The problem was that neither the Canadian nor American diplomatic corps leaders could conceive of a credible reason for any North Americans to be in Tehran after the hostage crisis had begun. Teachers, agricultural researchers, and others had all left. In the midst of the brainstorming, Mendez had a unique idea: to assemble a film scouting crew.

The plan was fleshed out as follows. Mendez would play the role of fictitious film producer Kevin Harkins from Canada and request a "location scout" trip to Iran for a Hollywood studio film. The concept seemed plausible because so-called Hollywood creative types might conceivably be oblivious to the situation in revolutionary Iran.

Focusing on finding the right backdrop for a new movie, perhaps a science fiction story in need of an exotic desert landscape, a Hollywood producer might just be crazy enough to scout out the view in Iran. Moreover, the Iranian government wanted the hard currency and might welcome this kind of business venture. A film production could mean millions of US dollars.

Pursuing this idea, Mendez needed partners. The cover story seemed plausible. But a great deal of work still needed to be done to fill in the details for an operation that could withstand scrutiny while manhunting Americans was in high gear. To prepare the foundation for this cover, Mendez flew to Los Angeles in mid-January to meet John Chambers, a veteran makeup artist who had won a 1969 Academy Award for *Planet of the Apes* and was also a longtime Mendez collaborator. Chambers invited makeup artist and special effects expert Bob Sidell to join the meeting.

Chambers found a well-suited script in the vast archives of submitted screenplays never filmed. Mendez gave the script a new title, *Argo*, the name of the vessel used by Greek mythology hero Jason (and his Argonauts) on his daring voyage across the world to retrieve the Golden Fleece. Mendez and Chambers designed a full-page ad for the film to run in key trade magazines *Variety* and the *Hollywood Reporter*.

Finally, Mendez obtained false Canadian passports for the six and flew to Tehran. Meeting the hostages, he explained the cover story and presented Jack Kirby's conceptual art, the screenplay, the ad in *Variety*, and the "Studio Six" business cards. With some reluctance, the houseguests agreed the ruse could work and set about memorizing their new identities to match their fake Canadian passports. Soon they were headed to the Tehran airport to make their dangerous escape from Iran—in plain sight.

After several tense moments at the gate, Mendez and his "film crew" boarded the plane. The plane took off, and Mendez and the six

escapees breathed a collective sigh of relief. Together they had successfully accomplished the most creative and improbable "exfiltration" of Mendez's career.

Teaming Across Boundaries

Mendez, the houseguests, the Canadians who sheltered them, and the creative artists in Hollywood who made it all believable had little in common. They came from different backgrounds, different organizations, different areas of expertise, and different cultures. Yet they collaborated to execute a remarkable and remarkably innovative operation. This kind of diversity involves boundaries between people from different identity groups.

Education (level and type), along with the socializing processes that occur when we interact with others in our field, contributes to unconscious beliefs that the knowledge shared by one's own group is especially important. The knowledge and skills we learn in a given field of expertise make up the visible curriculum. Most people take the knowledge that lies on their side of a boundary for granted. This can make it hard to communicate with those on the other side. But at its core, teaming is about reaching across or spanning such boundaries. To do this, we must first be keenly aware of what they are and what they do.

Taken-for-granted assumptions are hard to recognize. The first step in doing so is becoming aware that they exist, so you can be on the lookout for them.

Types of Boundaries

Three types of boundaries are particularly important in the context of teaming to innovate: physical distance (location, time zone, and so

on), status (perceived social value, hierarchical level, profession, and so on), and knowledge (experience, education, and so on).

Physical Distance

In many companies, work teams in globally dispersed locations—so-called virtual teams—are used to integrate expertise. They're virtual because they work together using communication technologies like email, phone, or Skype. The potential for innovation from such teaming is great; however, the challenges are equally so. Without face-to-face contact, taken-for-granted assumptions can be particularly tricky to recognize and address.

Status

The most common status differences at work are profession-based status and level in the organizational hierarchy. Professional status particularly influences speaking-up behavior. In health care, for example, physicians have more status and power than nurses, who in turn have more status than technicians. Yet members across these professions almost always have to team up to take care of patients. So patients are at risk if people don't learn how to team across status boundaries.

Knowledge

Teaming to innovate is most often about bridging across areas of expertise. In product and process development teams, in particular, bringing together people from different organizational functions for a limited period of intense teaming is increasingly common. In product development, engineering offers insight into design and technology;

manufacturing, into feasible production processes, accurate cost estimates, and pilot and full-scale production; and marketing, into customer receptivity, customer segments, product positioning, and product plans. Combining these diverse skill sets and perspectives is as crucial as it is challenging, because misunderstandings arise due to different meanings embedded in different disciplines, and mistrust often follows.

Organization and occupation are both important sources of knowledge boundaries. Organizational boundaries exist anytime people from different companies—or even sites within a company—have to work together. Occupational boundaries come from the training or education through which experts gain mastery over a specialized body of knowledge. This gives them a particular mindset, a way of knowing. And that mastery becomes taken for granted. The jargon acquired in specialized education and practice constitutes a kind of foreign language for others. This makes working together—across the "thought worlds" of occupational communities—vulnerable to misunderstanding.

Meanwhile, in most fields specialization is intensifying. The rate of new knowledge development requires people to invest considerable time just to stay current. This, of course, makes it even harder to master other disciplines. In technical fields the explosion of new knowledge makes narrow specialization especially likely. Fields spawn new subfields, and they in turn spawn even more specialized subfields.

Innovation requires teaming across knowledge boundaries. Whether developing a new cell phone or discovering a cure for diabetes, it is essential to find novelty and synergy from the unexpected combinations of ideas and techniques that can occur between fields of expertise.

What It Takes to Team

The time pressures we all experience today mean that a highly structured approach, in which managers plan each aspect of a large innovation project is unrealistic. Such planning becomes even less realistic when completed tasks are "thrown over the wall" to other functions or disciplines. Instead, the walls between disciplines have to come down, and simultaneous work on related tasks must be coordinated and negotiated.

Nowadays, it's just not possible for even expert individuals to develop important innovations all by themselves. The chances of individual parts coming together into meaningful, functional wholes without intense communication across boundaries are exceedingly low. How can the boundaries between diverse groups be overcome? Curiosity, psychological safety, and process guidelines are three of the key ingredients.

Mutual Curiosity

Genuine curiosity about what others think, worry about, and aspire to achieve is invaluable for crossing boundaries. By cultivating our own curiosity about what makes others tick, each of us can contribute to creating an environment where it's acceptable to express interest in others' thoughts and feelings. MIT professor Ed Schein, a preeminent researcher on corporate culture, uses the term *temporary cultural island* in his description of a process for sharing crucial professional and personal information in a multicultural work group. (Note that the term *culture* applies to nations, companies, professions, and other identity groups.) The process involves talking about concrete experiences and feelings and is fueled by thoughtful questions on the part of a leader acting as a facilitator. Schein explains that cultural assumptions related to authority and intimacy are crucial issues in culturally

diverse teams. When someone in one culture violates an authority rule that is taken for granted in another culture, for example by speaking in an overly familiar manner to a high-status person, someone may experience the behavior as jarring. When we share stories in which these issues are exposed, boundaries begin to dissolve.

Psychological Safety

Boundaries will not be spanned, and innovation cannot flourish in an environment that lacks psychological safety. Psychological safety describes an interpersonal climate where people feel able to express ideas, ask questions, quickly acknowledge mistakes, and raise concerns about the project early and often. They also feel responsible for doing so. It's not that it's easy for them to take these interpersonal risks; rather, they understand it's expected of them. It is part of collaboration. They recognize, too, that teaming up is as interpersonally challenging as it is rewarding. Without these behaviors—which can feel especially risky in hierarchies—successful innovation is unlikely. Table 10.1 depicts leadership actions that help build a climate of psychological safety where innovation can thrive.

Table 10.1 Leadership Behaviors That Build Psychological Safety

Behavior	Description
Acknowledge limits.	When leaders admit that they don't know something, their genuine display of humility encourages other team members to follow suit.
Invite participation.	When people believe their leaders value their input, they're more engaged and responsive.
Use direct language.	Using direct, actionable language instigates the type of straightforward, blunt discussion that enables learning.

In fast-paced, cross-disciplinary, cross-border teaming, it's not easy for people to quickly share their ideas and expertise. Some people worry about what others will think of them. Some fear that they will be less valuable if they give away what they know. Others are reluctant to show off. Even accepting others' ideas can be difficult if it feels like an admission of weakness. Because vital interpersonal exchanges don't always happen spontaneously, leaders must facilitate them. A basic approach to creating psychological safety as a leader is to model the behaviors on which teaming depends, such as asking thoughtful questions or acknowledging your own ignorance about a topic or area of expertise. Leaders who act this way make it safer for everyone else to do it, too.

Process Guidelines

In any complex teaming effort, it is important to establish process guidelines that everyone agrees to follow. A strategy for boundary management is essential. Guidelines are needed for specifying points at which separate teaming activities must come together to coordinate resources and decisions.

When Conflict Heats Up

Even when psychological safety, curiosity, and process guidelines are in place, the very nature of teaming is such that conflict will occur. In fact, conflict is desirable. Without conflict—the competing ideas from which new possibilities sometimes spring—innovation is less likely. But however appealing the idea of creative conflict is in theory, in practice managing conflict effectively is hard to do.

The trouble is, when we encounter differences of opinion, especially those based on values or beliefs we hold deeply, it can trigger strong

emotions. Emotions can hijack reason, temporarily of course, making it hard to sift through the differences and find the important questions, ideas, and new possibilities that may be lurking. It takes skill to cool one's own and others' emotions so as to put conflict to good use.

What set of skills is necessary to transform hot tensions into creativity and innovation? It starts with understanding the difference between hot and cool cognition.

Hot and Cool Cognition

Research by cognitive psychologists Janet Metcalfe and Walter Mischel showed that we each have two distinct cognitive systems through which we process events, which they called *hot* and *cool*. The hot system, when engaged, triggers people to respond emotionally and quickly. In this case they are often said to speak or act in the heat of the moment. The cool system, by contrast, is deliberate and careful. When using our cool system, we can slow down and gather our thoughts. The cool system is the basis for self-regulation and self-control. It is desperately needed to team effectively in the face of conflict. Think about the last time you found yourself debating an important issue at work, especially one you really cared about. Many such conversations go back and forth, with people repeating the same points over and over again. Conflicts heat up when people hold different values or belief systems, or have different interests and incentives. This can make it hard to process the conflict productively, and hard to find the seeds of something new and innovative.

Such conflicts often quickly reach an impasse, and the discussion gets personal. It's hard for people not to see each other's viewpoint as wrongheaded, and deliberately so. Each sees the other as stubborn or, worse, manipulative. They fall victim to what's called the *fundamental attribution error*, as we discussed in week 2. And whether blaming

each other's motives, character, or abilities, people in the midst of a tough conflict usually silently blame someone else for the lack of progress on the issues. Although very human, this spontaneous reasoning severely hampers innovation.

Three Practices That Cool Hot Conflict

The key question is this: how can people effectively use different perspectives to produce innovation rather than unproductive conflict? The answer lies in understanding how to cool hot topics in fast-paced conversations at work. I recommend three practices to cool down conflict.

Manage Self

This practice involves recognizing one's emotions for what they are: spontaneous personal reactions to a situation. Emotions let us know that we care about the discussion at hand, and we need to slow ourselves down to pay very close attention to what's happening. Managing self means learning how to quickly reflect—to turn our curiosity inward for a brief period and ask ourselves why we're feeling anxious, or frustrated, or angry. It's critical to remind oneself in these situations of two essential facts. First is the very real likelihood that you are missing part of the picture (the part that others see!). Second is that you too are contributing to the problem—in the same way you're convinced the other person is doing so.

Manage Conversations

This practice starts with realizing that conversations don't manage themselves. It takes a bit of guidance for a conversation that has

crossed knowledge boundaries and run into conflicting perspectives to go well and produce good results. To facilitate good communication in the face of heated conflict, it's necessary to slow the conversation down so as to combine thoughtful statements with thoughtful questions. This enables people to understand the true basis of a disagreement and to identify the rationale behind different positions. Doing this well also means inviting quiet voices into the discussion to bring new perspectives and new facts to light.

Manage Relationships

While the first two practices are skills that are needed in the heat of a disagreement, the third is the ongoing practice of building strong relationships that can withstand the temporary assault of disagreement. Managers who take the time to get to know each other as people and to understand the other's goals and concerns are less likely to attribute selfish motives to each other and more likely to be curious about others' concerns. Managing relationships is about building trust grounded in experience. Investing time in getting to know colleagues—new and old—helps lay the foundation for productive conflict, despite the emotions that will surely surface along the way.

It's not possible to manage conflict by simply avoiding emotions. Our emotions are spontaneous and natural. To suggest we avoid them in difficult conversations is a fool's errand. Instead, we have to learn how to be thoughtful and open about them. We have to be willing to dig a little more deeply into what they are telling us. This is essential because innovation almost always involves the effective use of differences. Learning how to talk about what makes us tick and what lies underneath our opinions helps to build the genuine, resilient relationships that are crucial to effective teaming.

Embracing the Risks of Teaming

Innovation involves people. And people, as we all know, are complicated creatures. Because innovation requires problem-solving on so many levels, from practical skills to expertise and creativity, teaming to innovate often involves a great deal of diversity. In fact, the greater the diversity among team members—in backgrounds, skills, and expertise—the greater the likelihood of success, but also the greater the likelihood of misunderstandings and problematic conflict. The teaming practices you learned this week can help innovation teams overcome these very real challenges to success.

Teaming to Innovate

Innovation is usually a team sport, but the composition of the team and how they work together matters a great deal. In this activity, you'll examine the need for the right team for innovation.

Activity

Reflect on the following questions:

Think back to the most successful team you've ever been a part of. What was the degree of diverse expertise or perspectives on the team? Could some members of the team be described as strange bedfellows? If so, why do you think the team worked so well?

_____

_____

_____

Of the three boundaries discussed this week that teaming can cross (physical distance, status, and knowledge), which do you think is the toughest to overcome? What strategies have you used in the past to get around this boundary?

_____

_____

_____

How important is it to you to feel camaraderie with your team? Do you believe it's possible to be a part of an effective team if there is no camaraderie? Why or why not?

_____

_____

_____

Of the three skills for cooling conflict discussed this week (managing self, conversation, and relationships), is there one that you often struggle with? What strategies could you use to gain mastery over this skill?

_____

_____

_____

Failing to Succeed

Benchmark goal: Fail well: See how failure sets the stage for success.

Every child learns at some point that failure is bad, and dodging blame is a winning strategy. By the time we're working adults, avoiding association with failure is all but second nature. This self-protective reflex may keep our reputation intact (or at least most people seem to think it does), but it harms the companies we work for. Why? It is nearly impossible to learn from failures if people don't admit and analyze them. In any industry where innovation is crucial for survival, an ability to learn from failure is an essential skill.

Learning from failure thus begins with unlearning. This is because childish notions of success are intimately twined with self-esteem, status, and the need for approval. As adults we understand that knowledge is in constant flux, technology insists on changing fast, and confronting new and unfamiliar situations is simply part of working in the twenty-first century. Expecting failure-free performance is illogical in this dynamic context. Moreover, if we want to innovate, we must unlearn spontaneous responses about failure. We must reprogram. Unlearning the idea that failure is bad starts with a deeper understanding of failure.

Unpacking Failure

Over the last 20 years of research and consulting within organizations in a variety of industries, I've seen managers really struggle to embrace the reality that failure is an essential prerequisite to innovation. In fact, the exhortation to fail well sounds to them like a nonsensical oxymoron. This is because they haven't fully recognized that failures come in several different types, not all (in fact, few) of them blameworthy.

I will describe three basic types of failure: basic, complex, and intelligent. I'll also talk about how to design intelligent failures and how to be courageous. Avoiding basic failures is both important and feasible. Complex failures can be hard to predict, but with vigilance they too can be largely avoided. By contrast, intelligent failures are in fact positive events. They're part of an essential strategy for creating new knowledge, developing ideas, and producing innovation. Failing well means engaging in intelligent failures. It also means learning quickly when complex failures occur, or nearly occur, so as to avoid any future recurrence. A primary aspect of failing well is avoiding the "blame game" so that you can use failure to promote innovation.

Many leaders worry that in the absence of blame there's no accountability, and without accountability employees won't work hard. The truth is, a culture that makes it safe to be honest, safe to report failure, and safe to admit mistakes is a culture in which a responsible adult can thrive and do their best work. Why? Because most people want to feel proud of the work they do, to be part of something larger than themselves, and to make a difference in the lives of colleagues and customers. Given the right conditions, they will.

Failure's Causes

Let's start with the obvious cause. Deliberate violation, in which a person chooses to violate a prescribed procedure or rule, clearly

anchors the blameworthy end of the spectrum. Inattention, in which someone inadvertently deviates from what's required because they lost focus or got distracted—well, that's a little less clear. Inattention could be due to texting when you should be looking at the road. That's blameworthy. Or it could occur when a worker is put in the problematic situation of working a double shift, and fatigue has made perfect attentiveness impossible. There's blame involved here, but it belongs to the manager who put the worker in that situation, not to the worker. Next on my spectrum is lack of competence. This describes a situation in which an individual doesn't have or hasn't been taught the necessary skills to do the job (hmmm, whose fault is that?).

Inadequate process describes a situation in which an individual, or a group, faces a faulty or incomplete set of guidelines. This often occurs when a process is new, and the kinks haven't been worked out yet. Task challenge describes situations in which the task at hand is simply too difficult to be successfully executed every time. For a simple illustration, consider the elite figure skater able to perform the extraordinary feat of a quadruple Lutz to embellish a winning Olympic routine. Given that no skater pulled off this extremely difficult move in a competition until 2011, it's clear that the quadruple Lutz is too challenging to support a realistic expectation that any skater can do it perfectly every time. When a failure to execute an exceedingly challenging task occurs, it would be just plain wrong to call that blameworthy.

Next, some situations are exceedingly complex. When Hurricane Sandy hit New York City in fall 2012, responding successfully meant bringing an enormous number of different people and actions to bear on a fast-moving problem with many affected people, buildings, and organizations. Even though good protocols were in place for hurricane response, complexity means that it was unlikely that everything

would work perfectly—that is, that no failures (small or large) would occur along the way. New York's emergency response system performed admirably, but this didn't mean that nothing went wrong and no one got hurt.

Relatedly, uncertainty means we don't have complete knowledge about future events. Given what they know at the time, people will take reasonable actions that nonetheless may produce undesirable results (failures). Note that it would be unreasonable to blame anyone for such failures; the appropriate reaction would be something like, "We did the best we could with the knowledge we had."

Finally, some failures happen as a result of experimentation. Consider two kinds of experiments. First, hypothesis-testing experiments test a specific prediction. They might be focused on whether a new packaging design will appeal to customers, for example. Sometimes our hypotheses are right. Sometimes they are wrong (failure again!). Either way, we've learned something. It's better to find out that customers don't like the packaging before we roll it out at full scale. Exploratory experiments, in contrast to experiments driven by a focused hypothesis, are conducted to investigate a possibility, without a strong sense of what we expect to happen. They expand our knowledge of some area through exploratory action.

Considering the range of causes along this spectrum, it should be clear that deliberate violation is the only action for which a person obviously deserves to be blamed. After that, from inattention all the way through to exploratory experiments, it would be harder to come to that conclusion. This would require us to ignore the effects of fatigue, poor training, poor management, or novelty (see Table 11.1). In fact, any failure resulting from honest effort or thoughtful experimentation is grist for the innovation mill and thus should instead be considered praiseworthy.

Table 11.1 A Spectrum of Potential Causes of Organizational Failures

Potential Cause of Failure	Description	Is Blame Appropriate?
Deliberate violation	An individual chooses to violate a prescribed process or practice.	Yes
Inattention	An individual inadvertently deviates from a prescribed process or practice.	Maybe
Lack of ability	An individual doesn't have the skills, conditions, or training to execute a job.	Unlikely
Inadequate process	An individual adheres to a prescribed process, but the process is faulty or incomplete.	Unlikely
Task challenge	An individual faces a task that is too difficult to be executed reliably every time.	Doubtful
Complexity	A process composed of many elements breaks down when novel interactions take place.	Rarely
Uncertainty	Lacking sufficient knowledge of future events, people take reasonable actions that nonetheless produce undesired results.	No

(continued)

Failing to Succeed

Table 11.1 *(continued)*

Potential Cause of Failure	Description	Is Blame Appropriate?
Hypothesis-testing experiment	An experiment conducted to test a prediction that a particular design or course of action will produce a particular result fails to confirm the hypothesis.	No
Exploratory experiment	An experiment conducted to expand knowledge and investigate a possibility leads to an undesired result.	No

I've shared this spectrum of causes with executives from a range of industries and asked them to estimate what percentage of the failures in their organization might be caused by blameworthy actions. Usually, they pick a number that is less than 5 percent. Then I ask how often failures in their company are actually treated as blameworthy. After a pause (or an uncomfortable laugh), they come up with a much higher number, say 70–90 percent. The discrepancy (between less than 5 and 90) is a far greater problem than most managers realize. If thoughtful managers understand that failures do happen, and that it's rare when an individual can rightly be blamed, then they'll also see that to engage in blaming is more than just illogical. It's counterproductive.

Why? Because valuable failures go unreported. Failure's lessons are lost. The real cost of blaming people for bad outcomes—when the real causes are uncertainty or complexity, for example—is that innovation is hampered. To understand this better, take a look at three kinds of failure.

Mapping the Failure Landscape

Although an infinite number of things can go wrong in organizations, they fall into three broad categories of failure: basic, complexity-related, and intelligent. The causes discussed in this chapter correspond roughly, and in sets of three, to these three failure types. In this 90-Day Plan, we are particularly interested in intelligent failures at the frontier (the frontier being where innovation occurs). But intelligent failures are best understood by contrasting them to the other types.

Basic Failures

Most failures in this category can indeed be considered "bad" in the sense that they were highly basic. They may involve unwarranted deviation from a well-defined process in a routine operation. In fact, they are particularly relevant in the context of routine operations, that is, when knowledge for how to do things "right" is available. Although rarely deliberate, such deviations are almost always avoidable. With proper training and support, steps in a routine process can and should be followed consistently. Failure to do so is usually due to one of the first three of the nine reasons for failure in the spectrum (violation, inattention, or lack of ability). When that happens, the causes can be readily identified and solutions developed.

In innovation projects, experiments that have been run before and failed but are inadvertently run again qualify as basic failures. Optimal practice for innovation is not to avoid failure, but it does avoid producing the same failure twice.

Complex Failures

Many organizational failures are the result of system complexity and are not completely preventable. When a particular combination of

needs, people, and problems has never occurred before—such as triaging patients in a hospital emergency room, troubleshooting in a major IT installation, or running a fast-growing start-up—at least some small failures must be expected. To assume otherwise would be illogical. System failure also is a perpetual risk in complex organizations like aircraft carriers, nuclear power plants, and air traffic control.

While serious failures may be averted by following risk management best practices, including a thorough analysis of all near-miss events (as I discuss in week 12), small process failures will inevitably occur. To consider them "bad" is a misunderstanding of how complex systems work. It is also counterproductive. It blocks the rapid identification and correction of small failures that is crucial to avoiding consequential failures. The majority of failures experienced by hospitalized patients—massive heparin overdoses that harmed babies in two separate hospitals a few years ago, for instance—occur as a result of a series of small process failures that unfortunately lined up in just the wrong way to allow patients to be harmed. Best practice means catching and correcting these small failures before this happens, because, again, small failures will occur in complex, customized work. Major failures, however, can be prevented through vigilance, good communication, and proactive learning. (For all of these behaviors, of course, psychological safety is critical.)

Intelligent Failures

The most important insight for managers seeking to promote innovation is that failures in this category aren't in fact "bad" at all. Indeed, intelligent failures can rightly be considered "good." They provide valuable new knowledge that can help a team to come up with innovative products and help a company to grow. Intelligent failures occur when experimentation is necessary—when answers are not knowable

in advance (because we've never been in this exact situation before and probably never will again). Discovering and testing new drugs, creating a radically new business, developing a new biofuel, creating a prototype for an energy-efficient vehicle, and testing customer reactions in a new market are examples of undertakings where this is the case. These are tasks that demand intelligent failure. And the faster the failures happen, the better.

This kind of experimentation is often referred to as *trial and error*, but that is a misnomer. *Error* implies that you could have done it right the first time and that not doing so constitutes a mistake. But a trial is needed precisely when results are not knowable in advance. For this reason, I call the experimentation process *trial and failure*. (We lack a word that means "unpreventable novel failures," which itself is telling.)

Failing Well—At the Right Scale

When you're exploring the frontier, the right kind of experimentation is one that produces good failures quickly and intelligently, which is why Professor Sim Sitkin at Duke calls them intelligent failures, despite the apparent oxymoron. Managers who work with failures in this fashion are more likely to get the most out of them—and also to avoid the unintelligent failure of conducting experiments on a scale that is larger than necessary.

As an example, in the late 1990s a major telecommunications company I'll refer to as Telco set out to innovate. To be positioned at what was then the forefront of new and some-what unproven technology, Telco decided to launch digital subscriber line technology, or DSL, to provide its customers with high-speed internet service. In its well-intentioned desire to innovate, however, Telco made the mistake of experimenting at too large a scale.

Despite the very real operational risks of the unproven new technology, Telco launched DSL throughout its entire market, all at once, and before the company was really able to deliver it reliably. The outcome, unfortunately, was a dismal failure. Customer satisfaction, usually in the high 80s, dove down to the teens. As many as 500 customers a day were waiting to hear back about some aspect of service. Twenty percent of complaints were taking 30 or more days to resolve. Customers were frustrated and angry, and employee morale suffered as well.

Of course, Telco's mistake did not lie in trying to innovate, or even in experiencing failure as part of the innovation process. The mistake was that it launched an experiment—an uncertain new service operation—at such a large and painful scale. By rolling DSL out to the entire market, rather than launching a small pilot that could help it see what worked (and what didn't), Telco lost the chance to make rapid changes as a result of thoughtful experimentation. The company converted what could have been an intelligent failure into a preventable (not-so-intelligent) failure. At that point in time, the process knowledge for how to deliver the new service reliably across diverse customer situations was simply underdeveloped. Not considering this mismatch, Telco was in a position of managing an initiative that should have been treated as a complex new operation, not as a routine operation.

By contrast, IDEO, the global product design consultancy, set out to launch a new kind of innovation strategy service. Traditionally, IDEO helped clients design new products within their existing product lines. The new service would assist clients in identifying new strategic product line opportunities. Knowing it had not worked out all the details for delivering the new services effectively, IDEO started with a small project with a low-tech manufacturing client so as to learn from an early small experiment. Although the project failed—the

client did not change its product strategy—IDEO learned from it. The company then figured out what it had to do differently, including developing new processes for understanding clients' businesses and hiring staff with MBAs who had experience diagnosing and developing business strategy. Today, strategic services account for more than a third of IDEO's revenues.

We can sing the praises of intelligent failure as much as we want. But that inner child, the one who wants to be right and is terrified of being wrong, doesn't just go gently into that good night. That's where leadership comes in.

Leading Failure

As we've seen, failing well means tolerating unavoidable process failures in complex systems and celebrating intelligent failures at the frontier of knowledge. Rather than promoting mediocrity, such tolerance is essential for any team or organization seeking the new knowledge that failure in complex and novel settings provides.

Strategically producing failures takes this one step further. Researchers in basic science know that once in a great while an experiment yields a spectacular success. However, more often (far more often!) experiments result in failure. Scientists can't succeed unless they learn to recognize failure as a step on the path to success. Remember from week 8 the chief scientific officer at pharmaceutical giant Eli Lilly who threw failure parties to celebrate clinical trials or scientific programs that were intelligent but that nonetheless failed? This odd ritual makes scientists more willing to take intelligent risks, but it also encourages them to speak up sooner rather than later about a failing course of action. Failing is neither blameworthy nor shameful, but part of a valiant effort to generate new knowledge.

Most managers in business, however, feel a great deal of pressure to make sure that their product or service is perfect when it goes out into the world. This pressure affects the pilot projects that are designed to test the new idea. Managers are so eager to succeed (understandably!) that they often design pilots that incorporate optimal conditions rather than representative ones. The result? Fragile successes. A pilot is meant to generate knowledge about what won't work, not simply affirm the genius behind an innovation. Pilots must be designed to fail.

To understand why, consider the Telco failure again. Before the full-scale urban launch, managers had run a small pilot in a suburb that housed well-educated, tech-savvy customers. The pilot was considered a soaring success. Unfortunately, pilot conditions were anything but representative of the large and diverse urban market in which the full-scale launch would take place. To make matters worse, the pilot was staffed by particularly expert and friendly service reps who were well versed in the new technology and could make it work for any customer's home computer setup. This small pilot was not so much a hypothesis-testing experiment as a demonstration project. It was designed to succeed—rather than to fail intelligently so that the subsequent full-scale launch could be a success.

What should Telco have done? First, the technology should have been tested in a small and unsophisticated market (old computers, fewer tech-savvy customers), with normal staffing levels to support it. The pilot should have been designed to uncover every little thing that could possibly go wrong—before announcing the new service to all customers. Managers would have been poised to reward intelligent failures and to help teams learn from them quickly to improve the product as well as the service that accompanied it. To generalize this lesson, I list a few questions that should be answered in the

affirmative when designing the right kind of pilot projects—the kind that fail intelligently.

As these questions demonstrate, managers hoping to successfully launch an innovative or novel product should not try to produce success the first time around. Instead, they should attempt to design and execute the most informative trial-and-failure process possible. This strategy for learning from pilot-size failures is a way to ensure that full-scale, online services will succeed.

Managers of successful pilots must be able to answer yes to the following questions:

- Is the pilot program being tested under typical circumstances instead of optimal conditions?

- Are the employees, customers, and resources representative of the firm's real operating environment?

- Is the goal of the pilot to learn as much as possible rather than demonstrate to senior managers the value of the new system?

- Is the goal of learning as much as possible understood by everyone involved, including employees and managers?

- Is it clear that compensation and performance ratings are not based on a successful outcome of the pilot?

- Were explicit changes made as a result of the pilot program?

Courage and Fear

Like the cowardly lion in *The Wizard of Oz*, we have to learn that fear and courage exist side by side. The lion didn't understand at first that courage does not mean an absence of fear but a willingness to act in spite of fear.

Confronting failure means confronting our imperfection. This takes courage because, of course, it is unpleasant. But acknowledging our limits with good nature and a sense of humor enables us to get on with things to be creative and innovative. Environments that discourage the reporting of problems, mistakes, and failures block this forward movement, this learning. Managers who ask employees to be brave and to speak up must not later express disapproval or even anger. Rather, gratitude is called for when an employee reveals the complex systems at work behind organizational failures. Then the real innovation can begin.

Managers are often concerned, as I've mentioned, that embracing failure will create a messy, anarchic, anything-goes environment in which nothing ever gets done. But this simply isn't the case. One does not follow from the other. The fact is, failure is inevitable, especially in today's complex knowledge economy. Learning from failure, even moving in that direction, will give any organization a competitive edge.

Tom Kelley (general manager of IDEO) and David Kelley (founder and chairman) have written about the importance of what they call *creative confidence*: "the natural ability to come up with new ideas and the courage to try them out." They put this into action in their company by giving employees "strategies to get past four fears that hold most of us back: fear of the messy unknown, fear of being judged, fear of the first step, and fear of losing control."[1]

No matter what kind of failure occurs, avoid playing the blame game—the pull to name culprits rather than causes. This game is deeply counterproductive. Get comfortable with the mindset that identifies failure as an inevitable, valuable part of the innovation journey.

Of course, failure is not worth much if we don't learn from it (and learn fast!). Let's look at what it takes to do that well.

Failing the Right Way

Failure can be a good thing, but only under the right conditions. In this activity, you'll take a look at productive failures.

Activity

Reflect on the following questions:

Three types of failure are discussed this week: basic, complexity-related, and intelligent. As you think of your own career, think of a time that you experienced each of these types of failures: which was the hardest? What "good" failures have you experienced? What did they enable you to do, subsequently?

_____

_____

_____

Of the three boundaries to teaming discussed in this week (physical distance, status, and knowledge), which do you think is the toughest to overcome? What strategies have you used in the past to get around this boundary?

_____

_____

_____

What does "failing at the right scale" mean to you?

_____

_____

_____

Do you agree that learning rather than demonstrating is the better goal for a pilot program? Why or why not?

_____

_____

_____

Learning from Failure

Benchmark goal: Learn fast: Make the most of your failure.

In companies, learning fast is a team sport. Although individual employees learn in a casual way all the time (having new insights, improving their skills), this type of learning doesn't automatically help the company to perform better. Individual participation in formal training programs doesn't either. Here, we look at what it takes for organizations to systematically learn from the vast array of experiences they have—especially from failure.

Everyone agrees that people and organizations should learn from failure. And yet organizations that systematically and effectively learn from failure are very rare. This is because learning fast requires discipline. It is systematic and effortful. I explicate four steps of the learning process that underlies innovation. Of course, there are barriers to learning inherent in each of these steps, and we'll take a look at how some companies overcome them. Finally, I give some tips for leading learning in the context of innovation.

Deliberate learning from experience starts with the right managerial mindset. I call it *organizing to learn*. It's a way of thinking and acting that is driven by the recognition that the world keeps changing, and that today's answers are almost certainly not tomorrow's. It means not having too much (unwarranted) faith in our first round of

ideas. For instance, recall the Telco DSL launch described in week 11. Senior management's (unsubstantiated) faith in the company's ability to deliver led to a premature full-scale rollout in a large and diverse urban market.

Learning as You Go

The Telco failure happened because the company went all out with an innovation without accurately assessing its own current operational capabilities. Imagine that instead of a full-scale, widely advertised rollout, Telco had engaged a few pioneering customers who tolerated some imperfections in the brand-new service and also gave the company feedback to help it improve the service quickly. As coinvestigators, these pioneers might have even enjoyed helping the company find the weak spots. Together, company and customer would learn as they went. Before long, the problems would be solved and the kinks worked out in an inevitable march toward a reliable, easy-to-use innovation, which future customers would take for granted. As one might roll out a carpet, a rollout implies that something is ready to go, just needing a bit of momentum to propel it forward. Cycling out, by contrast, is a journey punctuated with deliberate and thoughtful iteration and learning.

Any company trying to innovate must figure out a way to learn as quickly as possible from early experiences (preferably at a small scale) in the life of the project. There are no shortcuts. To provide a compelling new product or service that works and appeals to a wide range of customers, you have to be willing to start with one that doesn't work well. It means taking seriously the adage of nineteenth-century British philosopher G. K. Chesterton: "If something's worth doing, it's worth doing badly." Of course, just doing something badly (before you figure out how to do it well) isn't enough. To learn fast from experience, managers

have to deliberately frame the early-stage experiences as experiments. Experiments generate data—and data must be learned from.

On the innovation journey, each step is an experiment, and each experiment must be different from the one before. Its design must incorporate the knowledge gained in the prior cycle. In this way, an innovation cycles out, bumpily, improving as it expands. For example, Netflix introduced its Watch Instantly offering in successive waves of 250,000 customers, taking six months to cycle out its instant downloading technology; during this time, the company constantly checked in with customers via follow-up emails that inquired about the quality of specific movies watched. It also set up and actively monitored a Netflix blog to explain operations, step-by-step, and to respond to frequent customer posts regarding problems, requests, and suggestions. The service was essentially free for several years, until the problems were worked out. Once it really worked smoothly, Netflix asked customers to pay. This is the kind of practice that companies use to learn fast. Above all, innovation requires companies to fully use employee and customer experiences for learning.

How to Learn Fast

Learning in general, and especially for innovation, involves four essential steps: diagnosing the situation, challenge, or problem (including assessing what is currently known about it); designing initial actions; taking action (viewed as experimenting); and reflecting to gain the lessons from the experiment.

Diagnosis

Diagnosis involves sizing up the situation and the challenges that might lie ahead. It's about identifying the opportunities for innovation—the

subtle customer desires or pain points that haven't yet been addressed by viable products or services. Diagnosis may range from extended study of customer behaviors to behind-the-scenes analysis of large data sets to a quick exchange of ideas between colleagues about opportunities.

At Intuit, the financial software company, engineers directly observe customers as they interact with the software so as to evaluate how easy or difficult it is for them to use the features built into the product. This enables engineers to observe unmet user needs firsthand, needs that customers themselves lack either the experience or the vocabulary to voice. Another part of diagnosis for innovation is assessing what's feasible, given the current state of technology or the costs of inputs. Opportunities may be wide, but they are not infinite.

Design

The next step is to identify possibilities for action. Design is done when a team has a preliminary commitment to action—whether through a formal decision or plan, or by a gradual shift into agreement to try something out. The purpose of design in innovation is to guide action. That may sound oversimple, but design fosters learning by making action more deliberate and conscious.

At Motorola, one of the most successful innovations in the company's history was the RAZR phone, introduced back in 2004. That innovation was the result of a motivated team's efforts to brainstorm shapes and features for the phone and then to quickly try out mockups made of clay before getting too far down the path with real materials. As in this example, the design step in any innovation journey is often just a starting point. It may lead to only a single step forward, one that we expect to revise as soon as we learn more. Thus, in an innovation project, a focus group might be used to react to an

experimental new service or product idea before we figure out all of the details of execution.

Action or Experimentation

The shift from talking to doing, from considering to trying, also happens in teams. A key to effective action in execution-as-learning is making sure to track what actually happens as well as tracking the results of the action. Traditional management controls emphasize outcome data, which capture results. Execution-as-learning pays just as much attention to process data, which describe how work unfolds.

Rapid, unconstrained action is at the heart of innovation. It's called *experimentation*. Scientists, of course, routinely experiment, hoping to be first to make an important discovery in the process. Experiments range from those for which possible outcomes are all but unknown in advance to those in which strong hypotheses are being tested. In basic research, a scientist who has a 70 percent failure rate in the experiments they run might be in the process of earning a Nobel Prize. The RAZR team tried out several configurations before hitting on its revolutionary slimming design, by putting the battery next to the circuit board (prior phones had them stacked) to reduce thickness. Teams at IDEO routinely build quick prototypes to see what new products might look like in three dimensions. The point is simply to try things and see what happens. It's easy to stay in the conceptual plane—to talk about ideas and possibilities forever. A key to successful innovation is making frequent, small forays into action.

Reflection

After taking action, it's critical to take some time to understand what happened: what worked and what didn't. Reflection is about digging into failures, intelligent or otherwise. It's an analytic task.

Innovation teams have to learn fast from the trials and failures they produce so that they can conduct new trials as soon as possible. Reflecting on failure is rarely fun, but it's essential to figuring out the true causes of a failure in order to determine what gets tried next. Don't shortchange reflection in the desire to move quickly to the next experiment, because high-quality reflection can help avoid predictable failures in subsequent actions. Ed Catmull, founder and president of Pixar, lamented that Pixar employees would just as soon avoid post-project reflection altogether, preferring to relish the success of a film than to stop and identify what could have gone better. To get more out of this critical step, he instituted the following: participants are asked to list five things they would do again, and then to discuss five things they wouldn't do. According to Catmull, this positive-negative balance created a safe environment conducive to discussing every aspect of a project thoughtfully.

It's not easy for any company facing cost constraints (and who isn't!) to stop and reflect. Disciplined evaluation takes productive resources offline, and conventional management wisdom views this as lost productivity. Nonetheless, the only way to achieve and sustain excellence is for leaders to insist that their organizations invest resources in the reflection that makes innovation possible.

Overcoming Barriers to Learning

Learning from failure is a hallmark of innovative companies. But it requires an unusual mindset and systematic effort, and companies that do it well are rare. Why? Because there are barriers to innovation at each step of the learning process.

Barriers to Diagnosis

Diagnosis sets the stage for learning from the inevitable failures in any innovation process. This is where opportunities are assessed and

aspirational goals are revisited (remember "aim high"). Because most people experience strong negative feelings about failure, these kinds of conversations must be managed thoughtfully.

This story illustrates a pervasive and fundamental problem. Although many methods of surfacing current and pending failures exist, they are grossly underused in today's organizations. For instance, total quality management and soliciting feedback from customers are well-known techniques for bringing failures to light. But too many messengers—even the most senior executives—are reluctant to convey bad news to bosses and colleagues.

It's just not possible to diagnose or predict failure when people don't feel it is safe to express their full thoughts and feelings about the various issues on the table. Leaders have to go out of their way to avoid "shooting the messenger," and to instead encourage people to speak up. Mulally's applause is a great example of how to do that. People must feel able to speak up about both clear and ambiguous signals that something might be amiss. This is essential to innovation! Without evidence that the present is deficient in some way, the motivation to innovate is lacking.

Barriers to Design

For the purposes of organizational learning, the design step is a thoughtful pause that guides subsequent action. The most important barrier to design is a lack of psychological safety. When people are overly worried about what others will think of them, they become reluctant to raise potentially crazy ideas. But innovation benefits from crazy ideas. Sometimes it's the crazy idea—despite being impractical or useless in its own right—that triggers someone else to have a truly innovative and useable idea. It's important in innovation to make sure people feel uninhibited to dream and imagine all sorts of possibilities.

This points to a second barrier. Beyond feeling safe to speak up, people also have to reengage their imaginations, which can sometimes atrophy in corporate hierarchies. A lack of imagination is another important barrier to coming up with designs for action that are new enough—enough of a departure from the status quo—to generate worthwhile experiments. An important leadership task, therefore, is to provoke and nurture imagination, to help people think as broadly as possible about options. Thinking is free, whereas action can be expensive. So the design step should be used to conduct thought experiments through which obviously wrongheaded approaches can be skipped going forward.

Barriers to Action and Experimentation

A lack of psychological safety is also a barrier to the third step in the learning process: deliberate experimentation. If people don't feel safe, they will conduct only very low-risk experiments, where successful outcomes are relatively easy to predict. (This is why managers sometimes conduct pilots that don't yield much information, as described in week 11 in the examination of what it takes to "fail well.") But innovative organizations are willing to conduct (and learn quickly from) experiments that fail.

Consider the example of IDEO, the design firm that promotes internal experimentation through slogans such as "Fail often in order to succeed sooner" and "Enlightened trial-and-error succeeds over the planning of the lone genius." These statements are accompanied by frequent small experiments and much good humor over the associated failures.

In many companies, incentives (formal and informal) are inconsistent with stated values about learning from failure. This makes true experimentation difficult and rare. This obvious barrier to experimentation

must be mitigated—by aligning incentives with what it takes to innovate. Those who experiment should be celebrated, and companies must publicize both failures and successes internally, so that all employees can see that the idea of learning from failure is more than just "talk."

A final barrier to effective experimentation is the reluctance people have to call an experiment a failure, even after the data are clearly pointing in that direction. It's important to teach people when to declare defeat in an experimental course of action. The human tendency to hope for the best and avoid failure at all costs gets in the way, and organizational hierarchies exacerbate the problem. As a result, failing research and development (R&D) projects are often kept going much longer than is analytically rational or economically prudent. We throw good money after bad, praying that we'll pull a rabbit out of a hat. Intuition and experience may tell engineers or scientists that a project has fatal flaws, but the formal decision to call it a failure may be delayed for months.

Barriers to Reflection

Organizations cannot learn from failure, and other experiences, without thoughtful analysis and discussion. Again, a lack of psychological safety can be a major barrier to doing this well. Formal processes or forums for discussing, analyzing, and applying the lessons of failure involve direct language and straightforward confrontation of sometimes unwelcome facts. People rarely do this well unless they feel psychologically safe enough to leave their ego at the door and fully engage with the substance of the discussion.

A second major barrier (as we've seen) is blame. After experiencing failure, people typically blame other people or forces beyond their control (like traffic and weather). We tend to downplay our own responsibility and blame external or situational factors

when we fail, only to do the reverse when assessing the failures of others—a psychological trap we discussed in week 2 known as *fundamental attribution error.* Leaders have to help groups avoid the blame game and keep attention focused on what can be learned from the prior action or experiment and what that means for the next one. Expert outside (or internal) facilitators can keep a reflection process productive and bring new perspectives and insights that deepen the analysis.

Effective analysis of failure requires both time and space, along with skill in managing the conflicting perspectives that may emerge. Some organizations, like the military, set aside time for after-action reviews; hospitals use morbidity and mortality conferences to discuss significant mistakes or unexpected patient deaths as a forum for identifying, discussing, and learning from failures.

A third barrier is lack of technical or analytic skill. To learn from failed or successful experiments, people need to know how to use basic scientific tools, including the appropriate use of statistical analyses or qualitative data analysis. Relying exclusively on common sense, gut feel, or intuition can lead to flawed conclusions. Even without meaning to, we all favor evidence that supports our existing beliefs over alternative explanations. This is known as *confirmation bias.*

The final barrier is emotional. As previously noted, examining any failure is likely to be emotionally unpleasant. Left to our own devices, most of us will speed through or avoid failure analysis altogether. Reflection takes skill and patience. Yet many managers admire and are rewarded for decisiveness, efficiency, and action—not thoughtful reflection. It takes leadership to push forward against this cultural tide, ensuring that lessons are learned. In the long run, this saves time and promotes the innovation that is so necessary for tomorrow's success.

The goal in reflection is to go beyond first-order reasons (procedures weren't followed) to find second- and third-order explanations for a failure. One way to do this is to use interdisciplinary teams with diverse skills and perspectives. Complex failures in particular are the result of multiple events that occurred in different departments or disciplines or at different levels of the organization. Understanding what happened and how to prevent it from happening again requires detailed, team-based discussion and analysis. Although this takes patience and skill, the benefits for innovation are well worth the investment of managerial effort.

Leading Learning to Innovate

Overcoming the barriers to learning in the pursuit of innovation requires openness, transparency, and, yes, psychological safety. Leaders who wish to promote innovation must work to create and reinforce a culture that counteracts the blame game and makes people feel comfortable with and responsible for surfacing failures and learning from them. The leader's role is to insist on a clear understanding of what happened—not to ask "Who did it?"—when things go wrong.

Framing for Learning

Leaders should also send the right message about the nature of the work, such as reminding people in R&D, "We're in the discovery business, and the faster we fail, the faster we'll succeed." Many managers don't understand or appreciate this subtle but crucial point. To build a culture that is conducive to innovation, managers must create an environment in which everyone can put aside self-protective defenses and

approach the work with curiosity and a desire to learn from failure. We cannot underestimate the psychological and interpersonal barriers to this organizational learning process. Reframing failure from something associated with shame and weakness to something that is linked to risk, uncertainty, and improvement is a critical step in the learning journey.

Repeat (Learning Never Stops)

The secret to organizational learning and innovation is that the learning cycle never stops. Once the purpose (where the team is headed) has been established, the process (how we get there) can nearly always be improved.

Team sports have guidelines that move the game forward. Reflection, sharing insights widely in a psychologically safe environment, creating the next experiment, and learning from failures are all crucial steps that move innovation forward. In weeks 9 and 10, I described how to establish a goal and a process. In this week, I looked at how to continuously improve that process to move closer to the goal. Eventually, learning continuously from failure should become second nature—but for now let's just say that it's far more systematic and structured than it might first appear.

In organizations that innovate, learning must become a habit.

Learning from Your Mistakes

Most people take for granted an execution-oriented frame for getting work done. Reframing the work as a learning process is an essential driver of innovation. In this activity, you will examine the value of a learning mindset in innovation.

Activity

Reflect on the following questions:

_____

_____

_____

How did Netflix's rollout of "Watch Instantly" embody the learn-as-you-go approach? What do you think the results would have been if they had rolled it out to all customers for a cost immediately?

_____

_____

_____

What approach did Ed Catmull, founder of Pixar, take to get employees more comfortable with admitting and discussing failure? Do you think this approach would have worked at companies you've worked for?

_____

_____

_____

Do you agree that lack of psychological safety is a barrier to learning from failures? Why or why not?

_____

_____

_____

Wrap-Up

Performance goal: Innovate with teaming.

Teaming to innovate, as many of the examples in this part illustrate, is fueled by a commitment to create a better world in some small or large way. The size of the contribution depends on the kind of work you do and the kind of organization you work in. But no matter where you work, setting out to innovate is an act of hope.

Questions

1. How can people effectively use different perspectives to produce innovation rather than unproductive conflict?

2. Aiming high by setting a challenging goal is an important part of innovation. It means stretching beyond what seems initially feasible. Have you worked on such a goal in your career? Did it lead to innovation?

Activity

For this activity, get a paper and pen to write answers to these prompts.

Describe a time in your career when curiosity (or a lack of it) was an important factor in a team environment. How did it affect the team's ability to meet their goal?

Have you ever encountered a contentious situation on a team? Do you think using one of the key strategies for cooling conflict (managing self, conversations, and relationships) would have helped?

What barriers to learning have you encountered during your career? How do you think they affected your results?

Notes

Chapter 1

1. P. Senge, *The Fifth Discipline: The Art and Practice of the Learning Organization* (New York: Doubleday/Currency, 1990).

Chapter 2

1. L. Ross, "The Intuitive Psychologist and His Shortcomings," *Advances in Experimental Psychology*, Vol. 10, ed. L. Berkowitz (New York: Academic Press, 1977), p. 405.

Chapter 4

1. D. A. Harrison and K. J. Klein, "What's the Difference? Diversity Constructs as Separation, Variety, or Disparity in Organizations," *Academy of Management Review* 32, no. 4 (2007): 1200.
2. A. Tucker and A. C. Edmondson, *"Cincinnati Children's Hospital Medical Center,"* HBS Case No. *609–109* (Boston: Harvard Business School Publishing, 2009), p. 10.

Chapter 11

1. T. Kelley and D. Kelley, "Reclaim Your Confidence," *Harvard Business Review,* December 2012.

Conclusion

Congratulations! You've leveled up your teamwork skills in only 90 days. What you've learned in these 12 weeks will last you for a lifetime of teamwork. I recommend reviewing the weeks that you find most useful or most challenging to brush up occasionally.

Your 90-Day Plan to Level Up Your Teamwork Skills
Performance Goals
• Get ready to learn, innovate, and compete. • Team fearlessly with psychological safety. • Innovate with teaming.
Benchmark Goals
Days 1–30 Get ready to learn, innovate, and compete. Week 1: Understand how teaming is different than teamwork. Week 2: Learn the four pillars of teaming and why they work. Week 3: Lead through teaming. Week 4: Discover how to team across boundaries.

Days 31–60
Team fearlessly with psychological safety.
Week 5: Grasp the power of psychological safety.
Week 6: Make it safe to team.
Week 7: Frame your team for success.
Week 8: Create a fearless organization.
Days 61–90
Innovate with teaming.
Week 9: Aim high.
Week 10: Team up.
Week 11: Fail well.
Week 12: Learn fast.
Personal Goals and Vision for Success
What do you hope to achieve by leveling up?
How could your life change by reaching these goals?

Final Questions

- What tips or suggestions from your 90-Day Plan do you plan to implement in your day-to-day work life?
- Which goals will be most impactful to your career?
- What weeks were the hardest for you and why?
- How do you plan to stay motivated to boost your teamwork skills?

About the Author

Nearing graduation from Harvard College more than three decades ago, Amy Edmondson took a leap of faith and wrote a letter to a personal hero, seeking advice about employment. To her surprise, Buckminster Fuller wrote back. His letter arrived barely a week later with far more than advice. The legendary inventor, architect, and futurist offered her a job. Spending the next three years as Fuller's "chief engineer," she developed an intense and enduring interest in what leaders and organizations can do to create a better world.

Her book *A Fuller Explanation: The Synergetic Geometry of R. Buckminster Fuller* (Boston: Birkhauser, 1987) clarifies Fuller's mathematical contributions for a nontechnical audience. Edmondson received her PhD in organizational behavior, AM in psychology, and AB in engineering and design, all from Harvard University.

Today, as the Novartis professor of leadership and management at the Harvard Business School, Edmondson studies leaders seeking to make a positive difference in the world through the work they do in organizations of all kinds. The research described in this book captures the central thread that has run through her academic career: creating work environments where people can team up and do their best work.

Amy joined the Harvard Business School faculty in 1996 and has taught courses in leadership, organizational learning, and operations

management in the MBA and Executive Education programs. Her writings on organizational learning and leadership have been published in more than 60 articles in academic and management journals, and she has consulted widely on these topics for organizations around the world. In 2003, the Academy of Management's Organizational Behavior division selected Edmondson for the Cummings Award for outstanding achievement, and in 2000, it selected her article "Psychological Safety and Learning Behavior in Work Teams" for its annual award for the best published paper in the field. Her article with Anita Tucker, "Why Hospitals Don't Learn from Failures: Organizational and Psychological Dynamics That Inhibit System Change," received the 2004 Accenture Award for significant contribution to management practice.

Before her academic career, she was director of research at Pecos River Learning Centers, where she worked with founder and CEO Larry Wilson to design and implement change programs in large companies.

She lives outside Boston, Massachusetts, with her husband, George Daley, and their two sons.

Index

psychological safety and, 95
reframing, 200
strategically producing, 183
types of, 179–181
unlearning about, 173
unpacking, 174
unreported, 178
Fallible leaders, 98
False consensus effect, 39
Fear:
 as barrier to teaming, 36
 and courage, 185–186
 motivating employees with, 17–18
 teaming without, 75–87, 141–142
 working without, 123–139
Fearless organizations, 76, 123–139
 inviting participation at, 129–132
 psychological safety at, 123–129
 responses to risk-taking at,
  132–138
Feedback, soliciting, 53–54, 79, 94,
  98, 195
Feedback loops, 20
Firing employees, 102, 136
Ford, Henry, 16–18
Ford Motors, 52
Four pillars of teaming, 3, 8, 27–41
 barriers related to, 35–41
 collaboration, 30–31
 experimentation, 31
 for Motorola RAZR launch, 32–34
 reflection, 31–32
 speaking up, 28–30, 37–39
Foxconn, 17–18
Frames, 106, 108, 113–118.
  See also specific types
Framing, 4, 76, 105–121. *See also*
  Reframing
 for early-stage experiences,
  190–191
 of ideal employee, 119–120
 leader's responsibility for, 44, 105
 for learning, 107–113, 199–200
 for organizational change, 105
 tacit interpretations in, 106–107
 the work, 123–126
Frankl, Viktor, 107
Fundamental attribution error, 40,
  167–168, 198

G
Gibson, Charlie, 90
Globalization, 60
Goals:
 benchmark, vii–viii, 1, 8–9, 75–76,
  143–144, 205–206
 choosing worthy, *see* Aiming well
 performance, vii, 1, 7, 75, 143, 205
 personal, viii, 9, 76, 144, 206
 stretch, 154–155
Goffman, Erving, 78, 82
Google, 4, 132, 136–137
Groupe Danone, 66, 132
Groupthink, 91
g2g network, 132

H
Ham, Linda, 90
Harkins, Kevin, 159
Harrison, Dave, 61
Henríquez, José, 149
Here-and-now humility, 130
Hierarchy, 38, 54, 63, 67–68
Hirak, Reuven, 130
Hot cognition, 167–169
Hypothesis-testing experiments,
  176, 178

I
IBM, 99–100
Ideal employee, 119–120
Identity groups, defined, 58
IDEO, 182–183, 186, 193, 196
Ignorance, 79, 93
Imagination, 196
Inattention, 175–177
Incentives, values and, 196–197
Incompetence, 79, 94
Individual reframing, 120
Innovation, 203–204
 aiming well for, 147–150
 aspirations that motivate, 155
 expertise diversity for, 69–70
 failure and, 99–100
 getting ready for, 7–9, 73–74
 key concepts in, 4–5
 leading learning for, 199–200

213

Index

215

Index

OTHER BOOKS IN THE
90 DAYS SERIES

WILEY